SHROPSHIRE
Unusual & Quirky

HALSGROVE

First published in Great Britain in 2023

Copyright © Andrew Beardmore 2023

All rights reserved. No part of this publication may be reproduced, stored in a retrieval system, or transmitted in any form or by any means without the prior permission of the copyright holder.

British Library Cataloguing-in-Publication Data

A CIP record for this title is available from the British Library

ISBN 978 0 85704 346 7

HALSGROVE
Halsgrove House, Ryelands Business Park,
Bagley Road,
Wellington,
Somerset TA21 9PZ
Tel: 01823 653777
Fax: 01823 216796
email: sales@halsgrove.com
website: www.halsgrove.com

Printed and bound in India by Parksons Graphics Ltd

Shropshire – Unusual and Quirky

Welcome to *Shropshire – Unusual and Quirky*. This is the eighth book in the 21st century series that calls to mind that classic series of travel books called *The King's England*, written in the 1930s by Arthur Mee, since each volume in Mee's series was suffixed with *"There have been many books on <insert county>, but never one like this…"* Well the very same tag line could be applied to this book, as some of its elements are certainly unique. Having said that, the book still has plenty to offer in terms of conventional reference, but it delivers large parts of this in a lateral and humorous format never seen before.

Essentially, the book is comprised of two sections called *Conventional Shropshire* and *Quirky Shropshire*. The *Conventional* section kicks off with county maps along with key facts and figures relating to the county – such as county town, population, highest point, key industries and famous sons and daughters. The facts are then followed by a history of the Shropshire *area* from the Stone Age to the 11th century – by which time Shropshire, along with most of England's counties had been officially formed – after which the last one thousand years of county history is covered, bringing us up-to-date and into the 21st century.

Nevertheless, in keeping with the title of the book, the *County History* has many historical "Quirk Alerts" interspersed. Like a paragraph on how a prophecy about Harry Hotspur dying in Berwick came true, albeit not at the Berwick that Northumbrian, Hotspur, was expecting! Read also about a vicious 12th century storm in Morville which saw dozens of people and horses struck dead by lightning, or the 18th century hurricane in Wentnor that also killed scores. Alternatively, read about the Shropshire Chief Justice who hung a builder from one of his chimneys because it wasn't "the finest in Shropshire", or which Royalist Major took a do-or-die plunge down a steep 200ft slope, rather than surrender!

More quirky offerings include the stone in Norton-in-Hales on which people would be willingly beaten on a Shrove Tuesday, the steeplejack who "flew" down an 800-foot rope in Shrewsbury whilst blowing a trumpet, and a paragraph on why "disorderly women" were ducked into Marton Pool whilst strapped to a chair! Elsewhere, find out which Shropshire border village was home to "the oldest Englishman who ever lived", or read about the 19th century Shropshire rake who frequently hunted naked in the depths of winter, fed his 2,000 dogs on steak and champagne, and once set fire to his nightshirt to cure a bout of hiccups!

The *Conventional* section then hands over to the *Quirky* section… and it is here that we really begin to earn the *"… but never one like this…"* tag line – as the whole section is driven by a quirky poem known as a Shire-Ode! Told in rhyming verse, the Shire-Ode portrays imaginary inhabitants of Shropshire but, as an extra twist, the poem contains exactly one hundred place-names found within the historic county, each subtly woven into the tale – and it is these place-names upon which the *Quirky* section focuses. Firstly, the places have their location pin-pointed via a map. A series of chapters then follow in (largely) alphabetical order for each place featured in the Shire-Ode – and it is here that the strangest and most interesting facts and features about each place are explored. As a result, you get a random almanac of places that would never ordinarily appear together – along with population figures, earliest place-name recording and origins, famous sons and daughters, historic trivia, Quirk Alerts… and lots of accompanying photographs, too.

So, feel free to commence your obscure Shropshire fact-digging; to read about some famous people and their Shropshire exploits, to read about ancient battles and, quite frankly, some ridiculous legends, too… but to hopefully have a little chuckle along the way. For example, find out which Shropshire Lord became convinced that a ghost had invaded his vacuum cleaner, and which orange-haired Shropshire Lady, moved out of her hall into a nearby tree-house! Or discover which 16th century Guildhall was erected as the world's first flat-pack building, and then created some mobile stocks to parade offenders all around the town.

Ecclesiastically, find out which Shropshire church includes a bedroom window, which one has a life-sized memorial to a 7ft 3in tall man, and which one allegedly includes a brick from the Great Wall of China! Alternatively, find out which church's silver was hidden by its churchwardens in an ancient chest which remained undiscovered for hundreds of years, or which church's silver Tudor chalice was lost for centuries, before showing up at a curio shop in Yorkshire in the 19th century.

Finally, check out *The Hobbins from beyond The Bog*, the quirky Shire-Ode that drives the idiosyncratic *Quirky Shropshire* section and learn how a fictitious Shropshire lass faces her greatest fears!

Anyway, that's the introduction completed. As you have probably gathered by now, parts of this book are indeed "unusual and quirky"… so it's time to prime the quirkometer and pull up a pew at St Strangeways. Oh, and did I mention which Shropshire village was top of the national jam-making leaderboard in 1943? Or what about a monk called Frodo, the vicious Sleep Rouser of Claverley, the origins of the phrase "namby-pamby", the Great Bolas couple who married each other twice within a year, how acorns kept children out of school in 1868…

Contents

Introduction
　Shropshire – Unusual and Quirky 3

Conventional Shropshire
　Shropshire Facts and Figures 6
　Shropshire Maps 7
　Shropshire County History 8
　　Prehistory 8
　　Romans, Anglo-Saxons and Vikings 15
　　From the Conquest to the Dissolution 28
　　From the Dissolution to the Eve of the Industrial Revolution 56
　　Shropshire's Industrial Revolution 80
　　From the Late Victorians to Present Day 98

Quirk Alerts:
　　Wrekin Legends 8
　　Legendary Stones 10
　　Spring in the Step 25
　　Cave Life 27
　　Perrrin and Baggins 38
　　Chest Inflection 38
　　Music and Lightning 39
　　The Town that became a Village 39
　　The Bradling Stone 44
　　Tales of Shrewsbury 48
　　An Arrowing Wound 50
　　The White Stiffs of Condover 60
　　Perfect Pitchford 61
　　Trial by Chimney 62
　　The Bedroom in the Chancel 63
　　Flat Pack and Mobile Punishment 65
　　A Tall Story 65
　　Old Parr 66
　　Major's Leap 68
　　New Invention 71
　　Mind Your Scolding 71
　　The Sleep Rouser 73
　　Icarus of the Rope 75
　　Namby-pamby Fire Fodder 75
　　The Hurricane Gravestone 78
　　Hi Ho Tontine 82
　　"Mad Jack" Mytton 86
　　Heber's Hoard 87
　　Returns Policy 87
　　Pedlar's Parish 90
　　Matthew Webb 90
　　General Backacher 92
　　Tight Squeeze and the Tracts of Life 94
　　School's Out 96

The Wenlock Olympian Games *97*
Race to The Line. *99*
Brick or Trick?. *102*
Jam Today and Wartime Ghosts *103*
Fond of Barbirolli *103*
Undefeated *106*
The Break *106*

Quirky Shropshire

Introducing the Shire-Ode 108
Shropshire Shire-Ode: The Hobbins from beyond The Bog 108
Place-Name Table for The Hobbins from beyond The Bog. 109
Shropshire Location Maps for The Hobbins from beyond The Bog. 109
The Hobbins from beyond The Bog – A Shropshire Shire-Ode Almanac. 110

Three's Up: Anchor, Bache and Ball. 110
Badger 111
Bedlam 113
Battlefield 114
Bitterley 115
Bouldon 117
Clive 118
Three's Up: Comley, Crowsnest and Greete 120
Coton 121
Eaton 123
Great Bolas 125
Three's Up: Harton, Hints and Hoo 126
Highley 128
Hope 130
Three's Up: Howle, Inwood and Leigh 131
Knockin 132
More 134
Myddle 135
Three's Up: Mytton, Northwood and Overs 137
Nash 139
Pant 140
Preston 141
Ryton 143
Three's Up: Shelve, Sleap and Stanley 144
Stowe 146
The Bog 147
Three's Up: The Grove, The Hope and Trench 148
Tilley 149
Tong 151
Woore 153
The Best of the Rest 155

Bibliography 160

Conventional Shropshire

Shropshire Facts & Figures

County Status:	Ceremonial county and former non-metropolitan county
County Town:	Shrewsbury
County Population:	493,200
County Population Rank:	42nd out of 48 (so there are only six counties more sparsely populated than Shropshire)
Cities:	None
Largest Settlement:	Telford
Largest Settlement Populations:	51. Telford (142,723); 128. Shrewsbury (71,715); 558. Oswestry (18,743); 770. Newport (12,741); 786. Bridgnorth (12,315); 811. Market Drayton (11,773); 879. Ludlow (10,515); 930. Whitchurch (9,710); 1,232. Shifnal (6,240); 1,280. Wem (5,870); 1,370. Broseley (5,257); 1,453. Albrighton (4,829); 1,719. Church Stretton (3,698); 1,724. Ellesmere (3,686); 1,845. Gobowen (3,270)
National Parks:	None
Other Areas:	Shropshire Hills (AONB)
County Area:	1,346 miles^2 (3,487 km^2)
County Area Rank:	13th out of 48
Highest Point:	Brown Clee Hill (1,772ft; 540m)
Longest River:	River Severn; enters the county south-west of Melverley, flows through Shrewsbury, Ironbridge, Bridgnorth and Highley, before exiting via the south-east corner of the county
Football Clubs:	Shrewsbury Town (League One), Telford United (National League North, Tier 6)
Rugby Union Clubs:	Bridgnorth, Newport (both Midlands Premier/Tier 5); Whitchurch (Midlands 1 West/Tier 6); Ludlow, Telford (Midlands 2 West [North]/Tier 7)
Rugby League Clubs:	Telford Raiders (League 1/Tier 3)
Industries (Present):	Agriculture, Commerce, Distribution, Electronics, Engineering, Financial Services, Information Technology, Retail, Services, Tourism
Industries (Past):	Agriculture, Coal Mining, Engineering, Textile

Born in Shropshire: Sir Thomas Adams, Archibald Alison, Richard Allestree, Ross Antony, Lucy Appleby, Jesse Armstrong, John Astley, Ricky Balshaw, Michael Bassett, Richard Baxter, Wyke Bayliss, Mary Beard, Thomas Beddoes, John Benbow, Elliott Bennett, Kyle Bennett, Gerald Berners, William Betty, Emily Bevan, Paul Blackthorne, Colin Bloomfield, Peter Bottomley, James Bowen, Christian Brassington, Thomas Bray, Joseph Bromfield, William Penny Brookes, Shirley Brooks, Charles Burney, Mickey Bushell, Joe Butler, Katherine Chidley, Samuel Chidley, Mary Cholmondeley, Thomas Churchyard, Lizzy Clark, Ernie Clements, Robert Clive, Geoffrey Hornblower Cock, John Constable, Andy Cooke, Isobel Cooper, Philip Corbet, Thomas Corser, Lol Crawley, Michael Croft, Charles Darwin, Barry Davies, Walford Davies, Matt Done, Herbert Edwardes, Dave Edwards, Humphrey Edwards, Kelly Edwards, Emyr Estyn Evans, Hilary Evans, Paul Evans, Richard Evans, Robert Evans, Suzanne Evans, Thomas Eyton, William Farr, William Felton, Calum Ferrie, James Friswell, Raymond Froggatt, Ben Garratt, Henry Gauntlett, Sir Edward German, Martin Giles, David Gilford, Tony Gillam, Richard Gough, Sara Grant, Carl Griffiths, Danny Guthrie, John Gwynn, Harry Hampton, Joe Hart, Charles Hastings, Chris Hawkins, Christine Hawley, Mary Cecil Hay, Edward Haycock, John Haycock, Dick Heckstall-Smith, Christopher Henn-Collins, Rowland Hill, Thomas Holland, Edward Hopkins, Walsham How, Albert Howard, Ian Hunter, Eleanor James, Eglantyne Jebb, Thomas Johnes, Adrian Jones, Di Jones, Ivan Jones, Ivor Roberts-Jones, Norman Jones, Peter Jones, Reuben Jones, Stephen Jones, Fred Jordan, Julia Kennedy, Marion Kennedy, Charles Kingsford, Humphrey Kynaston, Stuart Langelaan, Cecil Lawson, Rosemary Leach, Samuel Lee, Stewart Lee, John Lewis, Natalie Lisinska, Andy Lloyd, Eric Lock, Sandy Lyle, Reginald Macaulay, Humphrey Mackworth, William Macmichael, Thomas Mackworth, Stephen Marchant, John Marston, Stuart Mason, Thomas Minton, Richard More, Charlie Morris, Fred Morris, Len Murray, John Mytton, Frederick Oakeley, Graham Oakley, Job Orton, Harold Owen, Wilfred Owen, Edith Pargeter, Thomas Parr, Owen Paterson, Thomas Penson, Thomas Percy, Suzi Perry, Arthur Purves Phayre, Robert Phayre, Ambrose Philips, Edmund Plowden, Thomas Poole, Dilys Powell, Roger Preece, Tim Preece, Thomas Farnolls Pritchard, Adam Proudlock, Malcolm Pryce, Barbara Pym, James Quibell, Adam Rayner, John Hamilton Reynolds, Richard of Shrewsbury, Gordon Richards, Herbie Roberts, Henry Robinson, Henry John Roby, Richard Rolt, Margaret Rope, Trevor Rowley, Scott Ruscoe, Sybil Ruscoe, Darren Ryan, Lorna Sage, Thomas Savin, Jonathan Scott, Owen Seaman, Alexander Stanier, Hesba Stretton, Sir John Talbot, Richard Tarlton, Francis Tate, William Griffith Thomas, Peter Vaughan, Edward Waring (not him!), John Weaver, Mary Webb, Matthew Webb, Harry Weetman, Edward Weston, Stanley Weyman, Abraham Wheelocke, William White, Harold Whitfield, Nicholas Whittaker, Charles Wicksteed, John Lloyd Williams, William Withering, Ian Woosnam, William Wood, Richie Woodhall, Billy Wright, Thomas Wright, William Wycherley, George Wynn.

Shropshire Maps

1. Administrative Counties of England 1889–1965

Although Shropshire and its surrounding counties didn't change between 1965 and 1974, others did, the most significant being the abolition of the administrative counties of Middlesex and City of London which were replaced by Greater London.

2. Ceremonial Counties of England 1974–1996

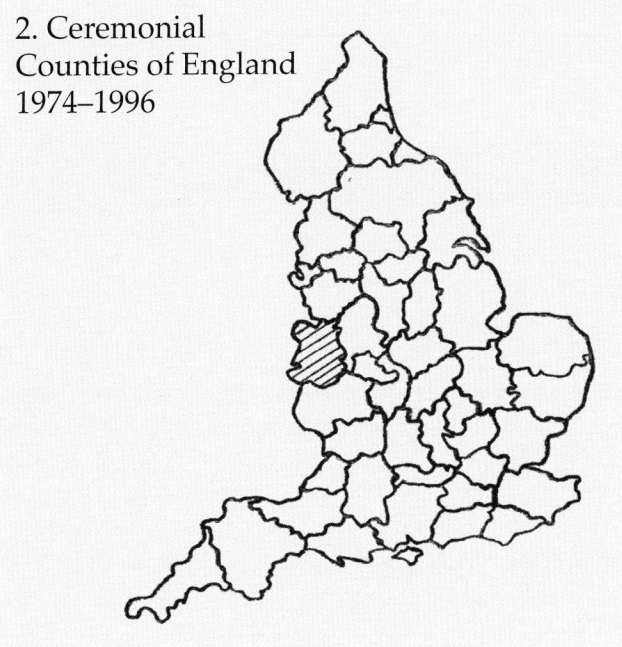

On 1st April 1974, several new counties appeared – including the merger of Herefordshire and Worcestershire on Shropshire's southern border. The new county – Hereford and Worcester – was then abolished in 1996 along with Avon, Cleveland and Humberside – and their former areas largely returned to the counties they took their land from in the first place (see top right).

3. Ceremonial Counties of England 1996–2019

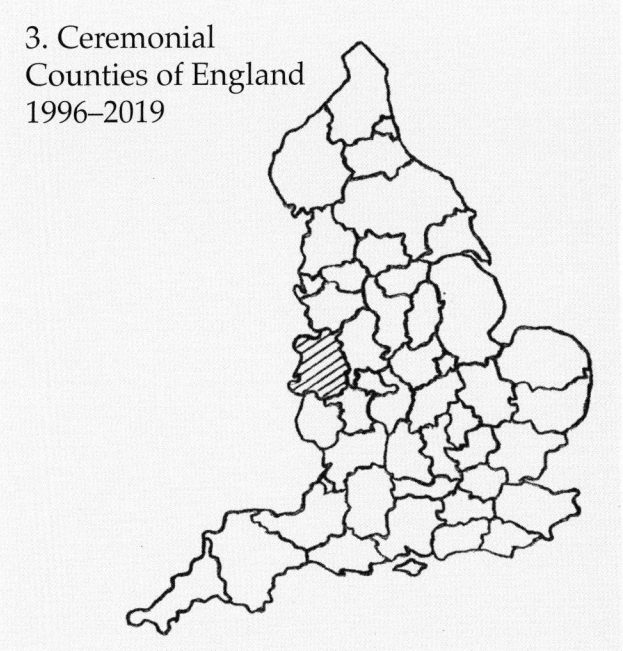

4. Shropshire Non-Metropolitan Districts 1974–2009

5. Shropshire Unitary Authorities 2009–2023

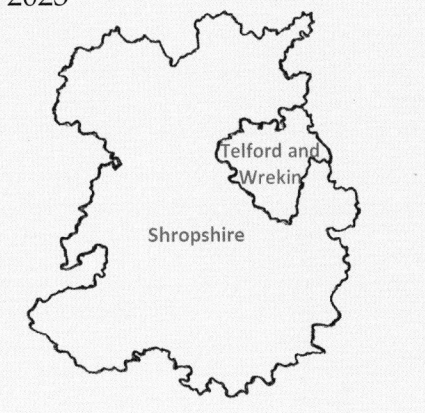

Shropshire County History

Prehistory

The county of Shropshire was created in the 10th or early 11th century, and is first recorded as *Scrobbescire* in 1006. By the time of Domesday Book (1086) it is recorded as *Sciropescire*, although it was also known as *Scrobbesbyrigscīr*, around that time, meaning "shire or district of the town of Shrewsbury". As for Shrewsbury, the name first appears as *Scrobbensis* in 901, as *Scrobbesbyrig* in the mid-11th century, and then again as *Sciropesberie* in Domesday Book (1086). The name probably means "fortified place of the scrubland region", deriving from the Old English words *scrobb* and *burh* (dative *byrig*), meaning "scrubland district" and "fortified place or stronghold", respectively. An alternative theory is "Scrobb's fort", with the former part deriving from an Old English personal name. Either way, the name gradually mutated over time, from *Sciropesberie*, to *Sloppesberie*, to *Schrosberie* and eventually to Shrewsbury.

Of course, Shropshire is also known as Salop, and this name derives from immediately after the Norman Conquest of 1066, when the county's new rulers named Shropshire and Shrewsbury as *Salopescire* and *Salopesbiry*, respectively. The abbreviated name survived from the Middle Ages as an alternative English form, while a Latin form, *Salopia*, was commonly used in documents in the 16th century, with legal records in subsequent centuries referring to the County of Salop, rather than Shropshire. That name was even revived as recently 1st April 1974, when the county was officially named as Salop – although this was altered back to Shropshire from 1st March 1980.

As for the *area* of Shropshire, that goes back much further and many of the most distinctive peaks in the county date from the Precambrian period, meaning they are constructed from some of the oldest rock on earth. To put this into perspective, the Precambrian period dates from 541 million years ago (Ma) to 4.6 billion years ago (when the earth was formed), and accounts for a whopping 88% of the Earth's geologic timeline. Indeed, the names Cambrian and Precambrian derive from the Latin name for Wales, *Cambria*, where rocks from this age were first studied. However, the peaks in question – such as the Wrekin, Lawley, Caer Caradoc and Earls Hill – date from the younger end of the Precambrian period, between 900 and 570 million years ago, and are formed of volcanic ashes and lavas.

The next oldest set of rocks formed during the Cambrian, Ordovician and Silurian periods (541 to 419 Ma), when Shropshire lay almost continuously under the sea, these being the mineral-rich areas around the Stiperstones, Wenlock Edge, Clun Forest and the limestones around Ludlow. These were followed by Devonian period rocks (419 to 359 Ma), such as the old red sandstone of the Corvedale and Clee Hills region, while the Carboniferous period (359 to 299 Ma) is represented by the coalfields of Coalbrookdale, Wyre Forest and Shrewsbury, and by the limestone belt which stretches north from Llanymynech Hill.

Moving forward to Permian and Triassic Shropshire (299 to 201 Ma), these periods are represented by the sandstones of the North Shropshire plains and the area east of the River Severn around Bridgnorth. That just leaves the clays, sands and gravels which cover much

> ### Quirk Alert: *Wrekin Legends*
> *Despite being formed of volcanic ashes and lava, there is no truth in the legend that the Wrekin was once an active volcano. Meanwhile, a stranger "legend" is that when that well-known traveller and memoirist, Celia Fiennes, visited Shropshire in 1698, it was claimed that the Wrekin was the highest point in England! Of course, it isn't even the highest point in Shropshire, as at 1,334ft, it is exceeded by the summits of Brown Clee (1,772ft), Stiperstones (1,762ft), Titterstone Clee (1,750ft), the Long Mynd (1,695ft) and Caer Caradoc (1,506ft).*

LEFT: The twin peaks of Lawley and Caer Caradoc. Along with the Wrekin, each of these mountains – which run from south-west to north-east through central Shropshire – date from the Precambrian period, over 570 million years ago and are amongst some of the oldest rocks on Earth. RIGHT: Ascending Lawley, heading in a south-westerly direction. The second "summit" is Lawley; Caer Caradoc is hidden behind it.

Lawley summit looking back north-east towards the Wrekin.

View from the summit of Caer Caradoc looking back north-east towards Lawley and the Wrekin.

And here are all three (Caer Caradoc, Lawley and the Wrekin), viewed from the summit of Bodbury Hill on a clearer day.

of the North Shropshire plains, which were deposited by ice sheets relatively recently – a mere two million years ago! When the ice retreated, the River Severn found itself cutting a new course. Previously, it had flowed into the Dee, but as the ice retreated, the Severn overflowed to the east and cut a passage through the Carboniferous and Silurian rocks – at what is now called Ironbridge Gorge. Also a legacy of the retreating ice, are the multiple meres and mosses of North Shropshire, extending from just south of Shrewsbury up to the Cheshire border.

For the oldest evidence of man in the area, we have to move forward to the Neolithic or New Stone Age period which ran from around 4500 to 2000 BC – as any earlier evidence of man was probably destroyed when the glaciers eroded their locations away. Neolithic evidence takes the form of scrapers and other implements made from local pebble flint, and found largely around the Wrekin, or on the county's south-eastern corner in parishes heading southwards from Worfield to Claverley and Alveley. Neolithic pottery and flintwork has also been discovered in the Wroxeter area dating from around 3500 to 3000 BC, but there is no further evidence of a settlement here at that time. Of the Neolithic arrowheads and stone axes found in the Wrekin area, some were made of stone from

The Mere at Ellesmere was carved out around 10,000 years ago by retreating glaciers during the last ice age, with the subsequent melt-water accounting for the water. The Mere is the largest of nine such meres in the locality. It is around 30ft deep (19m) and covers over 48 hectares – more than 70 football pitches!

Charnwood Forest, and others from stone as far afield as Cornwall.

Shropshire does have stone circles though, with the oldest dating from the late Neolithic (2500 to 2100 BC) or Bronze Age (2100 to 700 BC) periods. The best example is Mitchell's Fold stone circle. Located on the Welsh border at a height of 1,083ft (330m) above sea level, the circle is alternatively known as Medgel's Fold

Mitchell's Fold Stone Circle, a Scheduled Ancient Monument which dates from the Bronze Age – around 1500 BC.

or Madges Pinfold. Given the former part of the name, it is thought it may derive from the Old English word *micel* or *mycel* meaning "big" – in this case referring to the size of the circle. The stone circle was constructed using dolerite stones from nearby Stapeley Hill. Today there are 15 stones, arranged in a rough circle, but there may once have been as many as 30. The tallest stone was once one of a pair, and these would have formed an impressive entrance into the circle; there may also have been a central stone as well. The surviving stones range in height from 10in to 6ft 3in (1.91m), and are arranged in an elliptical shape 89ft (27m) on a north-west to south-easterly bearing by 82ft (25m). The tallest is at the south-eastern end of the major axis, standing close to the line of the southern moonrise.

As with other ancient stone circles, Mitchells Fold's purpose isn't fully understood, but it was probably of ritualistic importance to the people who built it, and may have provided a focus for funerary rites. Or perhaps it was used to mark important solar and lunar events with the stones deliberately aligned to emphasise such events.

The only other surviving stone circle in Shropshire is the Hoarstones located 1.5 miles north-east of Mitchell's Fold. The Hoarstones dates from a similar period to Mitchell's Fold, and is comprised of 37 (formerly 38) dolerite stones, all less than a metre high, while the circle has a diameter of 72ft (22m). There are also two small mounds in the north-west of the circle that may be the remnants of barrows. Interestingly, there are holes drilled in some of the stones, but these date from a much later period, thought to be when local miners would fill the holes with gunpowder and set it off as part of wedding celebrations!

The Hoarstones are located 1.5 miles to the north-east of Mitchell's Fold, and consist of 37 stones all less than a metre high.

Quirk Alert: *Legendary Stones*

As with many prehistoric sites, Mitchell's Fold Stone Circle is associated with a legend. This one states that during a time of famine, a fairy produced a magic cow that provided an endless supply of milk. Alas, one night an evil witch milked the cow into a sieve until it was dry, at which point the cow fled east to Warwickshire where she became the famous Dun Cow. As punishment, the witch was turned to stone and a circle of stones was erected around her, to ensure that she could not escape. Another legend replaces the fairy with a giant, while local folklore also suggests that this is the (yet another) place where King Arthur withdrew Excalibur from one of the stones in the circle and then became king of the Britons!

These two stone circles are also close to a late Neolithic or early Bronze Age picrite stone axe factory at Cwm-Mawr, where distinctive axe-hammers were produced and traded extensively into central Wales and England. Meanwhile, if you follow the path from Mitchell's Fold across Stapeley Common, you will find firstly the Cow Stone, a single standing stone or menhir, and secondly the Stapeley Hill Ring Cairn. It was probably also the folk of this period who made the dug-out canoes found in the mere country of north-west Shropshire, as well as the Perry Valley and Marton Pool on the mid-Shropshire border with Wales.

In addition to the stone circles, there is also plenty of Bronze Age evidence in Shropshire courtesy of multiple burial mounds or round barrows; in fact, there are 25 on the Long Mynd alone, most of them along the ancient trackway known as the Port Way. Elsewhere, Bronze Age burial mounds have been found on the gravel terrace south of Shrewsbury and the plain north of Ludlow. The latter area is thought to have been a site for burials from about 2560 BC and remained so for another eight centuries.

At Wroxeter, modern geophysical surveys have revealed a cluster of probable Bronze Age burial mounds dating from around 1500 BC, while contemporary flintwork along with a decorated fragment of an early Bronze Age 'pygmy cup' has also been found here, too. It is possible that the Wroxeter burial mounds were established at a time when the course of the Severn was being altered to its current alignment, with large amounts of silt deposited to form its new banks. It is thought that the silt was caused by massive and sudden deforestation further upstream, suggesting that much woodland clearance of the lowland Severn plain was taking place at this time. As a result, the Severn was transformed from a broad and shallow river, to a relatively narrow one that was difficult to ford.

In the south of the county, a vast number of Bronze Age flints have been found in fields and roadside verges which indicate a Bronze Age trading route which has been named as the Clee-Clun Ridgway. It stretched from Bewdley in the east, passed to the north of Ludlow and just south of Clunton and Clun,

Stapeley Hill Ring Cairn on top of Stapeley Hill dates from the Bronze Age.

then through Bettws-y-crwyn before heading north-westwards into Wales. Flints from the Marlborough Downs and East Anglia were traded along this route, and stone axes made at Hyssington near Corndon were exported from Shropshire territory.

From the 7th and 6th century BC, iron tools and weapons became more widespread and iron currency bars were used for trading. This heralded the beginning of the British Iron Age, which ran from around 700 B.C. to the 1st century AD. Wroxeter would later claim much greater importance, but in the Iron Age there were at least two ditched enclosures here. Elsewhere in the hinterland around Wroxeter a number of single-ditched enclosures have been found and, where excavated, these date from Iron Age and/or Roman times. The widespread nature of these enclosures indicates a settled and farmed landscape in the Wroxeter area with evidence for a mixed farming pattern of arable and pastoral agriculture set within a network of tracks and field boundaries.

The most prevalent legacy of Iron Age habitation is the hillfort, although a number show evidence of prior Bronze Age occupation too. The shropshirehistory.com website lists 68 Iron Age sites. Here is a brief summary of the most significant survivors, all of which are classified as Scheduled Monuments.

Iron Age Hillfort	*Features and Remains*
Beacon Ring, Pontesbury	Also known as Earl's Hill Camp. Buried remains of a small multivallate hillfort, sub-rectangular, with dimensions of 110m NW-SE by 280m SW-NE, enclosing c.2.9ha. Access from the north. Probably occupied by a large Iron Age community. Later altered to create two defended areas, one being an oval-shaped enclosure of c.1.1 ha constructed around the higher and rockiest part of the hill-top.
Berth, Baschurch	Two mounds of glacial deposits, originally surrounded by water, but now reduced to the Berth Pool. The larger mound is surrounded by a single rampart and the other by a single ditch, with both connected by a 120m causeway.
Billings Ring, Lydbury North	Situated on top of a ridge overlooking the River Onny to the north and east. Sub-rectangular in plan, 155m N-S by 225m E-W, enclosing c.1.7 ha.
Blodwell Rock Camp, Llanymynech	Situated on the cliff edge to the north of Llanymynech hillfort. Sub-rectangular in shape with an internal area of about 1.8ha. The defences are univallate for much of the circuit, doubled at the northern end.

Bodbury Ring, Church Stretton	Large univallate hillfort, believed to be a Bronze Age settlement reused in the Iron Age. It occupies a strong defensive position on the southern tip of Bodbury Hill. Roughly pear-shaped, measuring 120m NE-SW by 100m transversely, enclosing c.1ha. Strong NE-E facing rampart 6-10m wide, rising to 3.5m above base of outer ditch of 8m wide and 1.3m deep.
Burgs, Bayston Hill	Multivallate contour fort, sub-rectangular enclosing 2.1ha. Bivallate defences for most of circuit but on W/SW side are the remains of more complex arrangements of banks, 15m wide and up to 1.5m high – now in the gardens of various houses!
Burrow Hill Camp, Aston-on-Clun	Iron Age multivallate hillfort with an elongated tear-shaped trivallate enclosure situated on the brow of Burrow Hill.
Bury Ditches, Lydbury North	Small multivallate hillfort situated on the summit of a small but steep-sided hill at the NW end of Clunton Hill. Roughly oval measuring 374m SW-NE by 260m transversely, enclosing 3.3ha.

Some of the ramparts surrounding Beacon Hill (also known as Earls Hill), Pontesford.

The surviving northern rampart of Bodbury Ring near Church Stretton.

Ramparts at the top of Bury Ditches, located in the south-west of the county, just north of Clun.

Iron Age Hillfort	**Features and Remains**
Bury Walls, Weston-under-Redcastle	Large multivallate hillfort, occupying a well-defined promontory which forms part of the southern escarpment of an imposing sandstone ridge. Measures 380m E-W by 520m N-S, enclosing c.8ha.
Caer Caradoc, Church Stretton	Large multivallate hillfort with associated causeway and Caratacus' Cave, named after the legendary 1st century Welsh chieftain. Steep-sided hill just NE of Church Stretton, with hillfort lying along the spine of the hill, measuring 450m SW-NE by 160m transversely, enclosing 3 ha. Defences include well-defined inner and outer ramparts, in places incorporating natural rock outcrops.
Caer Caradoc, Clun	Roughly D-shaped, this Caer Caradoc measures 180m NW-SE by 390m SW-NE, enclosing c.2.1 ha. The defences were built on a massive scale with two ramparts separated by a rock-cut ditch on the SE and N sides, and with an additional outer ditch and counterscarp bank aligned with the latter.
Caerbre, Chirbury	Univallate promontory fort in a bend of the River Camlad, measuring 200m N-S by 100m E-W. Bounded to W by rocky cliffs falling to river 300ft below, and to S & N by steep natural slopes; E enclosed by large earth and stone rampart.
Caer Din Ring, Bishop's Castle	Enclosed settlement measuring 114m E-W by 122m N-S, enclosing c.0.85ha. Earthworks consist of earth and stone bank of between 6 to 9.5m wide and up to 1.8m high, and an external ditch between 3 to 4.5m wide.
Calcot Camp, Chirbury	Univallate hillfort sited on a promontory overlooking the River Camlad. Ramparts to N and E consist of steep scarp slopes, and the site was probably rectangular, measuring around 130m by 120m.
Callow Hill, Minsterley	Buried remains of a small triangular multivallate hillfort, measuring 96m NW-SE by 146m SW-NE, enclosing c.0.3ha. Slopes steeply on eastern and western sides, deep ravine to south; much of north destroyed by quarrying.
Castle Hill, All Stretton	A roughly sub-rectangular motte with a level platform, measuring 20m N-S by 22m E-W. Some earthworks remain.
Castle Ring, Meadowtown	Univallate hillfort, roughly oval, measuring 115m NW-SE by 185m SW-NE, enclosing c.1ha.
Castle Ring, Ratlinghope	Univallate hillfort incorporating a series of cross dykes. Roughly triangular measuring 160m E-W by 170m N-S, enclosing c.1ha.

Bury Walls, near Weston-under-Redcastle.   *Some of the ramparts towards the summit of Caer Caradoc, looking southwards.*   *Surviving ramparts on Callow Hill, Minsterley.*

Iron Age Hillfort	Features and Remains
Castle Ring, Snailbeach	Large univallate hillfort in a strong defensive position on the summit of Oak Hill, a steep sided spur at the north end of Stiperstones. Roughly triangular, it measures 280m NNE-SSW by 190m transversely, enclosing c.3.8ha.
Caus Castle, Westbury	Situated on a prominent hill at the SE end of Long Mountain. Roughly rectangular, measuring 200m NW-SE by 565m SW-NE, enclosing c.4.7ha.
Caynham Camp, Ludlow	Large univallate hillfort situated on the summit of a small spur at the western foot of the Clee Hill escarpment. Roughly oval, measuring 460m SW-NE by 190m transversely, enclosing c.4ha.
Chesterton Walls, Worfield	Large multivallate hillfort, occupying a slightly elevated position in an area of undulating land, within an angled, steep-sided bend of the Stratford Brook. Roughly D-shaped, measuring 340m N-S by 620m NW-SE, enclosing c.9.5ha.
Coed-y-Gaer, Rhydycroesau	Located on an isolated hill with steep drop on the north and west sides. Roughly oval, univallate hillfort with the long axis north-east to south-west.
Coxall Knoll, Bucknell	Buried remains of a large multiple enclosure hillfort, situated on the summit of a natural outcrop. Roughly oval, it has three enclosures with max dimensions of 570m E-W, and 200m N-S.
Ditches, Longville in the Dale	Also known as Wynbury Castle, this multivallate hillfort is sited in coniferous woodland and old coppice. Almost circular with three lines of bank and ditch. The ramparts are largely preserved and widely spaced.
Ebury Hill, Uffington	D-shaped univallate hillfort, measuring 230m NW to SE by 250m SW to NE, enclosing c.3.6ha. Ramparts of earth and stone have an average width of 12m; height varies from 1.5m to 3.2m externally and 0.7m to 2.1m internally.
Haughmond Hill, Uffington	Irregular polygonal univallate hillfort, measuring 155m N-S by 230m E-W. Interior rampart survives as a discontinuous earthwork incorporating the steep natural scarps and rock outcrops of the hilltop. SE rampart is c.17m wide and 1.8m high; less pronounced to the north and survives as a scarp about 0.8m high.
Lawley, Longnor	Small hilltop enclosure situated at northern end of Lawley; a NE-SW orientated razor-backed ridge of high ground. Earthworks lie along axis of hill, forming an elongated, hour-glass-shaped enclosure with internal dimensions of 85m long by 22m wide at the widest point, and 14m at the waist.
Linley Camp, Norbury	Small earthwork of a bank with outer ditch at the top of Linley Hill, measuring 21m each way. The bank is 6m wide by 0.3m high on the inside and 0.8m above the present base of the ditch – which is 4m wide and 0.5m deep.
Llanymynech Hill, Pant	One of Britain's largest hillforts, enclosing 57ha. Possible tribal centre housing large population. Mining location for copper ore used in manufacture of bronze weapons and implements; Bronze Age mining implements found in caves here. S and W sides very steep, with single rampart, later incorporated into Offa's Dyke. Some ramparts survive, but much damage caused by quarrying.
Nescliffe Hill Camp, Great Ness	D-shaped multivallate hillfort, enclosing 1ha, with a multivallate annexe of 0.1ha to the east. Constructed on a cliff edge which falls to the N & W. Defences are bivallate for much of the circuit except for the north side of the annexe where only part of a single rampart remains. Measures 185m N-S by 310m E-W, enclosing c.2.8ha. Its size suggests occupation by a large community.

Nordy Bank, Clee St Margaret	Univallate hillfort occupying strong defensive position on Nordy Bank, the tip of a spur of high ground running west from the main plateau of Brown Clee Hill. Roughly oval-shaped, earthworks measure 260m E-W by 198m N-S, enclosing c.3.2ha. Defences include well-defined rampart averaging 1.5m high around all but the east side, where it is up to 2.8m high. The outer face averages 4.2m in height, falling to an outer ditch varying between 8m and 5m wide and averaging 1.5m deep. There are five entrances with the main entrance in the NE corner.
Norton Camp, Culmington	Buried remains of large D-shaped multivallate hillfort above the Onny Valley, on a precipitous slope and cliff. Measures 350m NW-SE by 360m SW-NE, enclosing c.7ha. Size indicates large economic and social community.

Ramparts at the top of Nescliffe Hill Camp.   *Impressive ramparts at Nordy Bank.*   *Looking towards Nortonwood Camp.*

Iron Age Hillfort	Features and Remains
Old Oswestry, Oswestry	A striking and nationally rare multivallate hillfort, situated on a glacial mound. Flints and a stone axe suggest activity since Neolithic times; excavation revealed occupation from Late Bronze Age through to end of Iron Age. Incorporated into the line of Wat's Dyke in 8th century. Diamond-shaped, measuring 570m NE-SW by 420m NW-SE, enclosing c.8.4ha. Ramparts of five earthen banks and ditches, interrupted by two complex entrances on E and W sides. The inner two banks and ditches are the earliest, probably dating to the 6th century B.C.
Pontesbury Hill Camp, Pontesbury	Buried remains of small multivallate hillfort on Pontesford Hill, half a mile south of the hillfort on Earl's Hill. Constructed around a steeply-sided shelf, it measures 105m NW-SE by 140m SW-NE, enclosing c.0.3ha.
Radnor Wood Camp, Clunbury	Earthworks form three sides of a rectangle with rounded corners, all largely covered in bracken and bramble. North side is 40m, west 50m and south 60m. The lack of an eastern rampart suggests the site was unfinished.
Ratlinghope Hill Camp, Ratlinghope	A univallate enclosure towards the S end of steep-sided spur below Stitt Hill. Pear-shaped, measuring 130m NW-SE by 110m NE-SW, enclosing c.1ha.
Ritton Castle, The Bog	Buried remains of univallate hillfort constructed around a projecting shelf on the NW side of Brooks Hill, where the ground slopes steeply to N, W & S. Sub-rectangular, measuring 116m NW-SE by 215m SW-NE, enclosing c.1ha.
Roveries, Lydham	Small oval univallate hillfort on summit of Roveries Hill; 264m SW-NE by 110m NW-SE, enclosing c.2.5ha. Previous Neolithic occupation.
Titterstone Clee, Bitterley	Focus of ritual activity during Bronze Age, but probably not occupied as a hillfort until early Iron Age, when a system of defences encircled hilltop. Large site measuring 770m E-W by 450m N-S, enclosing c.28ha. Ramparts made extensive use of drystone walling, still largely visible as tumbled stone wall. Defences badly damaged by modern quarrying to S.
Wall Camp, Kynnersley	Large oval multivallate hillfort on elevated area of sandstone and boulder clay surrounded by extensive area of peat. Measures 590m N-S by 690m E-W, enclosing c.12ha. Earthwork defences of multiple banks separated by ditches, with the best-preserved to the W and N, standing at c.2m in height.
Walton Camp, Worthen	Oval bivallate hillfort on isolated knoll. Measures 120m E-W by 145m N-S, enclosing c.0.5ha. Two ramparts of earth and stone, bounded by external ditches with an outer bank enclosing all except NE. Defences tallest on W and S sides – combined height of inner rampart/ditch of 3.2m; combined measurement for outer rampart/ditch of 2.3m.

Wrekin, Little Wenlock	Large multivallate hillfort, encompassing the entire spinal summit of the Wrekin, measuring 150m NW-SE by 900m SW-NE, enclosing c.8ha. Pottery suggests a Bronze Age settlement of c.900 to 800 B.C., but the hillfort is Iron Age and dates from 700 to 500 B.C. Size indicates large community where centralised economic, social and ceremonial activities practiced. Earthworks of two ramparts with steep outer faces separated mainly by a narrow ditch – now infilled. Tops of ramparts and adjacent infilled ditches resemble terraces running around the sides of the hill. NE entrance known as "Hell Gate", where ends of inner rampart turn inward to form an entrance passage about 3.5m wide. SW entrance is 2m wide, flanked by a series of banks and ditches, now visible as low earthworks.

Some of the massive ramparts and ditches at the western end of Old Oswestry.

The Wrekin, site of an Iron Age hillfort and probably the capital of the Brythonic tribe known as the Cornovii.

Close-up of some of the natural western-facing defences at the top of The Wrekin.

Within many of these deep ditches and high, stockade-topped ramparts, there were closely-packed rectangular and round huts, some used for accommodation and some for storage. It is thought that these Iron Age hillforts could support around 210 people per hectare – hence some of the larger hillforts like that on the Wrekin supported around a thousand people. Meanwhile, more recent archaeology has proven that there were also many lowland Iron Age settlements too, such as a clutch of Iron Age farmsteads along the Severn Valley between Montford Bridge and Buildwas. Iron Age farmsteads usually took the form of large round dwellings made of a circle of timber poles with low wattle-and-daub walls and a thatched roof, with the property surrounded by a ditch.

Throughout the Iron Age in Britain, Shropshire territory was home to the Celtic *Cornovii* tribe. *Cornovii* territory stretched from the northern tip of the Wirral all the way down to northern Herefordshire and Worcestershire, and across from much of Cheshire and Staffordshire, through Shropshire to parts of eastern Powys, Flintshire and Wrexham. Indeed, the *Cornovii* capital of pre-Roman Britain, was almost certainly the large hillfort on the Wrekin, while Ptolemy's 2nd century *Geography* names two *Cornovii* towns: *Deva Victrix* (Chester), and *Viroconium Cornoviorum* (Wroxeter). As for the economy of the *Cornovii*, this was mainly pastoral, with some evidence of cereal crop cultivation, while they also created a network of paved and semi-paved roads which would have supported their product distribution.

Throughout the Iron Age, the *Cornovii* were involved in conflicts and tribal disputes with their neighbours, these being the *Brigantes* to the north, the *Corieltauvi* to the east, the *Dobunni* to the south, and the *Deceangli*, and *Ordovices* to the west. Alas, each tribe was unaware that a far stronger foe from afar was eyeing their territory and the riches within...

Romans, Anglo-Saxons and Vikings

The Romans invaded Britain in AD 43, and by AD 45 they had constructed the Fosse Way, which ran all the way from Exeter (*Isca Dumnoniorum*) in the south-west of Britain, to Lincoln (*Lindum*). The Romans controlled all areas to the south and east of that line, but they began to operate beyond it under the second and third Roman governors of *Britannia*, Publius Ostorius Scapula (AD 47 to AD 52) and Didius Gallus (AD 52 to AD 57). For example, a fort was built at Wall (*Letocetum*), just south of Lichfield in around AD 48, thus establishing a forward base for Roman forays westwards towards Wales, along the ancient Brythonic grassy trackway that they named as Watling Street.

Aerial photography has revealed a grouping of temporary Roman military camps, that are probably from this period, and are located around what would then have been the *Cornovii* capital on the Wrekin. This fits with the English Heritage view that "the legions appear to have stormed and set fire to the hillfort on the Wrekin which caused the tribal leaders to capitulate rapidly". The Romans then established a garrison in the region and continued its campaign to the west and north. As well as Roman encroachment via Watling Street, they also advanced westwards into southern Shropshire territory along the road from the fort at Greensforge, thus ensuring that both banks of the River Severn were covered. Further forts were established at Wall in south-eastern Shropshire territory, and at

Leintwardine (*Bravonium*), with a further marching camp established at Stretford Bridge near modern-day Craven Arms.

One of the most prominent characters of this period is the Briton, Caratacus, and it is likely that his famous "last stand" against the Romans in AD 51, took place in Shropshire territory. Caratacus was a chieftain of the *Catuvellauni* tribe, who were based around modern-day Buckinghamshire, Bedfordshire and Hertfordshire, and just prior to the Roman invasion, Caratacus is associated with the *Catuvellauni* expansion west into *Atrebates* territory (modern-day Berkshire). The ousted *Atrebates* queen, Verica, fled to Rome and appealed to the emperor Claudius for help. This was allegedly the excuse Claudius had been looking for to invade Britain in the summer of AD 43. Caratacus then led the defence of the country against Aulus Plautius's four legions of around 40,000 men, primarily using guerrilla tactics. Much territory was lost to the Romans, though, and *Camulodunon* (Colchester) was converted into the first Roman *colonia* in Britain, *Colonia Victricensis*.

According to Tacitus, Caratacus's next move was to lead the Welsh tribes of the *Silures* and *Ordovices* against Plautius's successor, Publius Ostorius Scapula (AD 47 to AD 52). It is thought that Scapula defeated Caratacus in AD 51, in a set-piece battle somewhere in *Ordovician* or *Cornovii* territory, with Caer Caradoc just north of Church Stretton a likely location – and hence its name, which derives from Caratacus himself. Caratacus allegedly fled north after this defeat, to the territory of the *Brigantes* where the *Brigantian* queen, Cartimandua, promptly handed him over to the Romans in chains! He was sentenced to death as a military prisoner, but allegedly made a speech before his execution that persuaded the Emperor Claudius to spare him. Back in *Britannia*, though, the capture of Caratacus saw much of southern Britain from the Humber to the Severn pacified and garrisoned.

The early AD 50s saw a small garrison of around 500 men established at Wroxeter in a fort which measured around 5.8 acres (2.3ha). It was located on the east bank of the Severn, probably to guard the ford there, and may also have been home to a detachment of cavalry. Meanwhile, several other temporary forts or fortresses are known in the immediate area of Wroxeter at this time, suggesting it was a very active base. However, in around AD 57, there was a concerted Roman attempt to subjugate the whole of Wales, and it was probably at this time that the 14th Legion (*Legio XIIII Gemina*) moved its headquarters further west from *Letocetum* (Wall) to Wroxeter, and the resulting legionary fortress and later settlement became known as *Viroconium Cornoviorum*. The fortress was located with its northern rampart on the highest point in Wroxeter on a gently sloping plateau between two streams running east-to-west that cut off approaches to the fortress from the north and south. To the west, the fortress was protected by the River Severn but to the east there was no natural defence.

The fortress was of conventional design with the main gate facing westwards, towards the enemy. We know little of the detail of this early fortress, although most of the buildings and the defences were made of timber. However, parts of some barrack blocks have been excavated as well as some storehouses, while a granary is also visible near a gate on the north side. Meanwhile, a small civilian trading settlement known as a *vicus* developed, close to the ford, south of the fortress. The initial inhabitants may have moved to the region by travelling up the River Severn, given finds from this period include pottery from the Malverns and coins issued by the neighbouring tribe to the south, the Dobunni. Another, more formal settlement under the control of the legion, may also have been established north of the fortress.

It is thought that the fortress at Wroxeter was occupied in three distinct phases, this being in-line with Roman military activity during this period. The initial phase ran from AD 57 to AD 66 when it was home to the 14th Legion, while the fortress was refurbished for a second phase of use from AD 66 to AD 78 – which was probably when the 20th Legion (*Legio XX Valeria Victrix*) replaced the 14th. The

The surviving Roman city of Viroconium Cornoviorum, *at modern-day Wroxeter. Founded in the mid-1st century AD, originally as a legionary fortress, the town or civitas was established here in the late 1st century and remained inhabited until the 7th century. The large wall is known as the Old Work, and was part of the Palaestra or Baths Basilica, the exercise hall of the bath house which measured 240ft by 69ft (73m by 21m). Symbolically, the Wrekin is in the background – the* Cornovii *capital before the Romans invaded!*

final phase appears to have coincided with the fortress being turned from an active base into a storage facility and reserve base. *Viroconium Cornoviorum* ceased as a primary military base at this time as it had been superseded by *Deva Victrix* (modern-day Chester) 40 miles further north, with the latter commencing as home to the 20th Legion for the next 300 years. Before they left *Viroconium* in the late AD 80s though, the 20th Legion ensured that they levelled the fortress defences. It is also thought that they were in the process of building a bath-house as a gift to the town, but they were never completed for reasons unknown.

Nevertheless, *Viroconium Cornoviorum* was gradually converted into a civilian town over the next two decades, and initially made use of the previous fortress street grid, and some of its buildings. The town soon became the tribal capital of the *Cornovii*, and although its town council would have been mostly comprised of local aristocrats, it would almost certainly have included some of the 20th Legions' veterans who had chosen to retire here. As for the town, it soon absorbed all of the fortress and its annexes, as well as both sides of the Bell Brook valley. A street grid of 48 town blocks was laid out, and it is thought that the first *mansio* was built at this time – a hostel where official travellers could stay and get a change of horses, a meal and a bath.

The development of *Viroconium Cornoviorum* accelerated in the AD 120s, possibly due to a visit by the Emperor Hadrian in AD 122. This is probably when both the baths and the forum were built, and the

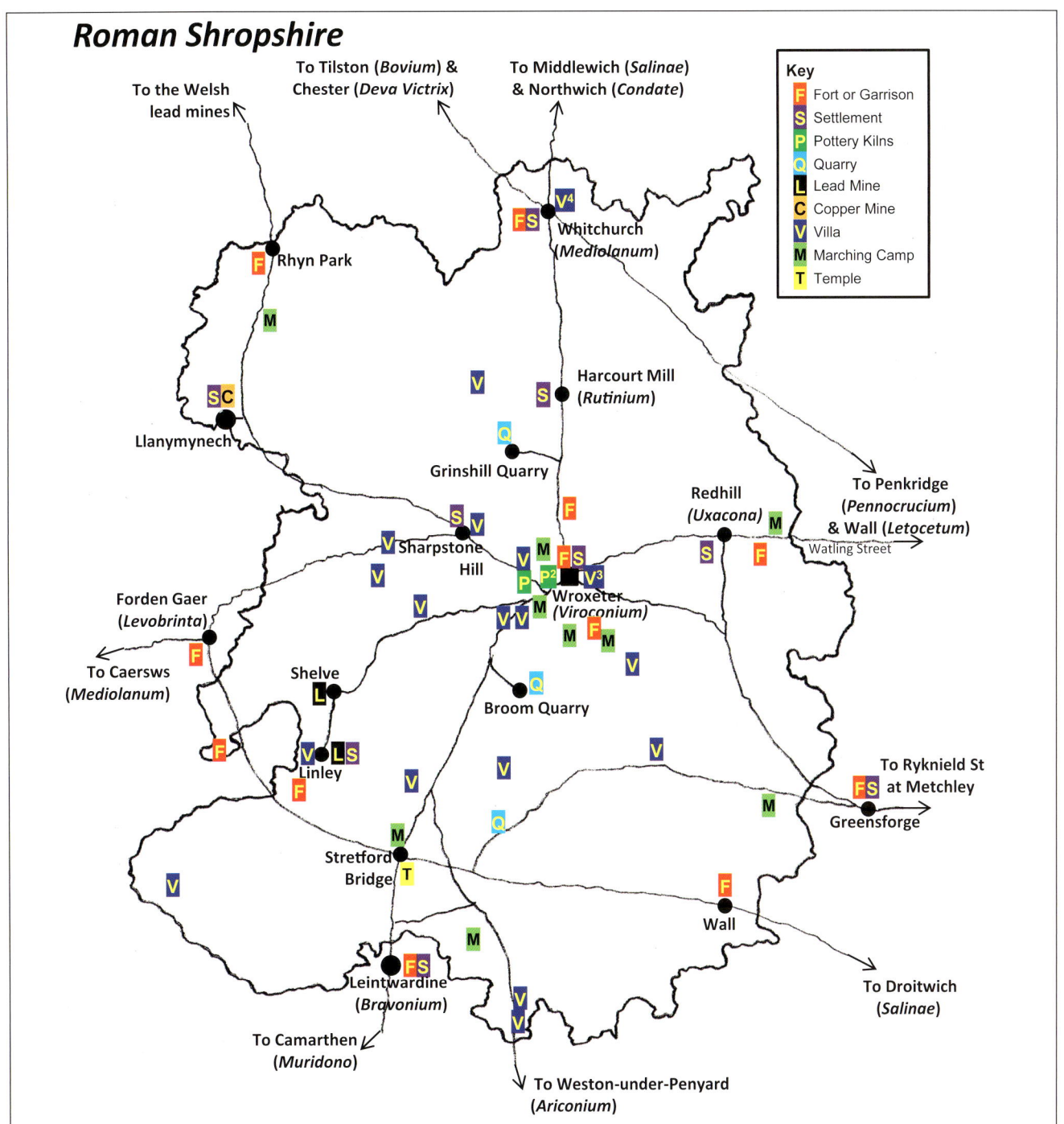

Stone from Viroconium Cornoviorum was re-used in subsequent builds of Wroxeter St Andrew's church. LEFT: Roman stone incorporated into the north external wall of the nave. CENTRE: This enormous stone font is probably the base of a former Roman column. RIGHT: These sandstone churchyard gate piers were made in the 19th century by re-using Roman masonry thought to have originated from Wroxeter's Roman baths.

impressive inscription that had been located above the main entrance to the forum actually survives, thus giving us the date of its completion – AD 129–30. The forum measured 242ft by 225ft (74m by 69m) which is large when compared to other forums in *Britannia* at that time. It followed a standard plan, with a range of shops along the street frontage, a courtyard behind with a colonnade around it on all four sides and, on the far side of the courtyard, a large basilican hall with a range of rooms behind it. However, although the foundations for the baths had been laid at around the same time, construction of the bath complex only really got under way in the AD 140s with completion in around AD 150. Meanwhile, on the south side of the east end of the hall, a shorter arm of the building provided the main entrance, which survives today as 'The Old Work', while beyond this were humid heated rooms like a Turkish Bath with symmetrical suites on either side.

Both forum and baths were laid out on either side of the main road through the town centre, which entered the town at its north-east corner and exited at the south-west, where the ford was located. The town's main temple was located to the north of the forum, which we know thanks to the discovery in the 1850s of colonnades of distinctive square-based columns at that location. The market was located at the highest point of the town, where the town's water supply arrived via a long V-shaped aqueduct, fed by the Bell Brook and which emptied into a huge cistern located just inside the town's defences. Elsewhere, were houses for the wealthy. Of those excavated, a mixture has been found, some with mosaics and floors of herringbone tiles, some with ornate plaster vaulting, and some with underfloor heating provided by the standard Roman *hypocaust* system. There is even evidence of doors being secured by locks and padlocks. And in the town, bronze busts and brooches were made by some of the many metal-working craftsmen who flourished in the town.

By this stage, the place had been promoted to a city (*Civitas Cornoviorum*). It was also the seat of government for the *Cornovii* and the fourth largest city in Roman Britain – almost as large as Pompeii.

Defences were constructed around the town towards the end of the 2nd century, enclosing an area of 63ha (180 acres), and consisted of a 2.5-mile double rampart, topped by a palisaded stockade. This was refurbished in the 4th century, when the rampart was enlarged and the external double ditch was replaced by a single wider one.

There is plenty of evidence elsewhere in Shropshire territory of Roman military activities from the 1st century AD – such as its own fortress called Wall, this one located in a small valley around 1.5 miles north-east of the crossing of the river Rea at Cleobury Mortimer. The fort was also aligned a menacing 6 miles due east of the Brythonic hillfort at Titterstone Clee! The Roman fort is thought to have been a simple and standard-sized defensive square enclosure of around 1.8ha. Roof and *hypocaust* tiles along with Roman pottery were discovered during road-widening in 1929, but it wasn't until 1953 that it was identified as a Roman military settlement which was then excavated in 1960/61. The defences were fronted by a stone revetment sometime in the 2nd century, while the earliest pottery finds there were Samian ware dating from the Neronian period (AD 54 to 68) or early-Flavian (commenced AD 69 to 96). The fort is thought to be Neronian, but was replaced by a larger Flavian fort, perhaps during the initial consolidation of Governor Gnaeus Julius Agricola (AD 77 to 85) prior to his march upon Anglesey (*Mona*) and his campaigns into Scotland (*Caledonia*). The fort at Wall was abandoned in around AD 160.

Further military buildings have been identified at Whitchurch (*Mediolanum*), while in the north-west of the county on the banks of the Ceiriog at Rhyn Park, a major camp of 48 acres (19ha) is thought to have been a 1st century camp used during one of the Welsh campaigns. *Mediolanum* was probably constructed in the early AD 50s, and would have formed part of the border with Wales, established by Publius Ostorius Scapula. The fort was demolished in around AD 100, but at *Mediolanum*, a settlement succeeded the fort. The place was home to two early 2nd century wells with small, rectangular buildings and surrounding fences at the well-head, while several timber-framed buildings of industrial character existed by the mid-2nd century. As the settlement prospered, more substantial stone buildings were constructed in the late 2nd and early 3rd century.

The fort at Rhyn Park wasn't discovered until 1975 when two overlapping encampments were spotted from the air. They stood on the English side of the River Ceiriog with the western side of the smaller camp overlying the eastern defences of the larger camp. Both were probably vexillation forts – rectangular with rounded corners – and both were occupied on a temporary basis by a campaigning army of between 2,500 to 4,000 men, comprised of varying proportions of legionary and auxiliary troops. Archaeologists are uncertain of the dates, but it is thought that the larger fort was constructed in the mid-1st century, probably to support the campaigns against the *Deceangli* of North Wales. It was actually an irregular quadrilateral, measuring 1,080ft on the north side, 1,240ft (south), 1,640ft (east) and 1,530ft (west). This fortress was succeeded by a smaller, but still large fort, and which probably dated from around AD 75. The eastern defences have been lost to erosion but the east-to-west dimension is thought to have been around 1,000ft while the north-to-south is around 750ft.

This clock in Whitchurch proudly announces the town's Roman name.

Other smaller Roman forts were built at Duncot, Eaton Constantine, Lydham, Pentreheyling and Shifnal. Most of these were early forts dating from the mid-1st century and soon fell into disuse. In addition, there were lots of marching camps in Shropshire territory. The network of roads on page 17 shows the routes that Roman soldiers took, and the location of the forts where they were based. Romano-British settlements or *vici* grew up around the forts at both Wroxeter and Whitchurch, while two other settlements grew up around the copper and lead mining locations of Llanymynech and Linley, respectively. The only other known Shropshire-based settlements of this period were at Redhill (*Uxacona*) and Sharpstone Hill.

As for the location of Roman villas, these are captured in the following table.

Villa	Description
Acton Scott	This villa had a *hypocaust* system and painted wall plaster, and was probably owned by the master of the lead mines at nearby Linley. It was located alongside what was known as Watling Street West, which ran from Wroxeter (*Viroconium*) to Camarthen (*Muridono*).
Ashford Carbonell	Two villas linked by an enclosing wall on their eastern side. The first measured 88ft by 36ft and the second 118ft by 46ft.
Atcham	Micaceous flagstones, roof slates and box tiles have been discovered, all indicative of a villa.
Berrington	Evidence of two villas. Finds at the first site include a pit containing pottery, while at the second, pottery, tiles and villa rubble were found.
Bettws-y-Crwyn	A villa is suspected here following the unearthing of pottery and an urn.
Cruckton	Much Roman evidence destroyed by modern housing, but excavations revealed a four-roomed building with a *hypocaust* system, along with other building remains dating to the 2nd century.
Lea Cross	Excavations have identified three phases of construction. The first was just a bath-house, while the second phase raised the floor-level by 2ft with an infill of rubble containing pottery from the turn of the 3rd century. The third phase saw industrial usage in the 4th century.
Linley	Two villas. Two mosaics from the first villa can still be found in More church. The second villa was large, measuring 32ft by 14ft and contained three rooms with pillared *hypocausts* of tile and roughly cut stone – although only one floor of lime and pounded brick remains. Along the outside of the east wall was a well-made stone drain, and beyond it, a channel of flue tiles with a small chamber 11ft by 8ft projecting on its east side, while a stone aqueduct ran along the west end of the building and was traced for a distance of 880 feet north-east.
Pimhill	Excavations in Alkmund Park revealed rooms with a *hypocaust*, possibly a bath-house, while a V-shaped ditch contained pottery and tiles.
Sharpstone Hill	Pottery, glass and tiles have been found, dating from the 2nd century. From the 3rd century to the end of the 4th century, the site or settlement was primarily involved in industrial activities.
Upton Cressett	Pottery found here dates from the 2nd to 4th century, and includes Samian, Rhenish and Severn Valley ware. Though covering an area at least 200 yards square, no building material has been found, except for one fragment of a tegula tile.

Whitchurch	Also known as *Mediolanum*, this Roman town was home to four villas.
Whitley Grange	Well-preserved remains of a *hypocaust* system suggest a bath-house complex dating from the 3rd century with 4th century additions. A mainly red, white and green mosaic was discovered which dates from the 4th century, with the central medallion originally decorated with a bust of Medusa. The residential part of the villa consists of a service corridor and three small rooms.
Wroxeter	Three villas. One of them had substantial masonry walls adjacent to the ramparts of *Viroconium*, while a cremation in a grey ware jar was found nearby. Another villa had building material including brick and tile fragments, and at least one tegula, with mortar and stone.
Yarchester	Discovered in 1957, the building consisted of rooms arranged around a central courtyard, while part of the villa had a *hypocaust* system. At least partly-roofed with lozenge-shaped slates, while a late 4th century mosaic was discovered in what was probably the dining room.

The Romans also had key lead mines at Linley and Shelve, and a copper mine at Llanymynech. The latter is known as the Ogof, and it was here that a group of schoolboys found 30 denarii (Roman coins) in 1965. Other Roman coin hoards have been found at Child's Ercall (2,800 coins in a grey coarse ware jar, dating from AD 253 to 282), Church Stretton (3rd century coins), Cleobury North (small hoard of silver coins), Hordley (362 coins dating AD 138-282 contained in a small black burnished vessel), Moreton Say (c.1000 coins dating between AD 253-279), and Wroxeter (many coins found dating from 364 to 383).

It is generally accepted that the Romans left Britain in AD 410. As for the incoming culture, this is easier to measure on the eastern side of England, where Anglo-Saxon encroachment and settlement was extensive. However, in the west of England it was a different story, and evidence of Anglo-Saxon settlement in Shropshire territory is rare before the 7th century – but it is clear that several hillforts were re-occupied by Britons in the post-Roman period. As for Roman Wroxeter, archaeology tells us that the baths were maintained until the late 5th century before they were systematically dismantled. Over the cleared ruins a number of building platforms were created, designed to support timber structures. These houses seem to have formed a nucleus of buildings clustered in the town centre. It is not clear when Wroxeter was abandoned, but it may have occurred in the mid-6th century, when a 'Great Plague' is known to have swept through both Britain and Western Europe. Alternatively, it may have been dismantled in the 7th century when the Anglo-Saxons took control of the region. Despite the abandonment of the town centre, though, a small village formed around the ford at the south end of the town.

The Roman departure had a severe effect on Britain's economy which didn't return to similar levels until the late Anglo-Scandinavian period. It is thought that the Roman bureaucratic system designed to maintain Roman laws and to levy taxes, soon disintegrated. Naturally, this had a negative effect on trading and the economy reverted overwhelmingly back to agriculture. Britain then gradually became settled by the Angles and Saxons of northern Europe. The traditional view of Anglo-Saxon colonisation is that groups of Angles settled in Lincolnshire before pushing their way up the Trent valley into the Midlands. A further Anglo-Saxon incursion arrived via The Wash and headed westwards, eventually settling in the Upper Avon valley as well as migrating along Watling Street which eventually brought them into Shropshire territory, as did a likely incursion up the Severn.

However, it is also known that the Romans used Teutonic migrants and German mercenaries known as the *foederati* to help them defend the countryside. After the Roman departure, many of these *foederati* were given land and allowed to settle in Britain. In Shropshire territory, a man called Cunorix was probably the leader of a group of mercenaries employed in warfare during this

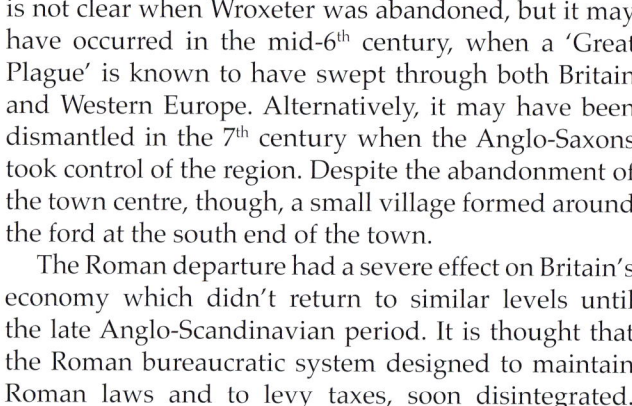

LEFT: *One of two mosaics inside More church, and which originated from the nearby Roman villa at Linley.* CENTRE: *The font at Shrewsbury Abbey is made from the base of a Roman column, which probably originated from Wroxeter.* RIGHT: *This sculpture can be found in Much Wenlock museum and is thought to date from Roman times, therefore providing evidence of an early religious water cult in the area. It was not uncommon for springs like that at Milburgas Well in Much Wenlock, to have been the site of rituals in Prehistoric times, and then adopted in the Roman period as the site of a shrine.*

period – although he was an Irishman whose tomb had been found at Wroxeter and dated from AD 460 to 480. His death and defeat may well have had something to do with the Romano-British war leader, Ambrosius Aurelianus, who re-established control from these mercenaries following the Battle of Badon in the late 5th century.

During the 6th century, Shropshire territory was subject to the rule of Urien of Rheged, whose lands stretched from Galloway all the way down to Wroxeter. However, by the 7th century, Rheged had disappeared, absorbed by the new kingdom of Northumbria, and hence Shropshire territory may have reverted to rule by Romano-British tribes. We can surmise this thanks to the *Tribal Hidage*, a census of Anglo-Saxon territories south of the Humber which was compiled sometime between the 7th and 9th centuries. The *Tribal Hidage* lists two tribes called the *Wrēocensǣte* to the north of Shropshire territory and the *Magonsǣte* to the south – both occupying territory which had formerly been part of the Iron Age *Cornovii* tribe. However, as the map right shows, the Anglo-Saxons were now largely encamped on their eastern doorstep. This probably explains why the *Wrēocensǣte* and the *Magonsǣte* retained strong links with the Celtic kingdoms of Gwynedd and Powys, to the west, both of which had emerged after the Roman departure and which also covered part of the lands previously occupied by the *Cornovii*.

In terms of territory, *Wrēocensǣte* lands stretched down from modern Cheshire into the northern half of Shropshire, including Wroxeter, and the name probably means "the Wrekin-dwellers". *Magonsǣte* territory largely covered southern Shropshire, Herefordshire, Monmouthshire and parts of western Gloucestershire. In around 616, though, it is thought that the *Wrēocensǣte* were defeated by King Æthelfrith and the Northumbrians at a battle fought at Chester between Northumbria and the kingdoms of Gwynedd and Powys. It is therefore possible that *Wrēocensǣte* territory became subject to Northumbrian rule for a short period, although there is scant evidence of Anglo-Saxon settlement within either Shropshire or Cheshire during this period.

By the 630s, though, the *Wrēocensǣte* had become aligned with both Gwynedd (under Cadwallon ap Cadfan) and Mercia (under King Penda) after their combined forces defeated the Northumbrians at the Battle of Hatfield Chase in 633. Then, in 642, Shropshire territory saw the Battle of Maserfield, near Oswestry, when King Oswald of Northumbria was defeated by the Mercians and the Welsh. The cause of the war is unknown, but if this location is correct, it would mean that Oswald was deep into the territory of his enemies, suggesting he was on the offensive. After his defeat, Oswald is said to have been crucified and dismembered – and it is this alleged event which led to the naming of Oswestry – meaning "Oswald's Tree" (Welsh, "Croes Oswallt", meaning "Oswald's Cross").

It is not clear whether the *Wrēocensǣte* and *Magonsǣte* tribes still had their independence in the 640s, but Welsh poems from this period suggest that they did. At this time, the ruler of the *Wrēocensǣte* was Cyndrwyn the Stubborn, probably the King of Powys and based somewhere in Shropshire territory, while a king called Constantine governed the *Magonsǣte* from Kenchester, which is in central Herefordshire, today. It is likely, therefore, that the later division between the dioceses of Hereford and Lichfield was the original dividing point between these two Romano-British tribes.

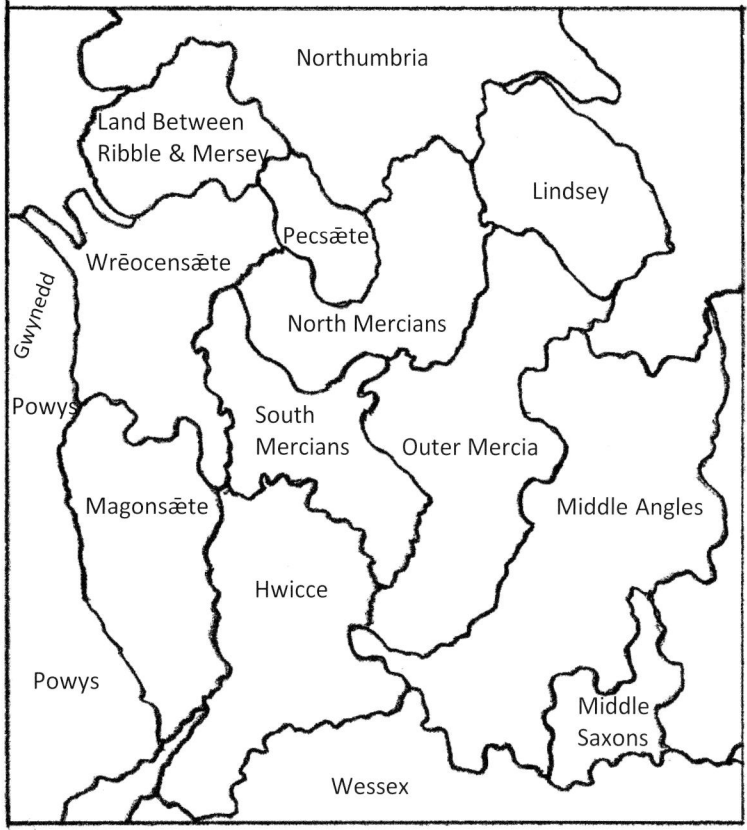

The independence of the *Wrēocensǣte* and *Magonsǣte* didn't last much longer though. Cyndrwyn's son, Cynddylan, is thought to have refused to pay tribute to Mercia in 655, and subsequently won a battle against a Saxon army at Wall, near Lichfield. However, Cynddylan was killed the following year when the Northumbrian army, led by King Oswald's brother Oswiu, overran Cynddylan's palace at *Llys Pengwern* in a surprise attack. According to later poetry, the entire royal family were slaughtered, except for Princess Heledd who fled to western Powys, and Shropshire territory finally succumbed to the Anglo-Saxons – albeit under the kings of Mercia based at Tamworth, rather than the more remote Northumbrians.

The Brythonic settlement of sub-Roman Britain known as Pengwern, was probably located east of

SAXON REMAINS AT ST ANDREW'S CHURCH, WROXETER

LEFT: This is the base of the south pier of the chancel arch at St Andrew's church, Wroxeter, and at the foot is part of a Saxon-carved stone; CENTRE: Outside on the south wall of the nave is part of an 8th or 9th century Anglo-Saxon cross shaft with carvings of dragons and foliage. RIGHT: This carved panel of a beast is thought to have once also been part of the 8th or 9th century cross.

today's border between Shropshire and Wales, but its exact location is uncertain. Some theories suggest it was a sub-kingdom of eastern Powys in the 6th century with its capital based at *Caer Guricon* – the site of the former Roman city of *Viroconium*, and modern-day Wroxeter. However, evidence suggests the abandonment of *Viroconium* in around 520, perhaps in exchange for a more defendable location further west, with one theory suggesting The Berth, the former Iron Age hillfort north of Baschurch. Regardless of its location, Pengwern is thought to have been the early seat of the kings of Powys, before that seat was later moved even further west to Mathrafal. It is certainly thought that the aforementioned Cyndrwyn was a king of Powys, who may have been based at a place called Pengwern. Welsh poems from the 9th century also place Cynddylan's seat at *Llys Pengwern*,

Anglo-Saxon herringbone stonework can be seen above at the eastern end of Clee St Margaret's church.

meaning the Court of Pengwern, while a 12th century Cambro-Norman archdeacon of Brecon and historian known as Gerald of Wales associates Pengwern with the site of modern Shrewsbury. That said, Shrewsbury isn't mentioned in recorded documents until 901, while the earliest archaeological evidence of a settlement at Shrewsbury dates from the early 8th century – some fifty years *after* Cyndrwyn was allegedly incumbent at Pengwern. That said, Shrewsbury's Anglo-Saxon name of *Scrobbesbyrig* suggests it was a fortress – so maybe it *was* Pengwern, after all.

For the record, the theory favouring The Berth as the site of Pengwern is based on a 7th century bronze cauldron which was found here, while after his death, one Welsh poem talks of Cynddylan being taken to the churches of Bassa. Meanwhile, Atcham, a couple of miles west of Wroxeter, has also been suggested, this based on the church having been dedicated to a 7th century Northumbrian bishop, St Eata, and the presence of cropmarks seen from the air. These revealed buildings of approximately 46ft by 26ft (14m by 8m) and 79ft by 26ft (24m by 8m). The larger building is similar to the great hall of a Northumberland palace built by King Æthelfrith (593-616), and remained in use until the time of Oswiu (642-670), whose Mercian contemporary, Wulfhere (658-675) brought an end to British rule over the *Wrēocensǣten*.

As for Mercia, the kingdom was centred on the Trent valley and its tributaries, with its capital sited at Tamworth. The most authentic source of information at this time is from the early 8th century Northumbrian monk and scholar, Bede, who describes Mercia as being divided in two by the River Trent. However, as Mercia expanded north-westwards towards North Wales, it brought the kingdom into conflict with its former ally, Gwynedd. As a result, Mercia could no longer allow the *Wrēocensǣte* and *Magonsǣte* tribes their autonomy, and the whole area therefore became absorbed into Mercia sometime in the mid-7th century. The Shropshire area thus became a frontier zone and was regularly subject to Welsh raids,

Anglo-Saxon long and short stonework can be found at the base of the chancel at Diddlebury St Peter's church, which dates from 1010 when the Saxon church was built. The north wall also has an unusual combination of herringbone masonry inside and squared masonry outside.

LEFT: Rushbury St Peter's has Anglo-Saxon herringbone stonework on the south wall, seen before entering the porch. CENTRE: Sidbury Holy Trinity church also has herringbone stonework on its south wall but which probably dates from the 12th century. RIGHT: Close-up of masonry at Sidbury.

All Saints' church at Culmington dates from the Anglo-Saxon period with 13th and 14th century additions. Here we see close-ups of Anglo-Saxon herringbone work on the north side of the church (left) and the south side (right), while the centre photo shows the Anglo-Saxon church in all its glory.

therefore accounting for the economic stagnation that occurred here during the 7th and 8th centuries.

Some of the earliest surviving Shropshire Anglo-Saxon evidence is provided by St Andrew's church at Wroxeter. The north wall was built sometime between the 9th and 11th century – albeit from reused Roman ashlar masonry taken from nearby *Viroconium*, while built into the south side of the church is an earlier monument, a carved Anglo-Saxon cross shaft which probably dates from the reign of King Offa of Mercia (757–96). This suggests that Wroxeter was still an important place at this time, while its parish uniquely straddled the River Severn, unlike all the other parishes along the Severn which were located on either the west bank and belonged to Hereford diocese or on the east bank and belonged to Lichfield diocese.

Meanwhile, 3 miles to the south-east at Cressage, the ancient parish church was dedicated to St Samson (c.485 to c.565), suggesting that Christianity may have still had a foothold in Shropshire territory from the end of Roman rule at the beginning of the 5th century to the establishment of Mercian authority in the mid-7th century. St Samson was born in Wales and travelled widely during the 6th century. Many churches in Cornwall and Brittany bear his name, and are usually places that he visited. His biographer relates that early in his itinerant life, he set up a church by a great river near a Roman camp – almost certainly *Viroconium* on the River Severn, hence the likelihood of him also spending time at Cressage. Indeed, the name Cressage means "Christ's oak tree" and derives from the Old English words *Crist* (Christ) and *āc* (oak-tree) and probably refers to a place where preaching took place.

Pagan Saxon burial sites in Shropshire are rare. However, one remarkable site was uncovered in Shrewsbury in February 2017. When archaeologists began excavating, they were expecting to find an Anglo-Saxon pagan burial site – but now say that it may be the country's oldest-known continuously used sacred ground, with finds suggesting it has been used during every era since the late Neolithic period, including early Anglo-Saxon times. This is thanks to carbon dating of a wooden post extracted during the dig, which revealed it was placed in the ground in 2033 BC.

Graves excavated at Bromfield near Ludlow also appear to be of the very early Christian Saxon period – as the inclusion of knives at the burial site suggests recently converted Saxons. The latter site is therefore likely to date from the mid-7th century, as it was 653 when religion in Mercia changed significantly. This was when Peada, son of King Penda of Mercia (626-655), converted to Christianity so that he could marry the Christian daughter of King Oswy of Northumbria. At this time, the Mercians also invited four priests to join the until-then pagan kingdom as missionaries.

Also discovered in 2017, was the site of an Anglo-Saxon hall on the estate at Attingham – a rarity in Britain. Archaeologists believe this to have been a high-status building, possibly a feasting hall or even a palace. The building had a wooden frame, dug into a trench with wattle and daub walls, samples of which were found during the dig. Also found were several Roman coins, three Roman brooches, Roman pottery, a Saxon loom weight and part of a Viking stirrup mount, as well as a probable Anglo-Saxon strap tag, meaning that the site was likely to have been of some importance throughout the Anglo-Saxon period.

One significant development in Shropshire territory occurred in the years before 690, when the monastery of St Milburga was established at Much Wenlock by the Mercian royal house. St Milburga was the daughter of Merewald, third son of King Penda, and she was also related to Æthelred I (675-704) and Ceolred (709-716). St Milburga headed the abbey which originally consisted of both monks and nuns, who appear to have worshipped in separate churches. The nuns eventually disappeared, but the order of monks evolved into a community of priests serving a minster church, all of this laying the foundations for the great Cluniac priory that was founded there in 1050.

Meanwhile, Welsh raids on Shropshire territory continued into the 8th century, resulting in Offa's Dyke, thought to have been constructed sometime during the 760s and 770s, by King Offa of Mercia (757-796). Offa's Dyke was a large linear earthwork which still delineates much of the England-Wales border and, back then, delineated the Mercia-Powys border – although claims that it stretched from the Irish Sea to the Severn Estuary are now disputed. Also disputed is the date of construction of the earthwork, with recent excavations suggesting at least part of the structure was built much earlier than the 7th century, with some of the lower parts probably dating to early post-Roman Britain, some 300 years earlier. Nevertheless, the final earthwork was up to 65ft wide (20m) when including its flanking ditch, and 8ft high (2.4m) – although some accounts state as much as 12ft at one stage (3.7m). It was constructed across low ground, hills and rivers, always traversing around hills to the western (Welsh) side. The ditch of Offa's Dyke was also placed on the Welsh side with the displaced soil piled up into a bank on the Mercian side. Today, sections of Offa's Dyke delineate three stretches of Shropshire's boundary with Wales, and also comprise some of the most impressive sections. Prime among these are the spectacular ascent southwards out of the Ceriog Valley, and the stunning stretches across the heights of the Clun Forest. It is therefore one of the most impressive memorials in Europe built during what is known as the Dark Ages.

Anglo-Saxon doorway on the north wall of St Peter's church at Stanton Lacy.

St Milburga's Well at Much Wenlock. The original abbey at Much Wenlock was founded by the 7th century king of Mercia, Merewald, and he installed his daughter, Milburga, as Abbess; she was later canonised, while the later 11th century Benedictine priory retained the dedication to St Milburga. Her bones were reputedly discovered at the priory in 1101, thus making the priory a place of pilgrimage. As for the well, it was later said to have cured sight impairments and helped Victorian women find a suitor!

In addition to Offa's Dyke, Wat's Dyke was also constructed in the Dark Ages, from Basingwerk Abbey on the Dee estuary to Llanymynech on today's Shropshire/Welsh border, six miles south of Oswestry, and hence has a good ten-mile run through Shropshire territory. However, the initial dating of Wat's Dyke to the 650s has also been disputed. Late 20th century scholars had suggested the later reign of King Æthelbald of Mercia (716-757), but excavations in the 1990s then once again theorised that lower-level construction took place in early post-Roman Britain, this thanks to pottery evidence and quantities of charcoal discovered that were dated to between 411 and 561. Then in 2006, further excavations swung back to a much later date of 792-852, with the earlier date now thought to relate to a fire site which preceded the dyke.

It was during Mercian occupation that many of Shropshire's villages were formed, many with place-name suffixes of –tun/ton and –ham, deriving from the Anglo-Saxon words *tūn* (farmstead) and *hām* (homestead), respectively. *Tūn* examples include Albrighton (farmstead of a man called Æthelbeorht), Alderton (farmstead where alder trees grow) and Alkington (farmstead of a man called Eastead or a man called Ealha), while *hām* examples include Atcham (homestead of a man called Ætti) and Caynham (homestead of a man called Cæga). The other common Anglo-Saxon place-name ending is –*ley*, deriving from the Old English word *lēah*, meaning "wood, woodland clearing or glade", and reflects the fact that during the early Anglo-Saxon period, much of Shropshire was thought to have been covered by forest, and the Anglo-Saxons were credited with founding villages and hamlets in self-created clearings.

A surviving stretch of Offa's Dyke as it heads towards Llanfair Hill.

Anglo-Saxon pilaster strips at St Peter's church at Stanton Lacy.

Between the 7th and 9th centuries, Mercia's fortunes ebbed and flowed, emerging as a great power in the first half of the 7th century under King Penda, but then losing North Mercia to Northumbria after his death in 655. Mercia then recovered its northern territory again in the second half of the 7th century under Wulfhere before gaining even greater strength under Æthelred. Then for a time throughout the 8th century, Mercia became the dominant power of England south of the Humber, led by Æthelbald (716–757) and Offa (757-796). Offa reformed the coinage, introduced the silver penny, constructed his famous dyke to keep the Welsh out, and consorted as an equal with European leaders such as Charlemagne. However, by 825, Wessex had taken over the dominant mantle, and by the mid-to-late 9th century, Mercia had lost its kingdom status and was ruled by ealdormen serving under the throne of Wessex.

> **Quirk Alert:** *Spring in the Step*
>
> *There is also a St Milburga's well near Stoke St Milborough, so-named because the 7th century granddaughter of King Penda (626-655) is alleged to have escaped a grave, but unrecorded peril here – this also being the point when the spring was revealed by a great kick from Milburga's horse's hoof!*

This decrease in power and status left eastern Mercia vulnerable when the Danes began to maraud in the late 860s, eventually destroying the Mercian capital at Tamworth in 873. By 877, the Danes had begun to partition Mercia, and the west of the kingdom, including Shropshire territory, was given to Ceolwulf II, a puppet king to the Danes. However, the Danes then suffered a major defeat at the Battle of Eddington in 878 against King Alfred of Wessex. The Danish king, Guthrum, was forced to sign the Treaty of Wedmore, which carved up England between Saxon and Dane – the south and the west to the Saxons of Wessex and Mercia, and the east to the Danes.

Despite the treaty, though, the Danes renewed their attacks on Mercia in the late 9th century, which included encroaching into Shropshire territory and building an

Looking through the nave towards the chancel in Stanton Lacy St Peter's church. Both the nave and the north transept date from around 1050.

This remarkable Saxon tympanum can be found above a doorway in the late 11th century tower of Stottesdon St Mary's church. Note the figures across the bottom of the carving – a cat, a cat or a dog and a deer – all upside down, while behind them is a portion of net which may represent a chase and capture.

encampment in 893 at Quatford, three miles south-east of Bridgnorth.

By this stage, Mercian links with Wessex had been cemented by the marriage of Earl Æthelred of Mercia to Æthelflæd, daughter of King Alfred of Wessex. On Æthelred's death in 911, Æthelflæd ruled Mercia as the 'Lady of the Mercian's' and set about fortifying Mercia's eastern borders. By 913 she had encroached deep into Danish territory, having established a *burh*

St Giles church at Barrow (left) is one of the most complete of Shropshire's oldest churches, and contains its only Saxon chancel (right).

at Tamworth – one of at least ten built between 912 and 918, which included strengthening the fortress at Quatford in 912, while another Shropshire *burh* may have been built at Chirbury, close to the Welsh border. Along with her brother (Edward the Elder), Æthelflæd then launched her first offensive foray in July 917 and expelled the Danes from the fortress at Derby and annexed the whole region back into English Mercia.

Æthelflæd died in 918 at which point the Mercians submitted to the rule of Edward the Elder. The Danes then hit back in 943, destroying the Mercian capital at Tamworth and massacring its inhabitants. The Danes were then driven out again only to return under King Sweyn of Denmark in 1013… but who only survived for another five weeks after which the formerly ousted Æthelred the Unready returned to reclaim his crown… only for the Danish King Cnut to invade in 1016 and claim it back! By 1035, though, what was now the Earldom of Mercia was back in Anglo-Saxon hands, under Leofric, Earl of Mercia.

It was during this period of Anglo-Scandinavian warfare that Shrewsbury first appeared, located in a part of West Mercia that was untroubled by the Danes. The town is first recorded in a document of 901, when a transaction is recorded as being made "in civitate Scrobbensis". This suggests a place of some authority, further corroborated by the establishment of a mint at Shrewsbury in the 920s. Of course, Saxon Shrewsbury (*Scrobbensis* or *Scrobbesbyrig*), gave its name to the county of Shropshire (*Scrobbesbyrigscīr* or *Scrobbescire*), which comprised the former southern territory of the *Wrēocensǣte* and northern territory of the *Magonsǣte* to make 2,400 hides. The first reference to *Scrobbescire* was in the Anglo-Saxon Chronicle of 1006, which records that Æthelred the Unready had "gone across the Thames, into Shropshire and received there his food-rents in the Christmas season."

Shropshire was then carved up into Anglo-Saxon "hundreds" for military and judicial purposes, probably in the early 11th century. A hundred had land which sustained approximately 100 hides (households) and was headed by a hundredman, usually a local nobleman, who was responsible for justice at a hundred court. He was also responsible for supplying and leading military troops. Hundreds were then further divided into tithings (c.10 households) and then subdivided into hides which became a unit of assessment for tax. There were 15 Shropshire hundreds recorded in Domesday Book (1086): Alnodestreu, Baschurch, Conditre, Condover, Culvestan, Hodnet, Leintwardine, Merset, Overs, Patton, Reweset, Rinlau, Shrewsbury, Wittery and Wrockwardine. During the first half of the 11th century, the area around Montgomery belonged to Shropshire, as did the hundred of Wigmore which is in present-day Herefordshire, while by contrast, much of Clun Forest was under Welsh rule. And not only were

LEFT: A carved figure of a Sheela-na-gig above the north doorway at St Laurence's church in Church Stretton. A pagan fertility symbol, it is thought that this figure was probably inserted into the original Norman wall by the local Anglo-Saxon builders! CENTRE LEFT: Another Sheela-na-gig, this time in the nave of St Mary's church at Stottesdon above one of the arch capitals. The nave there is Norman, although dates from around 1180, so the carving may date from the earlier Saxon period. CENTRE RIGHT: 10th century Saxon tombstones in St Mary's church, Shrewsbury – the only surviving remnants of the original Saxon church. RIGHT: This font is also Saxon and belongs to the beautiful timber-framed church at Melverley. It is the only surviving remnant from the church that was burned to the ground in 1401.

> **Quirk Alert:** *Cave Life*
>
> *In the rocky cliffs that rise above the Severn at Bridgnorth, there are a number of caves known as the Hermitage Caves. They were certainly inhabited back in Anglo-Saxon times, with one of them fashioned as a chapel, including a rough-hewn chancel arch and a recess used as a piscina. It was here that the brother of King Athelstan (927-939) is said to have lived a hermit's life. His name was Ethelward or Aethelard, the Grandson of King Alfred, and the Saxon name for the caves was Athelardetson. Later hermits are listed as living here during the reign of Edward III (1327-1377), while the* Magna Britannia *of 1727 also records an old cave that was inhabited by a hermit. Then in 1877, the town clerk recorded two cottages in the Hermitage Caves, one of which included a fireplace, chimney, window and doorway. He also records that one of the caves was 33 feet in length and used as a chapel. More recently, one of the caves was converted into a Custodian's Cottage, and was inhabited by the Norton family until 1939.*
>
> *There are also accounts of a tunnel from the cave that supposedly ran under the River Severn to the nearby Franciscan Friary as well as a second cave under the castle that connected with the hermitage caves – although this has never been found to date! Other records tell of a witch who dwelled in a large cave beyond the chapel who had the power to stop horses!*
>
> *Finally, from the caves, a wooded path leads to a high rock known as the Tailor's Stone. According to legend, it was so-named because a tailor vowed that he would make a coat while sitting up there, but lost his thimble as he was sewing on the last button. Alas, on stooping to find it, he fell from the rock and broke his neck.*

these hundreds adopted by the Normans after 1066, they actually lasted until the 19th century!

Finally, it is worth noting that while most of the Midlands counties to the east of Shropshire suffered at the hands of the Vikings from the 9th to the 11th century, and were considerably influenced and altered by them, Shropshire got off relatively lightly. In fact, there is not one place in Shropshire that ends with the most common Danish place-name suffix of – by, which derives from the Old Scandinavian word *bý* (farmstead, village or settlement). By contrast, there are 60 places ending in – by recorded in Leicestershire… and 225 in Lincolnshire! However, don't be fooled into thinking the folk of Shropshire were lucky; they had plenty to deal with from the west, particularly in the first half of the 11th century, and it is thought that these constant Welsh raids into Shropshire territory meant that it took many decades to recover. For example, the Anglo-Saxon Chronicle records that in 1053, the Welsh "slew a great many of the English wardens at Westbury". Harold Godwinson's response was to order that any Welshman found beyond Offa's Dyke, within the English pale, should have his right hand cut off!

Hundred House Inn at Purslow was built in 1685, and was a hundred court before it was a pub, thus sustaining the judicial system set up in late Anglo-Saxon times.

Nevertheless, despite this perennial animosity, both the English and the Welsh were shortly destined to be ground under the heel of another invader…

LEFT: Hundred House Inn at Norton was a later 17th century hundred court, while conveniently opposite (right) are the village stocks and whipping post!

From the Conquest to the Dissolution

Following the Norman Conquest of 1066, Shropshire was soon subjected to the same ruthless overhaul of ruling class and high clergy that was to be repeated in most other English counties. In other words, out went the previous Anglo-Saxon incumbents, to be replaced by Norman gentry and bishops. Domesday Book of 1086 reveals that among the disinvested English to have owned land in Shropshire, shortly before the Norman Conquest, was the King (Edward the Confessor) and his queen, Edith. Of course, Edward died on 5th January 1066 (before the Conquest) therefore Harold Godwinson acquired Edward's lands (alas, for a short nine months), while Harold also owned additional Shropshire manors already granted to him.

Also losing lands in 1066 were wealthy and important thegns such as Earl Godwin, along with Edwin and Morcar, earls of Mercia and Northumberland, respectively, while acquiring principal estates in Shropshire were Norman lords loyal to William I, such as Roger de Montgomerie, 1st Earl of Shrewsbury. Another of the Anglo-Saxon lords ousted was Eadric the Wild, who held manors in the south of Shropshire, including Clun. He refused to submit to the Normans, and was therefore attacked by Norman forces based at Hereford Castle, under the command of Richard fitz Scrob. Eadric's response was to align himself with the Welsh prince of Gwynedd and Powys, Bleddyn ap Cynfyn, and his brother Riwallon – somewhat ironic given historic animosities, but they were now united in a common cause. Together, they attacked Hereford Castle in 1067 – a castle only just repaired by William fitzOsbern, following its part-destruction after a Welsh invasion in 1055 into what was then Anglo-Saxon England! However, Eadric's attempt to take Hereford Castle from the Normans was unsuccessful and his forces retreated to Wales.

A Norman helmet in the museum at Battlefield, typically worn by soldiers between AD 1000 and 1200.

Eadric next surfaces as part of the widespread wave of English rebellions in 1069-70, when he burned the now-Norman town of Shrewsbury and unsuccessfully besieged Shrewsbury Castle, again helped by his Welsh allies from Gwynedd, as well as other English rebels from Cheshire. It was probably Eadric's forces who were defeated by William I in the Battle of Stafford in late 1069 – although, surprisingly, Eadric survived the battle and apparently submitted to William in 1070; indeed it is also thought that he assisted William in his invasion of Scotland in 1072 – although another account states that he was captured by Ranulph de Mortimer and sentenced to life imprisonment.

Eadric apart, Shropshire put up relatively little resistance to the Conqueror. This may have seemed a wise option when viewing the fate of neighbouring Staffordshire in 1070 – for William marched northwards through Staffordshire to include the county in his brutal "Harrying of the North", where vast areas were ravaged, the aim being to lay waste to the northern shires in order to eliminate further rebellion. As well as fortified buildings, William's army also destroyed the homes, stock and crops of ordinary people, as well as the means of food production and many starved to death as a result.

Despite the brutal suppression of rebellion in the north, William's position was still in the balance during the early years of his rule. He therefore commissioned the build of a series of Norman castles to which he could deploy garrisons that would be handily placed to quell any further uprisings, and these castles became the most symbolic representation of Norman power. One of these castles was built back in one of Eadric the

The Grade I listed ruins of Clun Castle, which was built by Robert de Say in the years after the Norman Conquest.

Effigy of Roger de Montgomery in Shrewsbury Abbey. He built Shrewsbury Castle in the early 1070s and Shrewsbury Abbey in 1083. He was also made First Earl of Shrewsbury in 1074.

Shrewsbury Castle was first built in 1070 by Roger de Montgomery, originally of wood. It was then rebuilt in stone during the mid-12th century, and the best surviving part of that build is the gatehouse, shown above left. Shown above right is the main hall in the north-western section of the bailey, and which was begun in 1164 and enlarged in 1300 and 1596.

The Grade I listed Ludlow Castle, pictured from the south-west. It was built shortly after the Norman Conquest, in around 1075, by Walter de Lacy.

Wild's former manors of Clun. It was built by Robert de Say, and was a substantial motte castle with two baileys. Robert held the castle and district from the Earl of Shrewsbury until 1102; thereafter, Robert and his descendants held their castle directly from the Crown. Robert's daughter then married the local Welsh lord, Cadwgan ap Bleddyn, and their son, Henry de Say, inherited the castle in 1098, with his son, Helias de Say controlling the castle until his death in 1165. It was also during this time that Henry I established a new castle-guard system at Clun, in response to constant Welsh attacks, while Henry II continued the royal focus on Clun as the regional centre for protecting the border, investing heavily in the castle between 1160 and 1164.

Shrewsbury Castle was also built shortly after the Norman Conquest. It was built in 1070 by Roger de Montgomery as a defensive fortification for the town, which was elsewhere protected by the River Severn, while the town walls were thought to radiate out from the castle and surround the town. In 1138, King Stephen successfully besieged the castle, which was held by William FitzAlan for the Empress Matilda during the period known as The Anarchy (1135-53), while the castle was also briefly held by Llywelyn the Great, Prince of Wales, in 1215. However, little of the Norman structure survives as the castle was extensively damaged during the English Civil War and then subsequently rebuilt.

Ludlow Castle was founded probably by Walter de Lacy, in around 1075. De Lacy had been part of the aforementioned William fitzOsbern's household during the Norman Conquest and, after fitzOsbern was made Earl of Hereford in 1067 and tasked with quelling unrest in the area, de Lacy became his right-hand man. Ludlow Castle was built at the heart of de Lacy's 163 manors, but also at a strategic crossroads over the River Teme, on a strong defensive promontory. However, Walter's son, Roger de Lacy, was stripped of his lands in 1096 after rebelling against William II and they were reassigned to Roger's brother, Hugh.

Ludlow Castle's Norman stone fortifications were completed by around 1115, based around what is now the inner bailey. It had four towers and a gatehouse tower along the walls, with a ditch along two sides, and would have been one of the first masonry castles built in England. During the mid-12th century, the Great Tower was constructed by converting the entrance tower, while an outer bailey was built to the south and east of the original castle. The entrance to the castle was also moved from the south to the east, to face the growing town of Ludlow, while the circular chapel in the inner bailey was also added.

Meanwhile, over in the east of the county, Bridgnorth Castle was built in 1101 by Robert de Bellême, son of Roger de Montgomery. Robert had already acquired lands in Normandy on the death of his father in 1094, but when his younger brother, Hugh, died in 1098, Robert also acquired lands in Shropshire. He also succeeded his younger brother as the 3rd Earl of Shrewsbury, while his 1098 acquisitions made him the wealthiest magnate in both England and Normandy. However, in 1101 Robert de Bellême was one of the great magnates who joined the Duke of Normandy, Robert Curthose's 1101 invasion of England to attempt to depose Henry I who had been crowned a year earlier. The invasion ended bloodlessly, but Henry soon drew up charges against Robert for unlicensed castle building, specifically of Bridgnorth Castle. When Robert refused to answer for them, Henry gathered his forces and besieged and captured Robert's English castles, stripped Robert of both his lands and his titles, and banished him from England. Meanwhile, Bridgnorth Castle's principal feature was a square great tower, built during the reign of Henry II (1154-1189). However, it was demolished during the English Civil War on the orders of Oliver Cromwell, due to it having been garrisoned by Royalist troops. The demolition left the surviving great tower leaning at a remarkable angle of 15 degrees!

Close-up of the western walls of Ludlow Castle. The tower on the left, known as Mortimer's Tower, probably dates from the early 13th century.

The only remains of the Norman castle after which Bishop's Castle is named – as it was built in 1087 by the Bishop of Hereford to defend the church and village from Welsh attacks.

Elsewhere, Shropshire became home to many more Norman castles, primarily due to its proximity to the as-yet untamed Welsh. In fact, Barrie Trinder in *A History of Shropshire* states that "more than 150 motte and bailey castles were built in Shropshire in the century or so after the Norman Conquest", and that "one group, situated between Montgomery (in Shropshire in those times) and Caus (modern-day Westbury), have uniform features, with mottes 3-6 metres high with diameters at the tops of 6-7 metres." The following table captures those Norman Shropshire castles of note.

Norman Castle	Description
Bishop's Castle	Built by the Bishop of Hereford in 1087 to defend the settlement of Bishop's Castle from Welsh attacks – although the most notable attack, in 1263, was by John FitzAlan, 6th Earl of Arundel and Lord of Oswestry and Clun, and which caused significant damage.
Bridgnorth Castle	Built 1101 by Robert de Bellême, 3rd Earl of Shrewsbury. Demolished during the English Civil War on Cromwell's orders, due to it having been garrisoned by Royalist troops.
Bryn Amlwg Castle	Built in the early 12th century as a wooden ring work, but reconstructed in stone in 1225. Occupied until 1377; thereafter fell into disuse. Only earthworks remain.
Caus Castle	Built by Roger Corbet in the late 11th century near Westbury as an earthwork motte with a tower and strongly defended inner bailey. Garrisoned by Henry II in 1165. Tower, keep and curtain wall re-built in stone in 1198. Garrisoned against Owain Glyndwr in the 15th century. Recorded as a ruin by 1521 but still used as a Royalist garrison during the English Civil War and hence destroyed in June 1645. Only earthworks now remain.
Clun Castle	Built shortly after the Norman Conquest by Robert "Picot" de Say. Prospered in the 13th century under the Fitzalan family, but suffered many Welsh attacks. Used as a hunting lodge in the 14th century but reported as ruinous by 1539. Survives as an impressive ruin.
Ellesmere Castle	Built in 1087 by Roger de Montgomery and later became a royal castle in 1138. Abandoned in the 14th century. All that remains today are the earthworks of the motte.
Holdgate Castle	Built late 11th century as a motte and bailey fortress by Helgot de Reisolent. Housed a college of clergy founded before 1210 and dissolved after 1373. Housed Royalist garrison during the Civil War, but demolished in June 1645. Earthworks still present. Remains of a 13th century semi-circular flanking tower are incorporated into a 16th century farmhouse.
Hopton Castle	Built late 11th century as a motte and bailey fortress by Robert de Say. Stone castle built 1276 by Walter de Hopton, with a rectangular three storey tower house, flanked by projecting angle turrets. Surrounded by a curtain wall, flanked with towers. Rare western castle held by Parliamentarians during the English Civil War. Captured by Royalists in March 1644 and garrison massacred after which the castle was destroyed. Grade I listed.

Ludlow Castle	Founded by Walter de Lacy, in 1075. Acquired by the Crown in 1461 as centre of admin for the Marches & Wales and underwent major rebuild. Besieged by Parliamentarians during the English Civil War, and the last Royalist castle held until capture in July 1646. Acquired by the Earl of Powys in 1811 and remains with his family today. Grade I listed.
Montgomery Castle	Built early 1070s by Roger de Montgomery. Then in Shropshire, the castle was given to Baldwin de Boulers in 1102. The de Boulers held the castle until 1215, when the fortress was destroyed by Prince Llywelyn ab Iorwerth. It was rebuilt in stone in the 1220s, only to be attacked by the Welsh in 1228 and 1233. After that, the castle became more of a military backwater and prison.

The remains of Bridgnorth Castle, built in 1101 by Robert de Bellême, 3rd Earl of Shrewsbury. The above is the remains of the precariously angled keep, which now leans at 15 degrees thanks to the demolition of the castle carried out on Oliver Cromwell's orders in 1646-47. That's a four-times greater "lean" than the tower at Pisa!

The ruins of Montgomery Castle, once in Shropshire, now in Wales. It was built between 1071 and 1074 by Roger de Montgomery, 1st Earl of Shrewsbury.

Norman Castle	Description
Oswestry Castle	Built late 11th century as an earthwork motte and bailey fortress owned by Rainald, Sheriff of Shropshire. Occupied by Madoc ap Maerdudd, Prince of Powys, between 1149 and 1157, who built the stone castle, adding a polygonal shell keep. Adopted by Henry II in 1165 for his disastrous campaign against Owain Gwynned, and by King John in 1211 against Llywelyn Fawr. Castle walls extended to include town by 1270, and was the scene of a parliament held by Richard II in 1398. In disrepair by late 15th century; demolished in 1648. Only fragments of collapsed masonry survive.
Ruyton Castle	Built in the 12th century but badly damaged in 1203 and 1212. Rebuilt in 1313 but finally abandoned at the end of the 14th century and the stone used to build the adjacent church.
Shrewsbury Castle	Earthwork motte and bailey fortress built in the 11th century by Roger de Montgomery, possibly replacing an earlier Saxon fortification. Replaced with a stone castle by Henry II in 1164 which encased the oval inner bailey with a curtain wall, pierced by a plain arched gateway. Edward I built the Great Hall and strengthened the castle with a rectangular outer bailey in the 13th century. Remodelled late 18th century. Acquired by the Shropshire Horticultural Society in 1924 and restored. Grade I listed.
Wem Castle	Built between 1135 and 1154 by William Pantulf. Rebuilt by Hugh Pantulf in the 13th century with stone buildings. In ruins by 1290 but rebuilt in 1313. Only a reduced motte survives that has been shored up on one side with a brick wall.
Whittington Castle	An Iron Age fort and possible Saxon fortification converted into an earthwork motte and bailey fortress in the late 11th century by William Peverel. Stone castle built in the mid-12th century by Henry II, crowning the motte with a rectangular keep. In 1221, Sir Foulke fitz Warine was granted a licence to crenellate and he surrounded the motte with a shell keep, flanked by five huge round towers. Two of the towers defended the gateway into the new inner bailey, with a twin-towered gatehouse defending the large walled outer bailey. Dismantled in the 18th century for road stone although the present outer gatehouse was restored in 1809. Grade I listed.

Whittington Castle was originally a timber-framed motte and bailey fortress built in the late 11th century. The later stone castle was built in the 1220s.

Hopton Castle, built in the late 11th century as an earthwork motte and bailey fortress by Robert de Say.

The year 1086 marked the creation of Domesday Book, a great survey of the majority of the lands in England and parts of Wales. We therefore know that most of the Shropshire parishes at this time were composed of several townships or hamlets. For example, Dawley comprised the townships of Dawley Magna, Dawley Parva and Malins Lee, while Leighton contained the mother township which included the church and the hamlet of Garmston. Large parishes contained many townships – such as Ruyton XI Towns, which is so-named because it contained 11 townships or hamlets at this time. As for boroughs, Domesday Book only records two for Shropshire: Shrewsbury and Quatford. Therefore, with the exception of towns which appeared during the Industrial Revolution, the rest of Shropshire's towns developed in the 200 years between the Norman Conquest and the mid-13th century.

Of course, a number of these towns grew up in the shadow of their castle – such as Ludlow, which was developed in the early 12th century by the de Lacy family in the ancient parish of Stanton Lacy, while Bishop's Castle was laid out in the late 12th century by the Bishop of Hereford in the parish of Lydbury North. Meanwhile, in the parish of Morville, Robert de Bellême transferred the castle, church and borough recorded against Quatford in Domesday Book, to the evolving settlement of Bridgnorth – this being in around 1101. And in the north-west of the county, Oswestry was founded by William FitzAlan in the late 12th century in the parish of Maesbury, again evolving in the shadow of the pre-Domesday Book castle there. Finally, to the north-east of the county, Henry I founded Newport in the early 12th century on the north-south route there, with burgesses committed to provide fish to the royal household on their passage! This also explains the three fishes on the town's coat of arms, and the dedication of the parish church to St Nicholas, the patron saint of fishermen. As for Market Drayton, the town was laid out in the mid-13th century by the monks of Combermere Abbey, while the town at Madeley was founded by the monks of nearby Wenlock Priory, also in the mid-13th century.

As for the county town, Shrewsbury pre-dated the Conquest, and hence doesn't follow standard medieval topography. That said, the borough of Abbey Foregate to the east of the Severn and town centre, and a separate jurisdiction under the abbot of Shrewsbury Abbey, was clearly planned, as were several other extra-mural suburbs of Shrewsbury such as Castle Foregate and Frankwell (to the north) and Longden Coleham (to the south-east). Domesday Book reveals that Shrewsbury had 252 houses in 1086, and also confirms that the four parish churches (St Alkmund's, St Chad's, St Julien's and St Mary's) were already established. It also reveals that 51 tenements were demolished to make way for the Norman version of Shrewsbury Castle, built a decade earlier.

The only remains of Oswestry Castle, a pre-Domesday Book earthwork motte and bailey fortress, owned by Rainald, Sheriff of Shropshire. These fragments of stone sit on top of the surviving motte.

For each new town that evolved from an older village, a distinct contrast can be observed between the formal layout of the new development and the haphazard pattern of the original settlement – both Clun and Wellington being good examples. Meanwhile, many planned boroughs failed to develop as towns. For example, the monks of Lilleshall Abbey probably laid out a new town by their toll bridge at Atcham where they were granted rights to hold fairs in 1269 and 1276,

SHROPSHIRE'S NORMAN SUCCESSORS TO SAXON MINSTERS

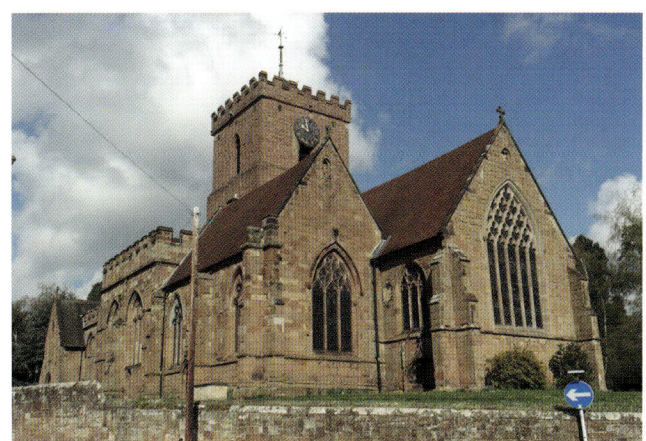

Shifnal St Andrew's church originated as a collegiate church in the 12th century, and its Norman chancel arch still survives.

St Peter's church at Wrockwardine dates from the 12th and 13th century, but retains several Norman features, including windows in the chancel.

St George's church at Clun dates from the 12th century with 13th and 14th century additions.

St Peter's church at Stanton Lacy dates from the 11th century and contains both Saxon and Norman work.

as did the monks of Shrewsbury Abbey at Baschurch – with their grant for fairs and markets dating to 1256. However, neither settlement developed into a town. Also, Newtown failed to develop as planned (and as named), almost certainly due to its proximity to Ruyton and its successful market.

In the late 11th century, each township had its own group of two, three or four open fields which were cultivated by peasants, each tenant having several strips scattered about each of the fields. For example, each hamlet in the hundreds of Ford and Condover had its own set of open fields, while the township of Ketley in Wellington parish consisted of the Great, Rock and Barn fields. Indeed, the three fields of Wrockwardine were still being cultivated as late as 1674 when they were called the Dale, Killstone and Wide fields, while in the mid-18th century, Samuel Garbet, in his *History of Wem*, is still able to name the open fields of most of the townships in the parish.

The medieval open field system lasted for centuries. However, evidence of this – which usually takes the form of ridge and furrow – is less common in Shropshire than elsewhere in the Midlands, with the best-preserved Shropshire ridge and furrow located around the deserted medieval hamlet of Lawton in Corvedale. Their emergence appears to be pre-Conquest, as excavations near Montgomery have shown that ridge and furrow pre-dates the Norman castle there, while similar evidence has been revealed at High Ercall in the north-east of the county. However, there is no evidence of this open field system in the north-western corner near Oswestry; instead, evidence suggests isolated farmsteads rather than nucleated townships. And, understandably, large tracts of Shropshire upland weren't cultivated either, such as the Long Mynd, Clun Forest and Brown Clee. Neither were wetlands, such as the Weald Moors and Whixall Moss, nor sandy heathland such as Northwood Common and Hind Heath, with these areas (wetland and sandy heath) being largely confined to the north and north-east of the county. Typically, these lands were used mostly for grazing or as sources for wood. For example, the parishes around Brown Clee shared grazing rights on the summit of the hill, while a similar arrangement served the Weald Moors.

Most medieval open fields were surrounded by extensive woodland and moor. However, these areas were gradually brought under cultivation by clearance, and new farmsteads were built, with a number of these being moated; 115 such sites have been found in Shropshire, many of which were located on the North Shropshire plain, and which were brought into cultivation in the 13th and 14th centuries.

The Normans were well-known for their hunting, and most English counties had royal forests – areas outside the usual system of law and subject to the monarch's personal authority. In Shropshire these included Brewood Forest in the east of the county, Claverley and Worfield, Morfe Forest, Shirlett Forest, and Wyre Forest in the south-east, and Haughmond, Wrekin Forest, Long Forest (including Stapelwood, Burswood, Lythwood and Stapleton), and the Long Mynd in central parts. That said, even by the late 11th century, parts of Long Forest in the hundred of Condover and Mount Gilbert Forest around the Wrekin were already under cultivation, and by the 14th century, most of Shropshire's royal forests had ceased to be forested at all! However, the harsh medieval forest laws still applied, so any form of encroachment – be it buildings, hedges, fencing or even cultivation – and the penalties would be severe. As for poachers, if they were lucky, they'd just have their eyes gouged out, but it was usually a hanging for them!

The role of the church during these times was all-pervasive, and individual churches and other monastic establishments were massively endowed. Cathedrals and abbeys were the most imposing buildings in the land, while even in remote parishes, the church was by far the largest and most enduring building. Consequently, as well as castles, the other main Shropshire survivors from Norman times are around one hundred churches, each of which retain varying degrees of 11th and 12th century stonework and features. Probably the finest church in Shropshire is Ludlow's Grade I listed St Laurence's church. Already large by the 12th century, much of it was re-built in the 15th century, with a spectacular crossing tower, nave, vaulting and misericords. However, surviving more-or-less intact from the 12th century in Ludlow, is the chapel of St Thomas, which was built in around 1190. Meanwhile Shrewsbury had four comparable chapels: St Blaise, St Catherine, St Mary Magdalene and St Nicholas, while St Chad's and St Mary's at Shrewsbury were collegiate churches at this time.

Norman archways, part of the surviving ruins of Haughmond Priory, which was first founded in the early 12th century.

The surviving Norman west doorway to Lilleshall Abbey which was founded between 1145 and 1148.

The superb Norman font in Holy Trinity church, Holdgate.

Another stunning Norman font, this time at St Mary's church, Stottesdon.

Another Norman font, this time at Morville Priory.

Norman font at Eaton-under-Heywood St Edith's church.

Norman font at Lilleshall St Michael and All Angels.

Norman font at St Mary's church, Knockin.

Norman font at All Saints' church, Berrington.

Norman piscina in Shrewsbury Abbey.

LEFT: Late 12th century doorway at Shawbury St Mary's. CENTRE LEFT: Norman south doorway of Heath Chapel. CENTRE: South doorway of Holdgate Holy Trinity church. CENTRE RIGHT: North doorway at Edstaston St Mary's (the wooden door is also probably the original 12th century door). RIGHT: 12th century south doorway at Llanyblodwel St Michael's.

Looking east towards the chancel from the Norman nave at Munslow St Michael's church.

The Norman nave of Shrewsbury Holy Cross Abbey. The lower two levels of arches are still the originals, built between 1083 and 1087.

The Norman nave of Shrewsbury St Mary's.

Looking through from the Norman nave to the Norman chancel at Much Wenlock Holy Trinity church.

SHROPSHIRE: UNUSUAL & QUIRKY

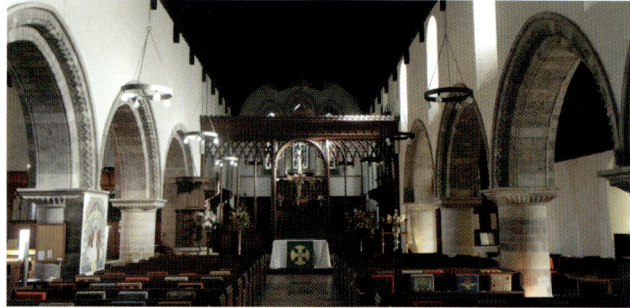
The Grade II* listed St George's church at Clun has a 12th century core.

Surviving Norman arches at Wenlock Priory.

The surviving Norman chancel arch inside St Andrew's church at Shifnal.

Norman windows in the north chancel wall of St Lucia's church in Upton Magna.

Norman tympanum above the south door at Aston Eyre church.

Norman capitals at Wenlock Priory.

Norman south doorway at Estatston St Mary's.

A close-up of the capitals of the Norman south doorway of Estatston St Mary's.

The shrine of St Winifred (or Winefride) at Shrewsbury Abbey, a Welsh saint whose bones were brought here in the 12th century. Henry V visited the shrine in 1416 to give thanks for his victories over the French.

St James's church at Stirchley in Telford is Grade I listed and has a surviving 12th century stone chancel (shown nearside). Originally a Norman chapel, it was partially rebuilt in 1741 and extended in 1838.

St Laurence's church at Church Stretton has a 12th century Norman nave and 13th century transepts.

LEFT: Norman carving of Christ on the lake in Wenlock Priory churchyard. CENTRE LEFT: More surviving Norman architecture at Wenlock Priory. CENTRE RIGHT: Norman Chancel arch at St John the Baptist church, Hope Bagot. RIGHT: The 12th century spire of St Mary's church at Cleobury Mortimer is renowned for its crooked spire, the combined result of the warping of its oak timbers, and damp-induced rot where the timber spire sits on the masonry tower.

Inside the Grade I listed All Saints' church at Claverley. Here we see the original Norman arches (left) that were part of the late 11th century church built by Roger de Montgomery, a close-up of the medieval wall paintings (centre) which adorn the walls above the arches and date from around 1200, and the church's Norman font (right).

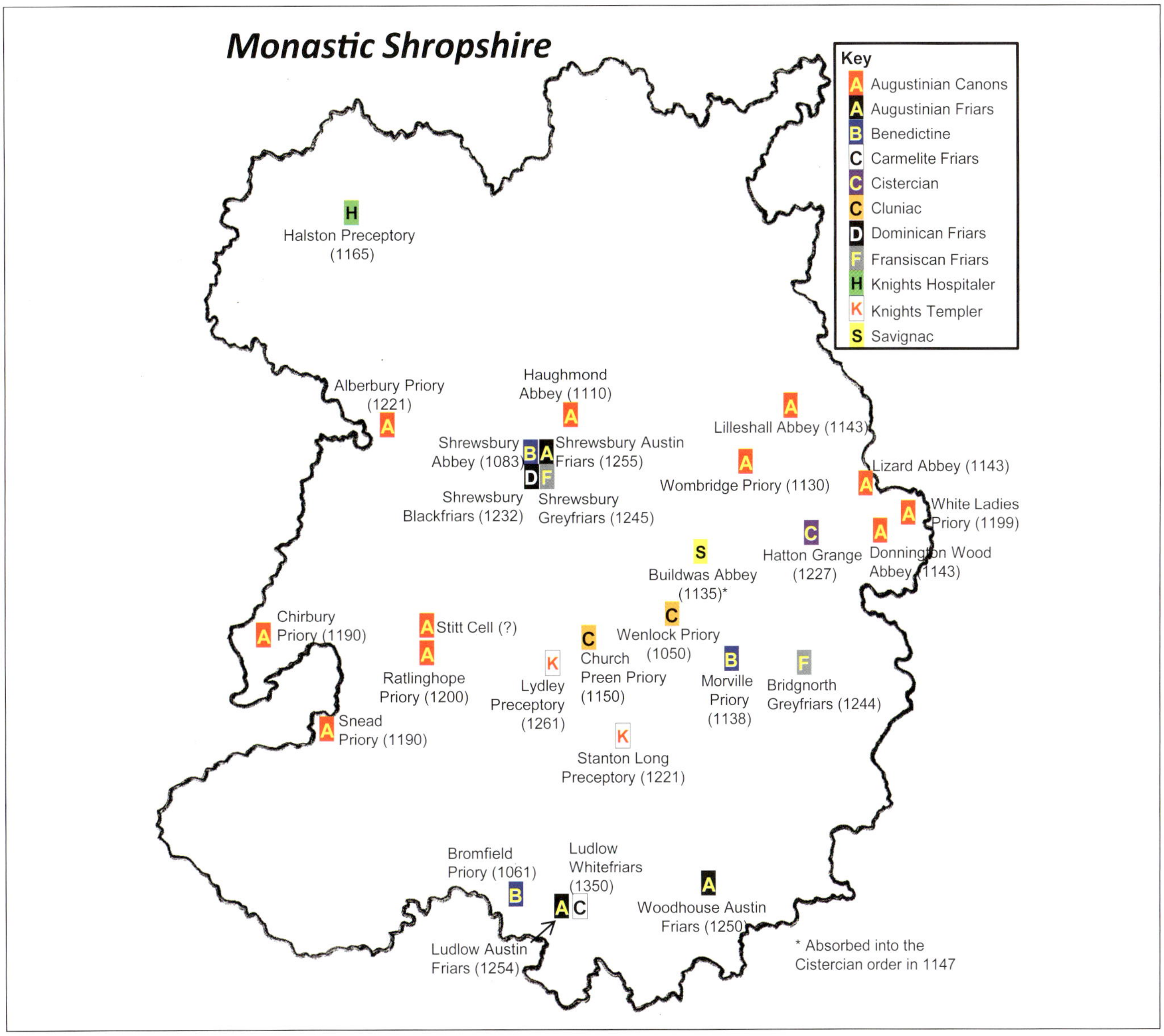

It was also in the early post-Conquest period that many new monasteries were founded in Shropshire, plus one nunnery (White Ladies Priory). The most important institutions were those at Much Wenlock and Shrewsbury, both founded by Roger de Montgomery, 1st Earl of Shrewsbury in 1079 and 1083, respectively, with the former built on the site of an earlier 7th century monastery. Both are Grade I listed.

The Anglo-Saxon monastery at Much Wenlock was originally founded in around 680 AD and it was still occupied by monks until after the Norman Conquest. However, in 1079, Roger de Montgomery replaced the abbey with a Cluniac priory for men. In the early 14th century, the priory church underwent a lavish rebuild, and was around 350 feet long (110m), making it the largest monastic building in the county. Its prominence is evident to anyone visiting the impressive remains today. Alas, many other features are lost without trace, like the clock tower for which Henry III gave six oak trees in 1233. Wenlock Priory once housed more monks than any other Shropshire monastic house; around 40 monks by the end of the 13th century. However, following its dissolution in the late 1530s, several buildings, including the late 15th century Priors House, were converted into a private residence later known as "Wenlock Abbey". The house was restored in the 19th century, and survives today.

> **Quirk Alert:** *Perrin and Baggins…*
>
> *When Roger de Montgomery, 1st Earl of Shrewsbury, founded Shrewsbury Abbey in 1083, the first two Benedictine monks to arrive were called Reginald and Frodo! They arrived from the great Benedictine abbey of Saint-Martin-de-Séez in Southern Normandy, and began to plan and build the monks' lodging.*

The Benedictine Shrewsbury Abbey initially incorporated a small pre-Conquest wooden church of St Peter, and it was generously endowed. It also gained considerable prestige when the monks acquired the bones of St Winifred from Basingwerk Abbey in Flintshire in around 1138. Shrewsbury Abbey was a monastery of medium size, housing between 12 and 18 monks in the later Middle Ages, while their abbots were entitled to wear mitres from 1397 onwards, and regularly attended parliaments. The abbey then grew to be one of the most important and influential abbeys in England, and an important centre of pilgrimage. Although much of Shrewsbury Abbey was destroyed in the early 1540s following the Dissolution, the nave survived as a parish church, and today serves as the mother church for the Parish of Holy Cross.

Buildwas Abbey was founded in 1135 by Roger de Clinton, Bishop of Coventry as a Savignac monastery, and was inhabited by a small community of monks from Furness Abbey. However, Welsh raids were not uncommon, and during the rebellion of Owain Glyndŵr in 1406, raiders from Powys kidnapped the abbot. The most notorious threat, though, came from within – this being in 1342 when one of the Buildwas monks, Thomas of Tong, murdered his abbot! Dissolved in 1536, the estate was granted to Edward Grey, 3rd Baron Grey of Powis, while in the 17th century, the abbot's house and infirmary were incorporated into a new private house. The impressive remains are now owned by English Heritage, and are considered to be among the best-preserved 12th century Cistercian survivors in England.

The monks of these institutions were also active in the colonisation of uncultivated land in Shropshire. Buildwas Abbey had granges at Hatton, Cosford, and Ruckley, and was responsible for pushing the limits of cultivation on its estate on the wild Stiperstones. At the same time, Shrewsbury, Haughmond and Lilleshall had fulling mills, and the houses on the fringe of Coalbrookdale coalfield were all operating bloomeries for making iron by the 1530s. Meanwhile, friaries arrived in England in the mid-13th century, and the Dominicans or black friars were the first to arrive in Shropshire in 1232, when they built a friary in Shrewsbury on the steep slope between the walls

> **Quirk Alert:** *Chest Inflection*
>
> *Shown right are two remarkable chests at St Gregory's church, Morville. The first photo is of the Crusade Chest, which is of ancient dug-out construction – in that it consists of a large, single main trunk of an oak tree. The information panel at the church states that "it is almost certainly 'bog-hardened', by immersing in mud and underwater, and it is too heavy to move other than being dragged by a horse". In terms of age, a chest with only one lock almost certainly pre-dates an edict issued by Pope Innocent III (1198-1216) which stated that all churches without secure storage should install one, and that such storage was to have three locks, and the three keys should reside one each with the Bishop, the Priest and a lay member (usually a churchwarden).*
>
> *The second chest dates from 1530-1560 and, therefore, has three locks! It is constructed of weathered oak boards that are tenoned into box form with legs. It is believed that this is the chest which was used to hide the church silver from Parliamentarian soldiers during the English Civil War. The chest was allegedly dumped into the Mor brook, but as both churchwardens who hid it were subsequently killed in the conflict, its location remained unknown until it was revealed decades later thanks to a long, dry summer – with all of its silver safe and sound inside!*

> ### Quirk Alert: *Music and Lightning*
>
> *In 1118, after the church at Morville was rebuilt, it was re-dedicated to St Gregory by Geoffrey, Bishop of Hereford. However, on completion of the ceremony, a violent storm broke out, and a group of three men and two women were caught out on the road home without shelter. As a record from the time states: "One of the women was killed by a stroke of lightning, and the other, being scorched by the flash from the navel to the soles of the feet, perished miserably, the men only narrowly escaping with their lives. Their five horses were also struck with the lightning, and killed."*

St Andrew's church at Stanton upon Hine Heath dates from the 12th century with 13th and 14th century additions. Although added somewhat later, check out the very large tower buttresses!

The nave and chancel at St Bartholomew's church at Moreton Corbet date from the 12th century.

and the River Severn, now the site of Blackfriars Crescent. They were followed by the Franciscans, or grey friars who arrived in Bridgnorth in 1244 and Shrewsbury in 1245 – again on the banks of the Severn, this time just west of English Bridge. The Augustinians arrived in Shrewsbury in 1255 and built their friary on the western loop of the Severn near to Welsh Bridge, while further Austin Friars set up friaries in Woodhouse near Cleobury Mortimer (1250) and Ludlow (1254); Ludlow also became home to a Carmelite friary (white friars) a century later in 1350.

One of the most unusual medieval religious institutions in Shropshire was the Palmers Guild of Ludlow, whose statutes date from 1284, although its foundation is older than that. The guild acquired extensive properties in Ludlow during the 14th century, while some of its richest members provided money for annual memorial services to be held on behalf of themselves and their kin. In 1446, it purchased in Bristol a hundred wainscot boards for the choir stalls in St Laurence's church in Ludlow, and which are still there. The guild also provided a grammar school for Ludlow in 1431, while between 1462 and 1482, guild member John Hosier endowed the almshouses which still bear his name. By the time the guild was dissolved in 1522, it possessed 152 tenements, 14 shops and 75 other premises in Ludlow, which passed to the borough corporation – and which therefore assumed the guild's former responsibilities for the almshouses and the grammar school, and for the maintenance of the clergy serving the parish church.

> ### Quirk Alert: *The Town that became a Village*
>
> *Ruyton-XI-Towns, formerly Ruyton of the Eleven Towns, must be one of the UK's most unusually-named places. It acquired the name when a castle was built here in the 12th century, and it became the major manor of eleven local townships, mainly situated to the north and west of Ruyton, these being: Coton, Eardiston, Felton, Haughton, Rednal, Ruyton, Shelvock, Shotatton, Sutton, Tedsmore and Wykey. Today, most of these places survive as either hamlets or – like Coton – a smattering of farm buildings, and only six remain in the modern Ruyton civil parish; the other five are now in the parish of West Felton.*
>
> *As for the castle, this was built in the early 12th century by John le Strange, suffered major attacks in 1148, 1203, and was then destroyed in 1212 by the Welsh. It was rebuilt in the early 14th century, but was recorded as ruinous again by 1364. Meanwhile, the town also lost its market in 1407, a charter which had granted Ruyton the same status as the County of Bristol, since its founding in 1308.*
>
> *By the time medical student Arthur Conan Doyle worked here, as an unpaid assistant in Ruyton for a Dr Eliot, the former town had reverted to a village. Conan Doyle lived at Cliffe House for four months in 1878, and later recalled Ruyton in his* Memories and Recollections *(1923) as "not big enough to make one town, far less eleven!" Today, the village is the location of the annual Ruyton-XI-Towns tractor pull event, which attracts contestants from all over Europe!*

St Lucia's church at Upton Magna has a 12th century nave and chancel, while the tower dates from the 15th century.

St Michael's church at Chirbury dates from the late 12th century with early 13th century aisles and a west tower dating from c.1300.

SURVIVING MEDIEVAL MONASTIC HOUSES IN SHROPSHIRE

Some of the surviving ruins of Haughmond Abbey, which was founded in the early 12th century by William fitz Alan of Clun.

Lilleshall Abbey was founded between 1145 and 1148 and belonged to the rigorist Arrouaisian branch of the Augustinian order.

Buildwas Abbey was founded in 1135 by Roger de Clinton, Bishop of Coventry, as a Savignac monastery, and was inhabited by a small community of monks from Furness Abbey. Note the surviving tower window in the right-hand photo.

The surviving beautifully vaulted and tile-floored chapter house at Buildwas Abbey.

Bromfield Priory Gatehouse. It belonged to Bromfield Priory, which was a college of secular canons, founded before 1061.

The only remains of Chirbury Priory, founded in c.1190 by Robert de Buthlers, Lord of Montgomery.

St Gregory's church at Morville was the priory church of Morville Priory, founded in around 1138 after its appropriation by Shrewsbury Abbey. Much of the church still dates from the 12th century.

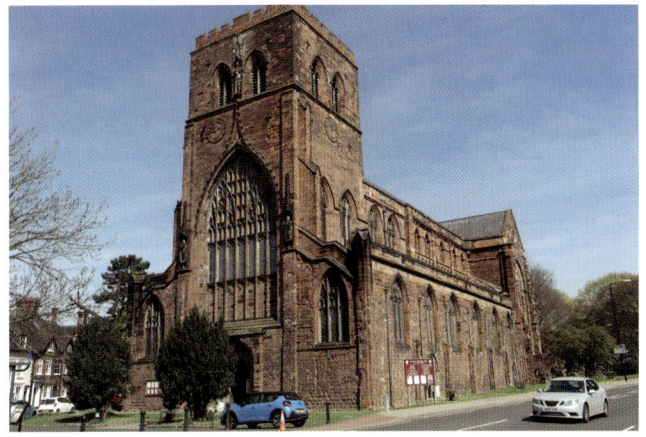

Shrewsbury Abbey. It was founded in 1083 as a Benedictine monastery by the Norman Earl of Shrewsbury, Roger de Montgomery. It is also the fictional home of Ellis Peters' Brother Cadfael.

Wenlock Priory dates from the 11th/12th century. Here we see the inside of part of the western façade.

White Ladies Priory was founded in the late 12th century. The name refers to the canonesses who lived here and who wore white habits.

Some of the remains of Wombridge Priory which was founded in the early 12th century, probably by William FitzAlan.

The surviving chapter house at Wenlock Priory.

Some of the surviving detail within the chapter house at Wenlock Priory.

Following on from the first raft of post-Conquest castles, were these medieval Shropshire castles:

Medieval Castle	Description
Acton Burnell Castle	A fortified manor house built in 1284 by Robert Burnell, Bishop of Bath and Wells, Chancellor of England from 1274-92, and friend and advisor to King Edward I for more than thirty years. On 12th October 1283, Edward held a Parliament at Acton Burnell, probably in the adjacent great barn, the only building large enough. Significantly, this was the first time in English history that the law-making process included the Commons as well as the Lords. It passed a law for the protection of creditors, which the King ratified and which became known as the Statute of Acton Burnell. As for the building, this was rectangular and three storeys high with a tower at each corner.
Alberbury Castle	Built in the early 13th century, probably by Fulk FitzWarine. Located 9 miles west of Shrewsbury, it was built to defend the English border against Welsh attacks.
Moreton Corbet Castle	A timber castle was built in c.1100 by the Toret family, eventually passing to the Corbet family in 1239. This was gradually replaced by a 13th century stone castle, which was dominated by the Great Tower. The process of extension and adaptation was completed in around 1580, by Robert Corbet, who built an impressive Elizabethan eastern range.
Red Castle	Built in 1227 by Henry de Audley, after which the village became known as Weston under Redcastle. The Audleys forfeited the castle when the 7th Baron Audley led a rebellion against Henry VII in 1497 and was executed. The castle fell into ruin and was replaced by Hawkstone Hall in the 17th century.
Shrawardine Castle	Motte and bailey castle built in the mid-12th century and completed by 1165. During the English Civil War, it was initially a Royalist garrison but was captured by Parliamentarians in June 1645 and then subsequently destroyed.
Stokesay Castle	A fortified manor house, built in 1281-91 by Laurence de Ludlow, a wealthy local wool-merchant. King Edward I granted a licence to crenellate in 1291. Largely unaltered since, although the Baldwyn family added a timber-framed gatehouse in the mid-17th century.
Tong Castle	Built in the 12th century and altered in the 16th by Sir Harry Vernon. Changed hands three times during the Civil War, but survived. George Durant demolished most of the original house in 1764 and replaced it with a Gothic castle, which was in turn demolished in 1954.
Wattlesborough Castle	Built in the late 13th century by Sir Richard Corbet, comprising a square two storey tower surrounded by a moated enclosure with a fishpond. Bought by the Leighton family in 1501 and used as their chief residence until 1711. Only the roofless tower remains.

During the 14th century, agricultural progress and population growth came to a shuddering halt, country-wide. A series of natural disasters were largely to blame, including the crisis years of 1315 to 1322 when it is estimated that the national population declined by at least 15 per cent. This period was marked by widespread outbreaks of sheep murrain and poor, wet summers, with the latter resulting in poor harvests and subsequent famine. However, all of these setbacks were nothing compared with the Black Death which first arrived in England in 1348 and is estimated to have taken up to half of England's population, returning it

Acton Burnell Castle, built in the late 13th century by Robert Burnell, Chancellor of England from 1274-92.

Alberbury Castle, built in the early 13th century, probably by Fulk FitzWarine.

Stokesay Castle is one of the finest surviving fortified manor houses in England, and dates from the late 13th century. It was built by Laurence de Ludlow on the site of an earlier castle built by the de Lacy's.

This view of Moreton Corbet Castle shows the Great Tower on the right and the Gatehouse on the left, both of which date from the early 13th century. The Great Tower would have dominated the medieval castle.

to its Domesday Book level of just over two million, some three centuries earlier. One result of this series of catastrophes was that by the 1350s, thousands of Shropshire fields lay uncultivated as there weren't enough peasants to till the fields.

The other effect of these setbacks was that a number of Shropshire hamlets and villages became depopulated during the 14th century, and are known today as deserted or shrunken medieval villages. Remarkably, the website shropshirehistory.com lists *several hundred* depopulated Shropshire villages, along with appropriate evidence. For example, in the hundred of Ford, of the 70 hamlets listed in Domesday Book (1086), 9 are now totally deserted and 33 are single farms.

There were other factors that led to depopulation though. For starters, a number of Shropshire villages, such as Berfield in the Clun area, were totally wiped out by Welsh raiders! In addition, ruthless landowners wiped out entire villages to accommodate their great houses (such as at Shipton), and ruthless "capitalist graziers" also drove out families to make money from their land. Some deserted villages, such as Abdon, Cold Weston and Heath, are still marked by isolated medieval churches, and many more are marked by house platforms, or rectangular earthworks resulting from the gradual collapse of houses. One of the best-preserved sites is Lawton, a township in Diddlebury parish, located by a bridge over the River Corve. A "main street" of house platforms runs through an orchard to the village pond, and a network of footpaths radiates from the bridge, while also still visible is the site of the local mill.

Ludlow is one of the best-preserved medieval new towns in Europe. The first component of this planned town was probably the tract extending from the castle along the top of the promontory between the rivers Teme and Corve. This was comprised of a wide market place with long strips called burgage plots running north and south, these being the original plots of land rented by the first inhabitants. Later growth followed the line of Old Street and Corve Street, with the lower part of the latter set out with burgage plots before 1186. The parish church was then enlarged in 1199, suggesting a sizeable town by this stage. By 1270, High Street was home to rows of market stalls which later became permanent structures, with cellars below and solars above. Similar in-filled market places have been suggested at Church Stretton and Wellington, while the pattern of a market place with a grid of streets to one side is identifiable on a smaller scale at Bridgnorth and Clun. However, Ludlow's configuration of burgage plots, filled with buildings at right-angles to the road behind the frontage, is duplicated in every medieval town in Shropshire, although it is at Bishop's Castle where Shropshire's medieval street layout is best-preserved, with the back lanes at the end of the burgage plots still largely intact.

Most of Shropshire's larger medieval towns were walled, and the oldest surviving wall masonry today dates largely from the 13th century. Ludlow's walls date from 1233, long after the basic pattern of the town's streets had been established – and most of the circuit survives, including one gateway, albeit in an altered form. Meanwhile, the north gate at Bridgnorth also survives, although this has been largely rebuilt twice, once in the 1740s and again in 1911. It is also possible to trace much of the town's walls even though only fragments remain. At Shrewsbury, one fine tower remains to the south of the town centre, and which is known as Town Walls Tower. Shrewsbury's town walls were built a number of times throughout the Middle Ages, always to protect the town against Welsh raids. One of the most significant builds occurred between 1220 and 1242, after Henry III issued a royal mandate urging the men of Salop to fortify the town, and the King stayed in Shrewsbury on several occasions during his campaign against the Welsh. By the late 14th century, though, the walls had apparently fallen derelict, and it was Henry IV who commissioned further rebuilding. It was probably at this time that Town Walls Tower was built. In fact, the town was still almost fully encircled by walls, featuring similar observation towers, as late as 1575. As for the town walls at both Oswestry and Wem, these are no longer visible.

LEFT: The Grade I listed Broad Gate in Ludlow is the original 13th century south gatehouse to the town walls – with 16th to 18th century additions. The building to the left dates from the 17th century, while to the right is the early 18th century Wheatsheaf Inn. Both are Grade II listed. CENTRE: The north gate at Bridgnorth retains some of its medieval stonework but has been largely rebuilt twice (1740s and 1911). It was once one of five gates used to enter the walled town; today, it is a museum. RIGHT: Town Walls Tower in Shrewsbury dates from the rebuild of Shrewsbury's town walls in the late 14th century; the lower course is 13th century.

Quirk Alert: *The Bradling Stone*

In the centre of Norton-in-Hales is a glacial boulder known as the Bradling Stone where, according to folklore, any male found working after mid-day on Shrove Tuesday was bumped or "bradled". The megalithic.co.uk website provides more insight, stating that the person would be "either beaten, bumped or rolled on this stone", while visitoruk.com suggests that it was on Shrove Tuesday (first celebrated in England in the late Middle Ages) and other holy days that offenders would be "bumped on the stone as punishment". The latter website also describes another legend, suggesting that the stone "marked the boundary of the parish and, on the occasion of Beating the Bounds, the younger members would be bumped on the stone so that they would remember the parish boundary."

More recently, itinerant teams of farm labourers, after taking refreshment in the local inn, would challenge each other to fights with the stakes being placed on the Bradling Stone!

In terms of medieval self-government, the larger Shropshire towns achieved this via charters and incorporation. Shrewsbury had a succession of charters with the first granted by Henry I (1100-1135), while during the reign of King John (1199-1216), the town was empowered to select bailiffs to head its government. Shrewsbury was also one of the first boroughs to be represented in Parliament, in 1268 and 1283. Bridgnorth, which had become a royal borough in 1102, acquired its first charter in 1157. However, this only happened two years after Henry II took the town during a siege, which became necessary because Bridgnorth had fallen into the hands of Hugh de Mortimer during King Stephen's reign (1135-1154). Following Henry's accession, Hugh was one of the Barons who objected to the King's demand for the return of royal castles in 1155, and he refused to give up Bridgnorth. Henry therefore launched a campaign in May 1155 against Hugh, simultaneously besieging his three principal castles of Bridgnorth, Cleobury and Wigmore. On 7th July 1155, Hugh formally submitted to Henry II at the Council at Bridgnorth, where he was rather generously allowed to keep his own two castles; Bridgnorth, of course, returned to the crown. As for the borough of Bridgnorth, it returned members to Parliament from 1295. Meanwhile, Oswestry received its market charter in 1190 and gained authority to administer its own affairs in 1399 after the Shrewsbury Parliament of the previous year had adjourned there, while Ludlow Corporation was granted a charter by Edward IV in 1461 and the borough returned its first MPs in 1467.

Although the town of Much Wenlock was small, the *borough* of Wenlock was, in area, the largest non-county borough in England. It was created by a charter of 1468 and comprised most of the

On the left is the surviving 13th century entrance gate tower to Wenlock Priory. The house nearside is on the road known as Bull Ring and dates from around 1600.

St Mary's church at Longnor is Grade I listed and dates from c.1260 to 1270, with early 18th century and c.1840 alterations and additions.

This is the Grade II listed Cruck Cottage at Upton Magna. The two internal pairs of crucks have been dated by dendrochronology to 1269, making them the second oldest standing crucks in Europe. The end gable crucks were dated to 1424-26, a time when the building was remodelled.

The Old Guildhall in Newport dates from around 1400, although it was extended to the north in the 16th century with a gable added to the north end of the street front in the 19th century. The frontage is also inscribed with the date 1615 alongside the name William Gregari.

extensive lands owned by Wenlock Priory. The borough courts had wide powers of jurisdiction, dealing with matters like coroners' inquisitions, which were usually the domain of Quarter Sessions, while by the 1490s, the borough was returning two MP's to parliament. As for Shrewsbury, the county town had become large and prosperous by the 13th century, with archaeological evidence suggesting a large rebuilding during this period. The poll tax returns of 1377 show that – with a population of around 3,000 – Shrewsbury was the 17th largest town in England, and with a population of around 1,700, Ludlow was 34th and Bridgnorth 41st. Much of the prosperity of these towns was based upon the wool trade, the main product of rural Shropshire – although the tradesmen who took most of the profit were town-dwellers! Indeed, of the 5,000 sacks of wool that England exported in 1273, 660 of them were provided by Shropshire wool merchants, the largest total of any inland county. The most powerful of these merchants was Nicholas de Ludlow – ironically from Shrewsbury! State papers from 1278 report that merchants from Flanders (the main importers of English wool) paid £2,022 to de Ludlow – a king's ransom back in the 13th century.

The most prolific survivor of medieval Shropshire is the period black and white timbered property. They are everywhere in the county, seemingly in every village, while the best town-centric examples are to be found in Shrewsbury, Ludlow and Much Wenlock. Alas, examples aren't so prolific in the towns of Bridgnorth, Newport, Shifnal and Wem – as these towns were hit by devastating fires between the 15th and 17th centuries. Meanwhile, it was also during the medieval period that most towns and a number of villages received their first market charters. The shropshirehistory.com website lists 51 places, and these have been captured in chronological order in the table below.

Note, that the dates appearing in blue text relate to the date that the first *fair* was granted to the place in question, as the date of the first *market* charter is deemed by shropshirehistory.com to be "Prescriptive". In other words, the markets became established or accepted over a long passage of time, with all of them established earlier than their first fair. Meanwhile,

Place	Date 1st Charter	Day Market Held	Place	Date 1st Charter	Day Market Held	Place	Date 1st Charter	Day Market Held
Ludlow	Anglo-Saxon	Thursday	Stottesdon	1244	Tuesday	Madeley	1269	Tuesday
Newport	Anglo-Saxon	Fri, Sat	Wellington	1244	Thursday	Worthen	1270	Wednesday
Quatford	Anglo-Saxon	Not known	Market Drayton	1245	Wednesday	Stanway	1271	Thursday
Shrewsbury	1094	Tue, Wed, Fri, Sat	Shifnal	1245	Monday	Tong	1271	Thursday
Much Wenlock	1138	Sunday	Knockin	1249	Tuesday	Wattlesborough	1272	Tuesday
Caus	1200	Wednesday	Lydbury North	1249	Friday	Rushbury	1283	Thursday
Clun	1204	Saturday	Pulverbatch	1254	Monday	Alberbury	1284	Friday
Church Stretton	1214	Wednesday	Baschurch	1256	Tuesday	Hodnet	1292	Tuesday
Whittington	1219	Wednesday	Betton	1256	Thursday	Wheathill	1300	Thursday
Ellesmere	1221	Tuesday	Culmington	1257	Tuesday	Cheswardine	1304	Monday
Holdgate	1222	Thursday	Prees	1259	Tuesday	Wistanstow	1306	Wednesday
Bridgnorth	1226	Fri, Sat	Shelve	1261	Friday	Ruyton-XI-Towns	1308	Wednesday
Cleobury Mortimer	1226	Saturday	Aston Botterell	1263	Tuesday	Adderley	1315	Thursday
Eaton	1227	Thursday	Burford	1266	Saturday	Chetwynd	1318	Tuesday
Much Wenlock	1227	Monday	High Ercall	1267	Monday	Leebotwood	1320	Thursday
Oswestry	1228	Tuesday	Lydham	1267	Friday	Whitchurch	1362	Friday
Albrighton	1232	Tuesday	Acton Burnell	1269	Tuesday	Bishops Castle	1394	Wednesday

the first three entries in the list don't have dates of first charter, mainly because they were established in Anglo-Saxon times, so these were also deemed to be "Prescriptive". Shrewsbury also belongs to this group, as the date of 1094 is the date that William I granted an annual fair to the town in addition to its weekly market, with the fair taking place each year on 1st August. Another four annual fair grants followed for Shrewsbury in 1205, 1267, 1309 and 1327.

We have already established that Shropshire territory was consistently subject to Welsh raids from the Iron Age through to the medieval period. Barrie Trinder in his *A History of Shropshire* surmises that "in some respects such disorders did no more than reflect the natural disaffinity between highlanders and lowlanders". He is referring to the harsh living circumstances of the more westerly hill-folk compared to the rich arable and pastoral lands of the English Midlands, and which presented "a continuing temptation, regardless of the political situation on the border" – particularly with regard to the seemingly "rich beyond imagination" towns of Shrewsbury, Ludlow and Bridgnorth. At the time of Domesday Book, Offa's Dyke still formed the border between Shropshire and Wales, except for one small Welsh area east of the dyke and the district around Montgomery which, back then, belonged to Shropshire. Despite this, large tracts of western Shropshire became a buffer zone controlled by the powerful Marcher lords; powerful because they had been granted the right by English kings to exercise almost regal powers in return for preventing further Welsh incursions. Marcher lords could therefore build castles, administer laws, wage war, establish markets in towns, and maintain their own chanceries that kept their records. They had their own deputies, or sheriffs, and sitting in their own courts they had jurisdiction over all cases at law save high treason.

It was during the 12th century that this gradual awarding of privileges by the Crown to the Marcher lords resulted in them acting almost as independent states; indeed, for some time, this resulted in the exclusion of the judicial authority of the monarch and of his representative, the Sheriff of Shropshire. One of the first Marcher lords was Roger de Montgomery, who was created 1st Earl of Shrewsbury in 1071, with powers bestowed upon him to bring peace to the borderland. He was succeeded in 1094 by his son, Hugh, who suffered a defeat to the Welsh army at Montgomery a year later in 1095. Also Marcher lords were the FitzAlans, who acquired lands in north-west Shropshire which became the lordship of Oswestry in 1114, and by 1155, they had also acquired the lordship of Clun in the south-west. In the second half of the 12th century, the FitzAlans withdrew Oswestry and the adjacent lordships from the authority of the Sheriff of Shropshire, and then repeated the manoeuvre at Clun. Meanwhile, from just after the Conquest until the early 14th century, the Corbets of Caus (near Westbury) dominated the central Shropshire borderland in between Oswestry and Clun. Caus Castle was built by Roger Fitz Corbet in the late 11th century, and it was from here that the Corbets ruled, withdrawing from royal jurisdiction large parts of the hundreds of Chirbury and Ford as early as the 1230s. Another of the great Marcher lords' families was the Mortimers, of Wigmore. They settled in the borderland a generation earlier than the FitzAlans, but it wasn't until Roger Mortimer was Lord of Wigmore, from 1246 to 1282, that his family's powers reached their zenith. This occurred when he took advantage of the Second Barons' War in the 1260s (Simon de Montfort's opposition to the rule of Henry III when de Montfort briefly became *de facto* ruler of England) to gain the manors of Cleobury Mortimer and Chelmarsh. Then in 1301, a later Roger Mortimer gained possession of Ludlow Castle through marriage, while in 1316, he was appointed Lord Lieutenant of Ireland. It was also this Roger Mortimer who led the Marcher lords in a revolt against Edward II in what became known as the Despenser War. Captured and imprisoned in the Tower of London in 1322, he later escaped to France, where he was joined by Edward's queen consort Isabella. A successful invasion and rebellion followed, Edward was deposed, and Mortimer became *de facto* ruler of England for three years before he was overthrown by Edward's eldest son, Edward III. Accused of assuming royal power and other crimes, Mortimer was executed by hanging at Tyburn. Nevertheless, in the 14th and 15th centuries, the Mortimers remained one of the most powerful families in the kingdom, and both they and the FitzAlans held the office of Sheriff of Shropshire at varying times, using it to increase their own powers.

A 14th century sculpture of the Virgin and Child in Holy Cross church, also known as Shrewsbury Abbey.

The refectory pulpit from Shrewsbury Abbey, which dates from around 1300. Today, it stands alone to the south of the abbey, in the middle of a car park! It is essentially a victim of the Dissolution, as the north and south transepts were demolished in 1540, while almost three hundred years later, Thomas Telford built a road through the abbey grounds, partitioning off the refectory pulpit from the main body of the abbey.

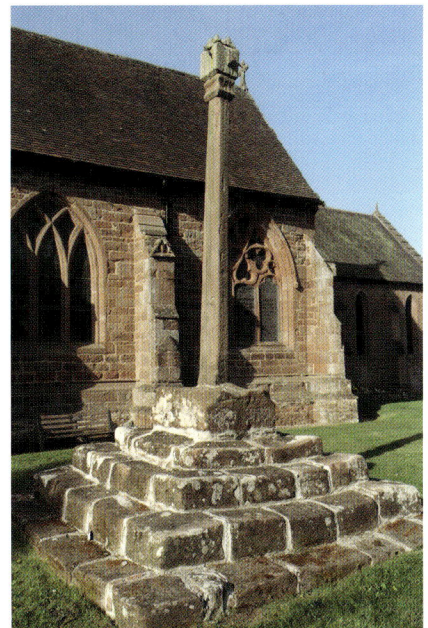

A Grade II listed medieval cross in Alberbury churchyard which probably dates from the 12th century when St Michael and All Angels' church was built. The head of the cross has been removed and replaced by a sundial – probably in the 17th century.

The Butter Cross at Newport was built here in High Street in around 1280 in memory of Roger de Pyvelesdon and is hence also known as the Pulestone Cross. The butter market was later built around it in 1632 by Richard Barnefield.

A buttercross located just north of Alveley. It was probably erected in the mid-14th century when the Black Death was rife, and folk were said to leave butter and other commodities here for the villagers to collect. Around 60% of the village's population perished from the disease.

Unsurprisingly, therefore, many of the principal dramas of national politics played out during the 13th century revolved around the borderland. In 1211, King John assembled an army at Oswestry and personally led two incursions into Wales, taking 20 hostages. The following year, the Welsh, under Llywelyn ap Iorwerth stormed John's newly-built castle at Aberystwyth. Alas, in response, a merciless John publicly executed his 20 hostages in Shrewsbury, including seven-year-old Rhys ap Maelgw. Unsurprisingly, Llywelyn the Great hit back and in 1217, his forces occupied all of Powys and took possession of Shrewsbury and its castle.

By this stage, John had been succeeded by a nine-year-old Henry III (1216-1272), and the latter would later go on to spend large spells of his reign in Shropshire either engaged in military operations against, or negotiations with the Welsh. In 1221, still during the King's minority, a treaty was signed at Shrewsbury with Llywelyn ap Iorwerth, but two years later Llywelyn had captured the castles at Kinnerley and Whittington. He followed this up in the early 1230s by laying waste to parts of the Marches, and in 1233 burnt Oswestry and Clun and occupied Shrewsbury. A peace settlement was then brokered in 1234 – again in Shropshire, this time at Myddle. However, when Llywelyn ap Iorwerth died in 1240, Henry III marched with an army from Gloucester the following year, to Shrewsbury, to counter the incursive threat now posed by Llywelyn's son, Dafydd.

We've already mentioned the Second Barons' War of 1264-67, when Simon de Montfort's forces seized Shrewsbury, Ludlow and Richards Castle, but alongside these events, Llywelyn ap Gruffudd (grandson of Llywelyn ap Iorwerth) began to threaten English authority in the borderland, too. With England weakened by internal division, a temporary peace was established in 1267 by the Treaty of Montgomery, which acknowledged Llywelyn ap Gruffudd as Prince of Wales, the only time an English ruler – Henry III in this case – recognised the right of a ruler of Gwynedd over Wales. The treaty also ceded Builth to Llywelyn, along with Brecon and Gwerthrynion in mid-Wales, while Llywelyn was also granted Whittington Castle, previously held by his grandfather in the 1220s.

Another frequent Shropshire visitor was Edward I (1272-1307), a very different proposition from Henry III. Edward declared war on Llywelyn at Michaelmas 1276, assembled his army at Worcester in 1277, and marched through Shropshire to secure bases at Oswestry and Montgomery. Indeed, for a number of months in 1277, the courts of the Exchequer and King's Bench sat in Shrewsbury. Llywelyn then submitted to Edward in November 1277, as the King's army besieged Snowdonia, while Edward also enforced the Treaty of Aberconwy, which superseded the stipulations laid down at Montgomery and severely curbed Llywelyn's power. Edward also began building his Welsh castles at this time, but fighting broke out again in the spring of 1282 when an English army under the Earl of Gloucester was defeated at Llandeilo and Oswestry was sacked immediately before Easter. A response came in December 1282, when an English army marched to Builth Wells from Montgomery Castle, to surprise and kill Llywelyn, allegedly by the hand of a Shropshire trooper called Stephen Frankton.

Edward followed this up by besieging Snowdonia in an attempt to starve the Welsh into submission, and who were now led by Llywelyn's brother, Dafydd – although he was captured in June 1283. A parliament was then summoned at Shrewsbury and adjourned to Acton Burnell. Here, the lords sat in the hall of the castle, and the commons in the neighbouring barn. The main focus was the trial of Dafydd ap Gruffydd who, as a baron of the English realm was accused of treason. He was found guilty, of course, and suffered a hideous death – dragged by a horse through the streets of Shrewsbury, to be hanged, to have his heart and intestines burnt, to have his head cut off and his body quartered. The four quarters were then exhibited in different parts of the kingdom, and the heads of Dafydd and his brother, Llywelyn, were displayed on spikes at the Tower of London!

Moving forward a century to 1398, Parliament was adjourned from London to Shrewsbury Abbey, where both the Lords and the Commons met. The following year, Henry IV usurped Richard II to claim the English throne, while shortly after this, further trouble flared up with Wales. This time, the Welsh were led by Owain Glyndŵr (Owen Glendower in English), who declared himself Prince of Wales on 16th September 1400 and instigated a fierce and long-running war aimed at gaining independence from the English. The uprising was initially very successful and rapidly gained control of large areas of Wales; indeed, it was even reported that Welsh scholars at Oxford and Cambridge had left to join the revolt! Then, on 22nd June 1402, the Welsh fought the English, led by Sir Edmund Mortimer, at Bryn Glas – a battle that opened with the Welsh archers in the English army turning their bows on their own side, butchering the English and mutilating the dead bodies.

Despite this, Owain Glyndŵr gained as an ally, a certain Henry Percy, Earl of Northumberland – who had actually been one of Henry IV's principal allies in the usurping of Richard II, and had initially supported Henry IV in his wars against both Owain Glyndŵr and the Scots. However, a wedge was driven between Henry IV and the Percys due to lands promised to them in return for their continued support, along with money and royal favour. This promise included lands in and around Cumberland but which were instead given to a rival, while the promised money allegedly didn't materialise, either. That said, Henry IV had still bestowed numerous civil and military offices on the Percys, and granted them numerous lands and castles, while other accounts mention that as late as March 1403, another large grant of land was made to the Percys as reward for their loyalty.

We must now introduce Henry Percy's son, also called Henry Percy, but known more commonly as Harry Hotspur. He was a one-time ally, friend and tourney colleague of the King, and supporter of Henry IV's overthrow of Richard II. He was therefore also richly rewarded, appointed as justiciary of Wales and Chester, and later lord lieutenant, all complemented by the grants of castles at Beaumaris, Caernarvon, Chester, Conwy and Flint. It was also Harry Hotspur who led the English to victory over the Scots at the Battle of Homildon Hill in 1402. However, the Percys had funded that war, but the King was slow to repay them, while he also denied them their ransom rights for the captured Scottish nobles – as was the chivalric norm. Furthermore, Hotspur was enraged at Henry IV's refusal to pay a just ransom to Owain Glyndŵr, for Edmund Mortimer, Hotspur's brother-in-law, whom Glyndŵr had captured in June 1402.

All of these factors, together with the promotion of Lancastrian interest in the north, meant that in the summer of 1403, Henry Percy, 1st Earl of Northumberland and Thomas Percy, 1st Earl of Worcester publicly renounced their allegiance to Henry. Furthermore, they charged him with imprisoning and murdering King Richard II, and also accused him of perjury because he claimed the throne in addition to his old lands and titles, and taxed the clergy despite his promise not to without the consent of Parliament. Harry Hotspur therefore led an army south where he was destined to meet Henry IV's forces on 21st July 1403; the scene was set for the biggest battle in Shropshire history.

> **Quirk Alert:** *Tales of Shrewsbury*
>
> *Apparently, the Battle of Shrewsbury took place in a field of ripening peas! Indeed, they are thought to have hampered the advance of the royal forces. Somewhat less light-hearted is this quote from Jehan Waurin in around 1450: "As I have heard tell by word of mouth and by writing…there was never in the kingdom of England, since the conquest of Duke William, so horrible a battle or so much Christian blood spilled as in this." (Thomas Walsingham, d.1422).*
>
> *On the eve of the Battle of Shrewsbury, having found that the royals held the town, it is known that Harry Hotspur retreated to Berwick, around 3 miles to the north-west of the town – and there is a popular myth about this. On the morning of battle, Hotspur was dismayed to find, whilst arming, he had left his favourite sword at the camp of the previous night, to which he is alleged to have said: "Now I see that my plough is drawing its last furrow, for a soothsayer once told me in my own country, that I should die at Berwick. Alas! He deceived me by that name, which I believed to mean Berwick in the north!"*

On his march south with around 200 men, some nobles joined Harry Hotspur, but he recruited most of his army in Cheshire, an area hostile to Henry IV and the sole county of England that had resisted the overthrow of Richard II. Hotspur was also joined by his uncle, the Earl of Worcester, and his army. Alas, Hotspur and Worcester weren't joined – as expected – by the self-proclaimed Prince of Wales, Owain Glyndŵr, as he was busy fighting in Carmarthenshire, although some Welsh forces from the Cheshire borders may have joined him.

The rebels then marched towards heavily-defended Shrewsbury. As for Henry IV, he had been heading north, believing he was going to be assisting the Percys against the Scots, but became aware of the southbound Percy forces on 12th July, whilst in Burton upon Trent. He therefore headed west to meet the immediate threat posed by the Percys, arriving in Shrewsbury before the Percys could capture the town.

As it turned out, both forces arrived in the Shrewsbury area on 20th July, with the Percy's setting up camp to the north of the Severn, and the King's forces to the south. The next day, the King's forces crossed the Severn at Uffington, about a mile to the east of Shrewsbury and the two armies took up position in a field about a mile south-west of where Battlefield Church now stands.

Estimates of the size of the two armies vary widely, although Henry IV's army is generally agreed to have been the larger. One report suggested 60,000 troops, but medieval chronicler, Thomas Walsingham, is more likely correct, estimating a royal army of 14,000 with some 9,000 to 10,000 rebels. What is generally agreed, though, is that the rebels lined up with three "battles", commanded by Hotspur in the centre, his uncle the Earl of Worcester on the right, and one-time enemy of the Percys, the Earl of Douglas on the left, while the King took the centre for the royals, Prince Henry the left and the Earls of Dunbar and Stafford the right.

Hotspur's army arrived first and formed up on a ridge of high ground which overlooked a field of ripening peas. For much of the morning of

THE BATTLE OF SHREWSBURY, 21ST JULY 1403
All photos are courtesy of the Battlefield Museum at Battlefield, Shrewsbury

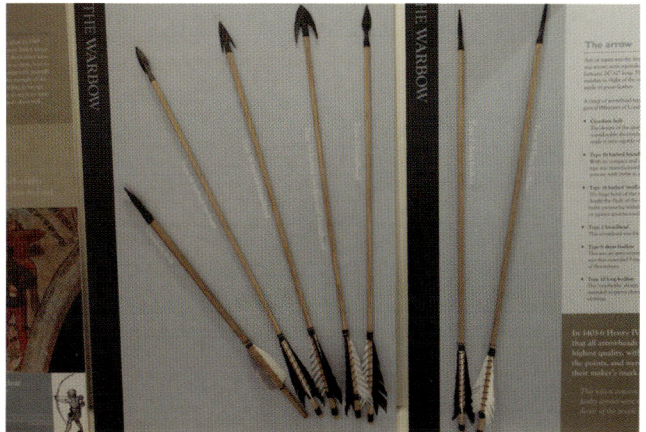 

LEFT: A selection of arrows that were in use at the time of the Battle of Shrewsbury. It was the first time that English archers had fought each other on English soil. One account by Jehan Waurin, c.1450, states: "For the sun which at that time was bright and clear then lost its brightness, so thick were the arrows." RIGHT: A close-up of a medieval arrow head (top) and a modern-day replica (bottom).

LEFT: This is the figure of Sir Nicholas Longford, dressed in armour from the early 1400s, which shows a late stage in the transition from mail to plate. The information panel describes all features of his armour enabling you to understand how ingenious the whole ensemble is. CENTRE: A mail coif which is made of thousands of linked iron rings and was worn underneath a helmet and on top of a padded coif. RIGHT: The "Great" helmet, which was passing out of use at the time of the Battle of Shrewsbury, having been a common item of battle between 1250 and 1400. It would typically have been worn on top of a mail coif.

Saturday 21st July, the two forces parleyed, with Thomas Prestbury, the abbot of Shrewsbury and the abbot of Haughmond presenting the King's terms. The headstrong and impetuous Hotspur, typically declined any terms and negotiations ended around noon. The battle, however, didn't commence until two hours before dusk, initiated by the King stating "proceed standard-bearer". In response, the right flank under Stafford advanced and was met by the left flank of the rebels under Douglas. There then followed a massive archery barrage from each side, with the rebels' Cheshire bowmen said to have proved superior. The royal vanguard therefore bore the brunt of the opening rebel arrow storm. Indeed, according to the *Dieulacres Chronicle* the King's right wing fled from the field, believed to be around 4,000 men, probably in response to their commander, the Earl of Stafford, having been killed early in the battle. It was probably also under this initial arrow onslaught that Prince Henry, Prince of Wales (and the future Henry V) was hit in the face with an arrow during the fighting, sustaining a terrible wound that would leave a permanent scar. Incredibly, he had the shaft removed, and carried on fighting with the arrow still lodged in his face and skull!

Despite these setbacks, enough of the King's men remained, particularly on the left wing, which was still under the command of the Prince of Wales. With things clearly going their way, Hotspur and the Earl of Douglas then led a rash charge aimed at killing the King himself. In the ensuing action, the Royal Standard was overthrown and its bearer, Sir Walter Blount, killed, Henry IV was unhorsed, and several royal-liveried knights slain. Crucially, though, Harry Hotspur was also killed in the charge, reputedly shot in the face with an arrow when he opened his visor. In the confusion of battle, though, the Northumbrian knights thought that Henry IV had been killed and proclaimed "Henry Percy King!" Henry IV thus retaliated by shouting "Henry Percy is dead", and with no reply to the contrary, the battle ended soon after – although other accounts attribute an outflanking manoeuvre by Prince Henry's reargard, which enveloped the smaller rebel force. Either way, the rebel force panicked and fled, although the Earls of Douglas and Worcester were captured, together with Cheshire captains, Sir Richard Venables and Sir Richard Vernon. Others scattered over a wide area, with the conflict degenerating into a murderous free-for-all. Nevertheless, as the King's forces sustained greater losses than the rebels, Henry IV was mighty close to losing both the throne and his life, and possibly would have done if Hotspur had shown more patience. Similarly, had Owain Glyndŵr shown up as planned, the result would have been even more likely to have gone the way of the Percys. Another case of history hanging by a thread!

As for Harry Hotspur, he was initially buried at Whitchurch, but rumours soon spread that he was not really dead – hence the King had him exhumed! According to the *Dieulacres Chronicle*, his body was preserved with salt and set up in Shrewsbury impaled on a spear between two millstones in the marketplace pillory, with an armed guard posted. The account also states that King Henry IV publicly berated the corpse before ordering it to be disembowelled, dismembered and cut into quarters – the latter parts being sent to and put on display in Bristol, Chester, London and Newcastle upon Tyne. His head was sent to York and impaled on the north gate, looking toward his own lands. Meanwhile, Thomas Percy, Sir Richard Venables, Sir Richard Vernon and Sir Henry Boynton were publicly hanged, drawn and quartered in Shrewsbury on 23rd July and their heads publicly displayed, Thomas Percy's on London Bridge where it was not removed until 18th December 1403!

Quirk Alert: *An Arrowing Wound*

Shown right is a model of the head of Prince Henry, the future Henry V, at the Battlefield Exhibition Centre. He was struck by an arrow during the battle which entered, at an angle, next to his nose on the left side of his face. After the arrow shaft was removed, the head of the arrow remained lodged in the furthermost part of the bone of the skull to a depth of around six inches. Nevertheless, the Prince fought on, helping to lead the royals to victory.

He was later treated at Kenilworth Castle, where the arrow was removed. Royal physicians treated him over several days, using honey as an antiseptic, and crafting a tool to screw into the broken arrow shaft to help extract the arrow without incurring further damage. The wound was then flushed with alcohol, while herbs from the nearby Kenilworth Priory's physic garden were used in his recovery.

Alongside the model, above, is a transcript from one of the physicians' treatise. It was written between 1403 and 1412, and details exactly how the arrow was removed. Note the replica of the tongs used on the table alongside the model of the head.

Elsewhere, Battlefield Church is said to have been erected over the site of the mass burial pit dug immediately after the battle. It was built initially as a memorial chapel in 1406, on the orders of King Henry IV and paid for by him, with prayers and masses held

This is St Peter's church at Melverley, viewed externally from the south (left) and internally from the western gallery (right). The church today sits on the eastern shore of the River Vyrnwy and hence the border with Wales. Alas, it was burned to the ground in 1401 by Owain Glyndŵr, the self-proclaimed Prince of Wales. The beautiful church shown above was rebuilt in its place in 1406. Melverley St Peter's church is a rare example of early British churches constructed of timber, wattle and daub, the timber being local Melverley oak. Notice how the white strips are narrower than the timber strips – a feature of early timber construction, while the entire structure is pegged together throughout, with not one nail being used! It has a Saxon font, too!

continually for the dead on both sides. The chapel was replaced in 1460 by a church. As for Shrewsbury, the town suffered considerably as a result of the battle, initially due to the occupancy of the royal army, and the subsequent deliberate burning of the town's suburbs beyond the gate, to prevent their capture by Hotspur's army. A petition was then made to parliament in 1407 as to its ruinous and impoverished state, but a plea for tax exemption was rejected.

Of course, Prince Henry was only sixteen at the time of the Battle of Shrewsbury, but he went on to become Henry V (1413-1422) and one of the most celebrated monarchs of all time, and perhaps the greatest warrior-king of medieval England. Both Henry IV and Henry V were later immortalised further by William Shakespeare. Indeed, Henry IV Part 1 opens twelve months into his reign and culminates with the Battle of Shrewsbury. That said, much of the play is about the coming of age of Prince Henry (nicknamed Hal). As for Owain Glyndŵr, his rebellion was brought to a standstill in 1406, and by 1409, the English had re-taken their former losses. There was one further raid into Shropshire in 1410, but thereafter, Glyndŵr fades away – although he remains the last native Welshman to hold the title Prince of Wales.

The Wars of the Roses of the second half of the 15th century also resulted in conflicts in the Marches. In the 1450s, Ludlow was the base of Richard, Duke of York, who challenged the rule of Henry VI. Then in 1459, Ludlow was also the selected rendezvous for the Earl of Warwick's forces with those of the Duke of York, Warwick's forces having crossed from Calais. Another Yorkist force based at Middleham Castle in Yorkshire, and led by the Earl of Salisbury, also marched south-west intending to link up with the main Yorkist army at Ludlow Castle. However, both Salisbury and Warwick had both just been indicted for rebellion by Henry's queen, Margaret of Anjou, so once she got news of the respective marches of Warwick and Salisbury, she sent a

Kynaston's Cave can be found on the western face of Nescliffe Hill. Ironically, at a time when order was gradually returning to the Marches in the late 15th century, this cave was home to outlaw Humphrey Kynaston. The son of Sir Roger Kynaston, the High Sheriff of Shropshire, Humphrey was outlawed following a conviction for murder in 1491. From this home, he is said to have lived a lifestyle comparable to that of Robin Hood.

force commanded by the Duke of Somerset to intercept Warwick and another under James Tuchet, 5th Baron Audley, to intercept Salisbury. Warwick successfully evaded Somerset, but Audley's forces successfully intercepted Salisbury's on 23rd September 1459, just

LEFT: Nos 5 and 6 Queen Street at Much Wenlock date from the 15th century. The core of the building is timber-framed throughout and incorporates three crucks, placed in parallel, including the one shown above, exposed in the gabled end of no 5. The building core is probably 15th century, too, and it is certainly the oldest timber-framed building in the town. A notable priest, Sir William Corvehill, lived here in the early 16th century. RIGHT: The stone part of Ashfield Hall on High Street at Much Wenlock, dates from the 15th century, while the building stands on the site of St John's Hospital, founded in the 13th century for "lost and naked beggars". It was later occupied in the 15th century as the private house of the Ashfield family – hence its name – while it was later called the Blue Bridge Inn, and Charles I is thought to have stayed here in 1642 on his way from Shrewsbury to Oxford.

before entering north-east Shropshire. The result was the bloody Battle of Blore Heath, which was won by the Yorkists, after Audley himself was killed – this despite the Lancastrians having a force of 10,000 men to the Yorkists' 5,000. The death-toll was around 2,000 Lancastrians to 1,000 Yorkists.

Following their victory, the Yorkists made a move towards London. However, a large Lancastrian army led by King Henry VI moved up to meet them, and hence the Yorkists fell back again to Ludlow, before making a stand at a fortified position near Ludford on 12th October. Barricades were constructed along with a defensive ditch which was dug on the opposite side of the River Teme from Ludlow, near a bridge – and hence why the pending battle became known as the Battle of Ludford Bridge. However, morale was negatively impacted by the sight of the approaching royal standard, as Richard and his supporters had always maintained that they were opposed only to Henrys "evil counsellors", yet here was the King in person – offering a pardon to any who would change sides, too! Sure enough, some 600 men did indeed defect to the Lancastrians. Faced with certain defeat, York, Salisbury and Warwick fled into Wales, leaving their abandoned army to kneel before Henry, and receive a pardon. York also abandoned his wife Cecily Neville, Duchess of York, his two younger sons George and Richard and his youngest daughter Margaret. The story goes that they were found standing at Ludlow's market cross when the Lancastrians arrived before being placed in the care of the Duchess's sister Anne, wife of the Duke of Buckingham. As for Ludlow, the town was pillaged by the drunken Lancastrian troops.

The following year, in December 1460, Richard, the Duke of York was killed during the Battle of Wakefield. This left his son, Edward, Earl of March, as the new Duke of York and Yorkist figurehead. In February 1461, Edward defeated a Lancastrian army at Mortimer's Cross, 8 miles south-west of Ludlow, and then proclaimed himself King Edward IV in March 1461. Meanwhile, Shrewsbury was later to become a town of great importance to Henry, Earl of Richmond, later King Henry VII (1485-1509), during his struggle to wrest the crown from Richard III (1483-1485). After landing

LEFT: The Council House Gateway at Shrewsbury dates from around 1610, whereas the Council House beyond the gateway (RIGHT) probably dates from the early 16th century.

The Grade II listed bridge over the River Clun at Clun – after a lot of rain!*

The medieval bridge over the River Teme at Ludlow.

The 15th century nave of St Laurence's church at Ludlow.

Close-up of the stalls in St Laurence's, which date from 1447.

from France at Milford Haven, Richmond found that Shrewsbury was the only town on the Severn not held by his enemies. He was therefore received favourably in the town on around 15th August 1485, before heading on to Bosworth Field in Leicestershire, for the most critical and decisive battle in the Wars of the Roses which took place on 22nd August 1485, and was won by the Lancastrians.

Ironically, alongside the Wars of the Roses of the late 15th century, order was gradually returning to the Marches thanks to the Council in the Marches and Wales. In 1471, Edward IV established a council to look after the affairs of the infant Prince of Wales, and then in 1476, it was given a judicial commission covering Shropshire as well as Herefordshire, Gloucestershire and Worcestershire. Shropshire regularly furnished the council with more members than the other three counties, and the base of its operations was at Ludlow, where memorials of its chief officers and their families are prominent at Ludlow St Laurence's church. However, the council also had a base in Shrewsbury, too – in the range of buildings which is still called the Council House today.

Later, Henry VII gave similar powers to the council to Arthur, Prince of Wales in 1493, while by 1501, a council for the Prince was formally appointed, and Arthur was sent to rule Wales from Ludlow. Then, under Henry VIII (1509-1547), Cardinal Wolsey sent Princess Mary to Ludlow in 1525, with a council which was both a household, responsible for the princess's education, and a court with the authority to administer justice. Later, in 1543, Thomas Cromwell appointed Rowland Lee, Bishop of Coventry and Lichfield, as its President – under whom public hangings were introduced for the crimes of both theft and murder. The council continued to exercise authority into the 17th century, but was suspended during the Interregnum. It revived under Charles II (1660-1685) but was finally dissolved in 1689.

As well as the break with Rome and the Dissolution, the 1530s was also a hugely significant decade in the history of England and Wales. Abolishing papal power was part of Henry's crusade to cement the sovereignty of the Crown throughout his kingdom, and another part was the abolition of the powers of the Marcher lords. The Laws in Wales Acts of 1535 and 1542 made Wales a full and equal part of the Kingdom of England and the legal system of England was extended to Wales along with the norms of English administration, and Wales became represented in parliament by 26 members, while justices of the peace were appointed in every Welsh county. The Marcher lordships were abolished as political units, and five new counties were established on Welsh lands (Brecknockshire, Denbighshire, Monmouthshire, Montgomeryshire and Radnorshire), thus creating a Wales of 13 counties, and ending the distinction between the principality of Wales and the Marcher lands; England and Wales now bordered each other much as they do today. The

This house was originally part of Oswestry School, founded by David Holbache in 1407, and the core of the building is still 15th century, re-modelled in the 16th century with considerable later additions and alterations.

The Grade I listed Llwyd Mansion in Oswestry. It dates from the mid-to-late 15th century, although it was re-modelled in 1604 with later additions and alterations; the date on the frontage also states 1604.

Tanners Wine Merchants on Wyle Cop, Shrewsbury. Parts of the building date back to the 1490s.

Nearside is 69a and 70 Wyle Cop, Shrewsbury, which is late 16th century, while in the centre is 71, 72 and 73, which date from the mid-15th century.

Fish Street in Shrewsbury. Nearside is Tudor House and the Three Fishes Inn, both dating from the late 15th century. Further up, the buildings are little more than an arms-width apart, with 15th century buildings on the left and 16th century on the right, including the 15th century Bear Steps Hall.

This building on the corner of Fish Street and Butcher Row is the oldest timber-framed building in Shrewsbury, dating from 1358-59. It is known as the Abbot's House and is Grade I listed.

lands which had formerly comprised the lordships of Clun, Ellesmere, Knockin, Maesbrook, Oswestry and Whittington were brought under the jurisdiction of Shropshire's county authorities, while other areas of the lordships were annexed to eight other English and Welsh counties. That said, the vicar of Whittington kept a Welsh-speaking curate until the late 18th century, while Welsh services were also maintained at Oswestry parish church until 1814; thereafter, a chapel was built at nearby Trefonen in 1821 to accommodate the Welsh in the parish. Welsh services also continued in Llanyblodwel church and Nonconformist Shropshire border chapels until at least the 1880s.

The border wars also affected Shropshire's ecclesiastical allegiances. In the 11th century, Shropshire lay within the dioceses of Hereford and Lichfield, but in the second half of the 12th century during a period of Welsh predominance, the parishes around Oswestry became part of the diocese of St Asaph, and remained so until 1920 when the Church of Wales was disestablished.

Rushbury Manor at Rushbury dates from the 16th century.

Bishop Percy's House at Bridgnorth dates from 1580.

This is 46, 47, 48 and 49 Corve Street in Ludlow. The homes date from the 16th century and are Grade II listed.*

Grade II listed and dating from the same period – albeit with a partial 18th century re-fronting – are numbers 106 and 107 Corve Street.

Also in Ludlow, on King Street, is the Tolsey – now known as the Fish House. This Grade II listed building dates from the late 14th century.

Alongside the Tolsey are these magnificent range of buildings. The two left-hand gables belong to the Old Bull Ring Tavern, which is Grade II listed. The building has the words "CIRCA 1365" etched below the timber frames.*

LEFT: Sticking with Ludlow, here is another Grade II* listed house on the corner of King Street and Broad Street, which dates from 1462.

RIGHT: Part of the medieval Grade II* listed St Thomas's chapel in Ludlow. The left-hand side of the house dates from the 18th century.

From the Dissolution to the Eve of the Industrial Revolution

The changes brought about by the Dissolution of the Monasteries in the 1530s and 1540s, and the so-called Acts of Union of 1535 and 1542 were probably at their most momentous in Shropshire. The Marcher lordships had gone after several centuries of vice-like domination, and the new councils in the region brought new levels of stability. Towns in the county finally began to prosper, no longer having to worry about warfare and constant Welsh raids; indeed, 20th century research has suggested that the second half of the 15th century was a period of catastrophic economic decline in Shrewsbury when trade may have fallen by as much as 70 per cent. Furthermore, a statute of the early 16th century numbered Shrewsbury, Bridgnorth and Ludlow amongst towns where many tenements were "in great ruin and decay". However, this new-found prosperity began to emerge in the mid-16th century, and is represented today by so many fine Shropshire town buildings that survive intact…

16TH CENTURY SHROPSHIRE BUILDINGS

The Old Market Hall, Shrewsbury, dates from the 1590s, built at a time when the town was recovering from centuries instability.

This building in The Square, Shrewsbury, also dates from the late 16th century and was formerly the Old Plough Inn.

Looking through to Wyle Cop in Shrewsbury. The three-storey building on the left-hand side also dates from the late 16th century.

The Old Tudor Steakhouse on Butcher Row, Shrewsbury, dates from the mid-16th century.

Castle Gates House in Shrewsbury dates from the late 16th century with later modifications and a major restoration in 1912.

The right-hand two sections of this building on Shrewsbury's High Street are known as Owen's Mansion and were built in 1569.

The Guildhall on Wilmore Street, Much Wenlock. A Grade II listed timber frame and plaster building, it dates from around 1557.*

Also dating from the late 16th century in Much Wenlock is Church House.

Tudor Cottage in Church Stretton is a Grade II listed building which dates from the late 16th century, with later alternations.*

The Black Bear in Whitchurch dates from the late 16th century, with later 17th and 19th century additions.

LEFT: The Bear Steps in Shrewsbury take you up through Bear Steps Hall from Fish Street to St Alkmund's Place. The hall dates from 1576-77. CENTRE: St Mary's Cottage, St Mary's Place, another late 16th century building in Shrewsbury. RIGHT: The Guild Hall of the Shrewsbury Drapers, St Mary's Place, was built 1576-80 – although the guild has been meeting on this site since 1485.

LEFT: The Grade II listed Butcher's Arms in Oswestry dates from the mid-to-late 16th century, albeit with considerable later additions and alterations. RIGHT: The Merchant House on Corve Street, Ludlow, is Grade II listed and dates from the 17th century. Next door is Tanners Cottage, which dates from the 16th and 17th centuries, while at the top end of the row is the Unicorn Inn, which dates from the 18th century built around a 16/17th century core.

The Feathers Hotel in the Bull Ring, Ludlow, dates from the early 17th century built around an earlier core.

Old Idsall House in Shifnal is Grade II listed and dates from the late 16th century.

The former White Lion public house in Ellesmere dates from the late 16th century. There is also a Black Lion and Red Lion in Ellesmere!

April Cottage on Church Hill in Ellesmere dates from around 1600 and is also Grade II listed.

This is a side-on view of the 1462 Grade II* listed building on the corner of Ludlow's King Street and Broad Street, also shown on page 55 from its King Street façade. Alongside on Broad Street are numbers 2 and 2a, which date from the early 17th century.

And a little further down Broad Street is The Angel Inn, another beautiful Grade II listed early 17th century Ludlow building.

Following the Dissolution, many of the dissolved monasteries were being keenly eyed by Shropshire's wealthy and ambitious, for those who inherited these now-redundant buildings from the Crown would substantially increase their social standing, thus enabling their descendants to dominate local society for many centuries to come. Prime amongst them was James Leveson, a Wolverhampton wool merchant who acquired the ruins of Lilleshall Abbey as early as 1539, and built a grand house here. Lilleshall later became the centre of a great estate, and Leveson's descendants were successively created Barons Gower in 1703, Earls Gower in 1746, Marquesses of Stafford in 1786 and Dukes of Sutherland in 1833.

The Grade II listed Kings Head in Bridgnorth dates from around 1600.

Also Grade II listed in Bridgnorth is the Town Hall, which dates from around 1645.

Grade II listed and dating from the 17th century is 103 and 104 Corve Street, Ludlow – also known as Tudor House and Tudor Cottage.

Similarly, the manor of Madeley was acquired in 1544 from Wenlock Priory by Sir Robert Brooke, who later became Speaker of the House of Commons. He built his house here in 1553 on the site of the former monastic grange, incorporating part of the original masonry, with the oldest part of his house thus dating from the 13th century. The manor eventually passed to Abraham Darby III in the 18th century. By the 1970s, though, the house was largely ruinous until Telford Development Corporation embarked on a restoration project in 1973. The property was later converted into a hotel.

Another mid-16th century country house that evolved from a former monastery was Morville Hall, just west of Bridgnorth. The house stands on the site of the abandoned Morville Priory, and was built in around 1546 after the site was acquired by Roger Smyth. The 16th century two-storey house was built of grey stone with projecting wings. However, a third storey was added as part of an 18th century enlargement. The property has belonged to the National Trust since 1965.

In central Shropshire, Shipton manor was granted by the Crown to Sir Thomas Palmer in 1548 – although he only enjoyed his acquisition for five years, as he was executed for high treason in 1553! After passing through several hands it eventually came into the possession of John Lutwyche in 1580, while it was Richard Lutwyche who built the current Grade I-listed Shipton Hall in around 1587, replacing an older timber-framed house which had burned down. The hall was then significantly rebuilt in the Georgian style in the mid-18th century.

Cheshire gentry also acquired some significant Shropshire estates, such as Thomas Egerton who bought the 30,000-acre Whitchurch estate in 1598, and the 9,000-acre Ellesmere estate in 1600. Meanwhile, John Weld bought the Willey estate in 1618, the manor of Marsh in 1619, and a large part of the manor of Broseley in 1620, making him one of the principal landowners in the Shropshire coalfield.

Of course, many grand new Tudor houses were built during the 16th century. Benthall Hall, just west of Broseley, was built in around 1580 for William Benthall, probably on the same site as the preceding 12th century medieval manor house. The Tudor hall's most significant period occurred during the English Civil War of the mid-17th century when it was garrisoned at varying times by both sides – more on that shortly. The house did pass out of Benthall control for over a century, but was re-acquired in 1934 – and then sold to the National Trust in

The Grade I listed Shipton Hall dates from around 1587.

Madeley Court dates from 1553.

Benthall Hall, just west of Broseley, was built around 1580, probably on the site of an earlier 12th century medieval manor and manor house.

Castle Lodge in Ludlow is a mix of medieval, Tudor and Elizabethan architecture. It has some of the largest collection of oak panelling in England, dating from the early 13th century, and was once the residence of Catherine of Aragon whilst she was married to Prince Arthur.

1958 – although the hall is still occupied by the Benthall family, while it retains much of its fine oak interior, and an elaborate 17th century staircase.

The Grade I listed Condover Hall, four miles south of Shrewsbury, is a three-storey Elizabethan sandstone building, which has been described as the grandest manor house in Shropshire. Condover was a royal manor in Anglo-Saxon times, and thereafter in and out of Crown ownership, but in 1586, it was purchased by Thomas Owen and it was he who built Condover Hall. The hall remained under Owen ownership until the late 1860s when it passed to the Cholmondeley family. The novelist, Mary Cholmondeley (1859–1925), briefly lived in her uncle's house in 1896, while another literary visitor in 1873 and 1879 was American writer Mark Twain.

We have already covered Moreton Corbet Castle in the medieval section. However, in around 1560, Sir Andrew Corbet made many alterations, including the building of a two-storey range between the Great Tower and the gatehouse. But it was his son, Robert Corbet, who commenced the construction of the Elizabethan range in around 1578, which was inspired by his extensive travelling. Unfortunately, he died of the plague in 1583, so his two brothers and successors, Richard and Vincent Corbet, completed the build of the new manor house which was one of the most splendid buildings of its period in England; it was described by antiquarian William Camden (1551-1623) as "a most gorgeous and stately house after the Italian model." Moreton Corbet Castle was then garrisoned for the Royalists in the English Civil War where it was subject to a number of sieges during which time it was badly damaged. The Elizabethan range was repaired after the war, but fell into ruin during the 18th century as the Corbets chose to live elsewhere.

Also built in around 1560 was Pitchford Hall in central Shropshire, built by John Sandford, "carpenter of Salop". This striking timber-framed, two-storey building with rendered red sandstone panels, was

> **Quirk Alert:** *The White Stiffs of Condover*
>
> *According to local legend, no heir to Condover Hall will ever prosper. This is due to a condemned butler falsely accused of stabbing to death his master, Knyvett, but who had actually been murdered by the butler's accuser, Knyvett's son. The butler's last words were: "Before Heaven I am innocent, though my master's son swears me guilty. And as I perish an innocent man, may those who follow my murdered lord be cursed."*
>
> *The story also goes that as the mortally wounded Knyvett had stumbled down the basement stairs, his bloodied hand had left an imprint upon the wall which defied all attempts to wash it away — and the marked stone eventually had to be chipped clean.*
>
> *Meanwhile, in 1930, a Great Western Railway Hall Class 4900 steam locomotive was named Condover Hall, and remained in regular service until 1965. It might look familiar if you saw it today, as the Hogwarts Express from the Harry Potter films is an identical Hall class locomotive!*

built for Adam Ottley, a Shrewsbury wool merchant, and incorporated elements of the previous medieval building. The floor plan is E-shaped round a courtyard to the south with a Victorian service wing to the west, while the roofs were decorated with many spectacular star-shaped chimney stacks. Inside, the drawing room panelling and ceiling are amongst the finest of their type and date back to 1626. A stretch of the Roman Watling Street runs through the estate, while 100 metres north of the hall, there is a naturally occurring pitch well by the Row Brook within the grounds. It is one of only a few such wells in the country, and gave the place its name (recorded as *Piceforde* in Domesday Book) as it is located opposite a ford across the Row Brook. Naturally, the pitch (or bitumen) was once used for waterproofing and protecting the exposed timbers of the house.

LEFT: The Grade I listed Condover Hall was built in the late 16th century. RIGHT: The eastern range of Moreton Corbet Castle was begun in around 1578 by Robert Corbet, and completed by his younger brothers in the 1580s.

LEFT: Morville Hall dates from the 16th century, although it was re-modelled in the early 18th century. RIGHT: The Grade I listed Pitchford Hall was built 1560 to 1570 for Adam Ottley around an earlier medieval core. This long-distance view of the eastern façade doesn't do the property justice, though, as is revealed by airborne views on www.pitchfordestate.com.

Quirk Alert: *Perfect Pitchford*

Pitchford Hall is home to ghosts. However, we're talking a vast number of ghosts; possibly the most anywhere in the country! If you don't believe me, check out: www.pitchfordestate.com/pitchford-ghosts, where several pages of tales are recounted by Caroline Colthurst who inherited the hall in 1972. Tales include the "Whiff" courtesy of imported South American cigarillos, mystery piano players, a cavalier, a footman, a butler, a housekeeper, a labrador, wildly excited maids, little old ladies, boys, girls, a man in a black cloak, and a docile serf in blue breeches and a bright yellow coat with silver buttons! Then there is the red-faced, tweedy man wearing braces, a woman seated in a chaise longue, another woman who hated the bath, and a pompous and overbearing character who inhabits another of the bathrooms! Another butleresque figure is seen chivvying young boys and cuffing their ears, while another old man with gnarled hands is seen struggling up and down stairs. And not forgetting other ghosts in the pantry, kitchen, passage, bathroom, attic, stairs, laundry room, library, sitting room, and bedrooms. Not that the tales are a source for amusement; many will spook you good and proper, while a psychic visitor once confirmed that the hall was "protected by a shield, which won't last forever…"

Meanwhile, in the grounds of Pitchford Hall, there is a Tudor-style tree-house which sits in a large lime tree and is believed to be the oldest tree house in the world, having stood here since the 1660s. Indeed, Queen Victoria stayed at Pitchford in 1832, aged thirteen, and records in her diary that she watched a visiting pack of foxhounds from the treehouse.

Finally, during World War II, the hall was one of the pre-prepared bolt holes to be used by the royal family in the event of a German invasion of London. I guess no one told them of the ghosts…

In north Shropshire, Soulton Hall was built in about 1550, around the shell of an older, medieval building. It was built by Sir Rowland Hill (MP), who was the first Protestant Lord Mayor of London in 1549, while as Sheriff of London, he was also involved in the case which established Parliamentary Privilege. Meanwhile, Upton Cressett Hall is an Elizabethan moated manor house built in brick, and dates from the 16th century. Again, the hall was built on the site of an earlier hall which, like the Elizabethan version, was built for the Cressett family. The first part of the 16th century version, built in the 1540s, was timber-framed with a great hall, a solar wing and a cross-wing. However, in 1580 the house was substantially remodelled by Richard Cressett, who encased the building in brick, added large brick chimney-stacks and created a false ceiling in the great hall allowing the creation of first-floor rooms.

The exterior of Soulton Hall dates from around 1550, but incorporates traces of an older, medieval building.

Upton Cressett Hall was built for the Cressett family between 1540 and 1580, although the Great Hall survives from the 14th century build.

Finally, the Grade I listed Wilderhope Manor at the north-eastern end of Wenlock Edge, is another Elizabethan period manor house, this one built of local limestone and dating from 1585. It was built for Francis

> **Quirk Alert:** *Trial by Chimney*
>
> *Plaish Hall in central Shropshire became the first brick-built Shropshire mansion when it was built for Chief Justice William Leighton in the 1580s. Local legend has it that Leighton employed a man who had been condemned to death to build the house's ornate chimneys, on the promise of a free pardon if the chimneys proved to be the finest in Shropshire. However, upon completion of the job, it is said that the labourer was hanged – allegedly from one of the chimneys he had built! Make your own mind up…*

Smallman and the manor remained in the Smallman family until 1734 when the estate was sold. Thereafter, it fell into a poor state of health, and by 1936, it was uninhabited. However, it was purchased by the WA Cadbury Trust who donated it to the National Trust on condition that it was used as youth hostel – which it has remained as ever since. The house still has many of the original Elizabethan features, including the oaken stairways, oak spiral stairs and plaster ceilings.

Returning to the Dissolution for one last time, part of Shrewsbury Abbey, as well as the former monastic churches at Battlefield, Bromfield, Chirbury and Morville, each became parish churches, while Shrewsbury Abbey and Much Wenlock Priory were, for a time, under consideration as potential cathedrals. Following the 1536 abolition of the authority of the Pope, the clergy were instructed to teach in English, using the Coverdale Bible, and to remove images from their churches. However, on the accession of Queen Mary I in 1553, the Latin Mass was restored, and at St Mary's in Shrewsbury, the altar and rood were re-erected – only to be removed again on the accession of Queen Elizabeth I in 1558. Further losses occurred in 1584 when some stained-glass windows and a stone altar were removed from St Mary's and during the 1580s, when the crosses outside St Mary's and St Julian's were destroyed.

Following the Reformation, some of the educational functions which had been performed by religious institutions were continued by other

The Grade I listed Wilderhope Manor was built in 1585 for Francis Smallman.

Today's library in Shrewsbury, but originally one of the buildings of Shrewsbury Grammar School, founded in 1552. Later pupils included Sir Philip Sydney, Judge Jeffreys, Sir Fulke Greville and Charles Darwin. The building continued to function as a school until 1882.

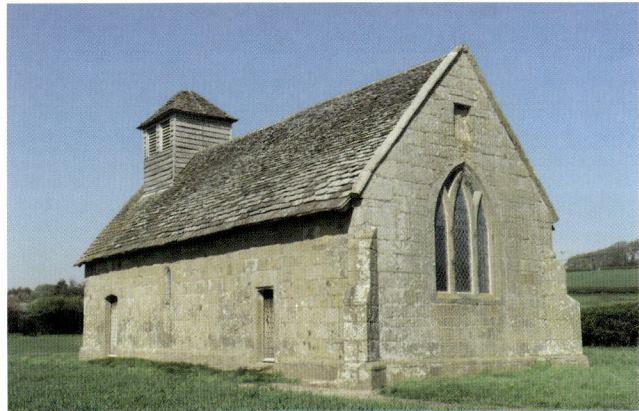
The Grade I listed Langley Chapel in central Shropshire was built in around 1564 on the site of a former chapel.

The isolated Langley Chapel is notable for having a complete set of original 17th century wooden furniture, including these pews.

In Market Drayton, both the Old Tudor House Hotel (left) and the Sandbrook Vaults (right) just around the corner, date from the mid-17th century.

means – like Bridgnorth Grammar School, founded in 1503, surviving until the mid-16th century thanks to benevolent endowments. Oswestry's school, founded in the early 15th century, was being supported in 1548 by money which had previously maintained a chantry in the parish church and was controlled by town bailiffs. In Ludlow, the corporation supported their grammar school after it received the properties of the Palmers' Guild in 1552, while in Newport a school which had been taught by a chantry priest survived with a small endowment until 1878. Finally, in Whitchurch and Market Drayton, schools were founded by Sir John Talbot and Sir Rowland Hill, respectively, both in the mid-16th century. Indeed, by the end of the 16th century, there were schools in most Shropshire towns, and also in a few villages like Bitterley, Donnington, Worfield and Wroxeter.

However, the most important post-Reformation school in the county was founded in Shrewsbury in 1552 by Edward VI, following a petition to Henry VIII in 1542 by the townsfolk of Shrewsbury for a free grammar school. It was first endowed with £20 a year from the estates of the colleges of St Mary's and St Chad's, which was augmented in 1571 by the rectory of Chirbury and various other tithe-based incomes which had belonged to Chirbury Priory. In 1561, a Cambridge graduate called Thomas Ashton was appointed headmaster, and under his guidance the school grew rapidly in both size and reputation. The school attracted large numbers of pupils from Protestant families in Shrewsbury, Shropshire and North Wales, with 266 boys on its roll at the end of 1562. In 1581, there were 360 pupils, and five years later it was said to be the largest school in England. This led to new buildings being built in the 1590s that were on the same scale as those at Oxford and Cambridge, although it took until around 1630 to complete them. However, by the 1680s, the school had entered a period of decline.

> **Quirk Alert:** *The Bedroom in the Chancel*
> *When Charles Foxe acquired Bromfield Priory, following the Dissolution, he used the chancel as part of his new house, making a bedroom of the top half and installing a new Tudor window to light it. However, around a century later, the house was destroyed by a fire – which the owners took to be an act of God, for they promptly returned the chancel to the church – thus leaving St Mary's church at Bromfield as the only English church containing a bedroom window!*

The Crown in Market Drayton dates from around 1600, with late 18th century alterations. It was also a brewery during the mid-19th century.

A few buildings further down the A529 is the Salopian Star, which dates from 1669 with late 19th century alterations.

The twin medieval issues of land enclosure and the conversion of arable land to pasture continued into the 16th century. However, whereas 250-plus Acts of Parliament relating to land enclosure had been passed by 1760, this legislation only affected seven Shropshire parishes – probably because the majority of land enclosure in Shropshire, between 1450 and 1700, was enclosed through stealth! Indeed, in 1597, Sir Thomas Coningsby urged that Shropshire should be exempted from enclosure bills because it was "the dairy-house of the whole realm". Meanwhile, open field farming on the great estates of Ellesmere and Whittington was in poor health by 1600, while in 1612, a church document refers to numerous hedges and enclosure within the three open fields of Leighton parish, and another suggests enclosure at nearby Buildwas. Similarly, so much enclosure had taken place at Oswestry by 1602, that a surveyor noted which remaining lands were *un*cultivated, and suitable for enclosure. Another document written in 1693 speaks entirely in terms of an enclosed landscape, all trace of open fields having apparently disappeared, hence in most townships of Shropshire, communal cultivation had ceased by 1700.

These strong hints continue in Myddle parish, where 1,000 acres of mere, marsh and sandy waste were brought into cultivation between the late 15th century and the mid-17th – presumably because all former common land was now enclosed and unavailable and they had to make the best of a bad hand – while in nearby Myddlewood, 241 acres were cleared by renting plots to freeholders and tenants in the adjacent townships in lieu of common rights. Similarly, the nearby glacial lakes known as Myddle Pools were drained in around 1570, and Harmer Moss was cleared of its water and turf – but here, the reclaimed land was converted into a meadow and pasture in the years after 1617.

Nevertheless, despite the harm it did to the common people, land enclosure was also one of the most important enablers to the Agricultural Revolution, as this allowed farmers to invest in land that they owned. Of course, only the wealthiest could afford to do it, while clearly, this activity removed much land from the communal system and often provoked violent opposition from evicted tenants. It also had social consequences, leading to the depopulation of some parishes and an increase in vagrancy.

It was also during the late 16th and early 17th century that much of the distinctive character of Ludlow was forged, with many splendid timber-framed buildings from this period surviving today; typically ornamented by herringbone struts, intricately carved star panels and beam ends, and elaborate barge boards. The town's

The Grade II listed Blackgate at Oswestry dates from 1621 – and is now the Black Gate Restaurant.

Also dating from the 17th century and Grade II listed is this timber-framed house on Chapel Street, Wem.

Yolande Court in Ellesmere is Grade II listed and dates from the early 17th century with later alterations.

This Grade II listed barn at Norton dates from the 17th century.

> ### Quirk Alert: *Flat Pack and Mobile Punishment*
>
> *The extensive timbered frame of Much Wenlock's 16th century Guildhall was allegedly erected in just two days. Apparently, all of the timber had been cut, laid out and numbered, so all the carpenters had to do was to peg it together! Meanwhile, the old stocks were kept at the Guildhall, and were unusual in that they were fitted with wheels – so that offenders could be paraded around the town!*

local services, and this helped to counter-balance the decline of Ludlow's cloth industry after 1600. During the 16th century, cloth production in Ludlow ranged from 400 to 800 pieces per year, much of which was a coarse cloth known as "Ludlow Whytes", and which was selling in London in the 1590s for £2 10s. 0d. each.

The cloth trade also flourished in Shrewsbury, thus further increasing the town's burgeoning wealth. At its heart was the Drapers' Company which had been founded by Edward IV and came to dominate the town's affairs during the Elizabethan period. In the 1580s, drapers were buying Welsh cloth in Oswestry, bringing it to Shrewsbury, having it finished by shearmen in the town, and then transporting it to London for export to Europe. The Shrewsbury Drapers' Company also successfully excluded the Shrewsbury Mercers' Company (dealers in textile fabrics) from any share in their trade, while Oswestry was also excluded from the trade, so by 1621, the Drapers' had a virtual monopoly.

> ### Quirk Alert: *A Tall Story*
>
> *Burford's church is home to one of the finest Elizabethan triptychs in the country. Painted and signed by Italian artist, Melchior Salaboss, it has two panelled doors painted outside with the Twelve Apostles, and inside with coats-of-arms. They open to show life-size portraits of three of the Cornwall family: Richard and Jenet and their son, Edmund, who lies full-length at the foot of the triptych – which is something to behold, as he was 7 foot 3 inches tall!*

Having ascended the throne in 1625 King Charles I believed in the Divine Right of Kings, therefore he ploughed on with unpopular religious policies, deeply unpopular taxes, costly intervention in Europe, and disastrous campaigns against Scotland. Furthermore, between 1627 and 1642, Parliament had spent more time dissolved than active, because they refused to support many of Charles' policies.

The inevitable English Civil War was fought in three distinct phases between the Parliamentarians and the Royalists. The first phase ran from 1642 to February 1646 when the King surrendered. Alas, Charles refused to accept Parliament's demand for a constitutional monarchy, and temporarily escaped

wealth at this time was due in large part to the Council in the Marches. With wealthy judges, attorneys and clerks living in the town, there was a good market for

Three stunning Grade II listed 17th century houses at Upton Magna. From left to right: Walnut Cottage, The Corner House and The Gatehouse.

captivity in November 1647, and hence the second phase of the war (1648-1649), but which again resulted in his capture, this time by Oliver Cromwell's now established New Model Army. This time, he was tried, convicted and executed for high treason on 30th January 1649. The monarchy was subsequently abolished and the Commonwealth of England established in its place. However, the third phase of the war took place between 1649 and 1651, when supporters of Charles II battled with Parliamentarians, and which ultimately resulted in Royalist defeat at the Battle of Worcester on 3rd September 1651.

Nevertheless, in 1642, much of Shropshire declared for the King, as did eight of the county's 12 MP's. Control of the area was important to Charles as Shropshire was a gateway to predominantly Royalist Wales, while Shropshire's ironworks were also an important source of munitions. Therefore, the week after raising his standard at Nottingham, Charles headed for Shropshire, arriving in Wellington on 19th September where he was met by Sir John Weld. On the 20th, he issued the Wellington Declaration promising to preserve the Protestant religion, laws, and liberties of his subjects, and the privileges of Parliament, while he also inspected his troops below the Wrekin. From Wellington, Charles then marched to Shrewsbury. Prior to his arrival, though, there was some doubt as to how he would be received, given Shrewsbury folk had been somewhat aggrieved at his imposition of Ship Money on the town in the 1630s to help raise funds for his unpopular wars. It was later revealed that Sir Richard Newport had brokered the peace ahead of Charles' arrival…in return for a peerage!

During Charles' subsequent three-week stay in Shrewsbury, the royal court was set up at the Council buildings. Courtiers were lodged with leading citizens and the surrounding fields were used for the drilling of soldiers under the command of Prince Maurice and Prince Rupert. On 21st September, it was estimated that the King had a force of 6,000 men at Shrewsbury. Shropshire gentry travelled to Shrewsbury with gifts of plate and money, while the plate belonging to Shrewsbury Grammar School was handed over to the King, personally, by the headmaster. From these donations, Charles established a mint in Shrewsbury under the supervision of Thomas Bushell. Charles renewed the town's charter, while he also issued his Solemn Protestation, blaming any future hostilities on others!

Charles left Shrewsbury on 12th October 1642, when he marched to Bridgnorth. From here, he continued to Wolverhampton and ultimately to Edgehill, in Warwickshire, where the first pitched battle of the war was fought on 25th October. In his wake, Shrewsbury was garrisoned as one of the King's principal strongholds. The castle was strengthened and houses in its vicinity

> **Quirk Alert:** *Old Parr*
>
> *Thomas Parr, or "Old Parr" as he is also known, was born in Great Wollaston on the Shropshire border with Wales. He is said to be the oldest Englishman who ever lived – although had he been born a mile further to the west, he'd have been the oldest Welshman who ever lived! There is a plaque to Old Parr in Wollaston's church, claiming that he was born in 1483 and died in 1635, aged 152 years and 9 months. The plaque names the ten monarchs that sat the throne during his lifetime – from Edward IV to Charles I.*
>
> *The story also goes that he didn't marry his first wife until he was 80, with whom he had two children – who sadly died in infancy. He took his second wife aged 122. He was then discovered by the Earl of Arundel in his final year, who took him to London to meet the King. When Charles I asked him his secret, Old Parr stated: "I did penance in the church when I was 100 years old!"*
>
> *Alas, he died shortly after, possibly succumbing to the rich diet of London, or the loss of his clean Shropshire air. His post-mortem declared all organs to be healthy and those of a vigorous man. He was buried in Westminster Abbey.*
>
> *Elsewhere, Shifnal church has a stone in the nave asking us to believe that two townsfolk had a combined age of 251 years. William Wakeley (born 1590) is said to have died in 1714, aged 124, and Mary Yates died a little later aged 127.*

The Old Barn (left) and the Kings Arms (right) in Church Stretton, both date from the 17th century.

demolished, while the town walls were refortified and an artillery base established at Cadogan's Fort above Frankwell.

In March 1643, Colonel Lawrence Benthall, who had already fortified Benthall Hall for Charles, commanded the Shrewsbury garrison in a successful attack on a Parliamentary plundering party led by Colonel Mytton of Wem. In August 1643, Wem was garrisoned by Parliament under Mytton, as he and his colleagues set about building an earthen rampart around the town, surmounted by a palisade of stakes. The garrison was soon threatened by Royalist forces under Lord Capel, but they were forced to retreat by a Parliamentary army arriving from Chester. Wem subsequently became the centre of the Parliamentary cause in Shropshire, and its garrison was deployed to subjugate towns and castles of far greater eminence.

One incident which demonstrates how the common folk were mere pawns, happened when Sir Paul Harris summoned the men of Pimhill hundred aged between 16 and 70 to assemble on Myddle Hill. Here, Robert More, brother of the rector of Myddle, stood by three or four pikes which had been struck into the ground, and offered 14 groats a week as wages for those who would serve the King. Meanwhile, Shropshire's furnaces were contributing strongly to the Royalist cause, while munitions from Bouldon furnace in Corvedale were supplied to the Royalist garrison at Ludlow.

On 28th December 1643, Tong Castle was captured by Parliamentarian troops – although it was later re-captured on 6th April 1644 by Prince Rupert. A few weeks earlier, on 13th March 1644, Hopton Castle was also captured by the Royalists, although the Parliamentary commander didn't surrender until after the final assault. His reward was that the Royalist commander, Sir Michael Woodhouse, decided not to exercise mercy, and all of his prisoners were killed – apparently clubbed to death, according to normal military practice! Longford Hall was also captured by the Royalists on 3rd April 1644.

However, the most significant struggle in Shropshire in 1644 revolved around Oswestry. Both sides were well aware of its strategic importance as it controlled several key routes into North Wales. Under the direction of the Royalist Colonel Edward Lloyd of Llanforda, and with a garrison composed entirely of Welshmen, a new gate and drawbridge had been erected, the steeple of the parish church demolished, and the walls of the castle heavily repaired. The Parliamentarians had made two previously unsuccessful attempts to take the town, firstly in January 1644 when they tried to lure Colonel Lloyd out of the town on the promise of a sumptuous meal, and secondly in March 1644 when an open attack was repulsed. However, on 22nd June 1644, a small Parliamentary force under the Earl of Denbigh took the town when the governor and part of the garrison had gone to Shrewsbury escorting prisoners. Denbigh captured 400 of the garrison, among them Sir Francis Newport. The fall of Oswestry was one of several events in the summer of 1644 which turned the tide of the war against Charles. As for the unfortunate inhabitants of Oswestry, they had to donate £500 to prevent the Parliamentary soldiers from plundering. That said, within a month, Oswestry was besieged by Royalists, under Colonel Marrowe, attempting to take the town back, but they didn't, thanks to the intervention of Sir Thomas Middleton.

Also garrisoned for the King was Shrawardine Castle, held by Sir William Vaughan. However, in October 1644, Vaughan was captured by Thomas Mytton

This row of cottages at Acton Burnell date from the 17th century.

Church Farmhouse at Rushbury also dates from the 17th century.

while receiving the sacrament in Shrawardine church. He was allowed back to his castle on the understanding that he would negotiate the garrison's surrender, but on entry, he promptly raised the drawbridge and broke his promise. Shortly afterwards, Vaughan was appointed general of Shropshire, and quartered his regiment around the county, leaving his parson brother, James, in charge of Shrawardine.

The next Royalist stronghold to be taken by the Parliamentarians was Apley House in early February 1645. However, the most important Royalist bastion to fall was Shrewsbury, which was captured on 3rd February 1645. The Parliamentarians from Wem had previously been repulsed by two attacks on Shrewsbury, but on this third occasion, they had probably been given inside knowledge that the garrison would be weakened following the despatch of an expedition into Cheshire. So, on 3rd February, a group of carpenters approached in a small boat and cut down the stake fence between the castle and the River Severn. Forty-two dismounted cavalry, under the command of Lieutenant Benbow and accompanied by a Puritan chaplain, stormed up the rampart beneath the Council House, while a large force of infantry poured into the town through St Mary's Water Lane gate, finding no resistance. The Royalist Guard in the market place was subdued, and once the north gate had been occupied, the drawbridge was lowered to let in the main body of Parliamentary cavalry. The governor, Sir Michael Earnley, was killed having refused quarter, after which the garrison surrendered on the condition that its English members should be allowed to march to Ludlow, leaving the Irish as prisoners. The only bright spot for the Royalists was that Prince Maurice had been able to escape without capture.

Thereafter, one Royalist stronghold fell after another: Benthall Hall in February 1645, Bridgnorth in March (when many buildings were torched by the retreating Royalists), Caus, Shrawardine and Stokesay in June, Lilleshall Abbey and Dawley Castle in August, and Moreton Corbet Castle in September. Of these, the Parliamentarians particularly valued the Benthall garrison as it offered a convenient base from which to patrol the River Severn crossings in the gorge, and also to prevent the river's use for carrying coal to the Royalists at Bridgnorth and Worcester. Clearly understanding the hall's strategic value, the Royalists launched a daybreak attack on the hall in an attempt to win it back, but they were eventually forced to withdraw. Naturally, serious damage was caused to the hall.

Particularly badly hit during the First English Civil War was High Ercall Hall. At that time, there were two halls: a fortified 13th century manor built by the Arkle family, and a mansion built in 1608 by the Newport family – who were still incumbent when the war

> ### Quirk Alert: *Major's Leap*
> *The owner of Wilderhope Manor during the English Civil War was Major Thomas Smallman. Like most Shropshire gentry, he was a Royalist officer. On one occasion, he was forced to flee on horseback from Cromwell's approaching troops, but as he was carrying important despatches, the Parliamentarians gave chase, and he was cornered on Wenlock Edge. However, rather than surrender, he took a do-or-die plunge down a steep 200ft slope. Smallman survived thanks to an apple tree breaking his fall; alas, the poor horse did not survive. Remarkably, Major Smallman then made his way to Shrewsbury on foot, where he delivered the despatches and roused a force of Royalists to claim back his home. Of course, the Parliamentarians had assumed the Major had died in the plunge – so imagine their surprise when Royalists, led by Major Smallman, launched an attack on them at Wilderhope Manor, a few hours later!*
>
> *From that day onwards, the location of the incident became known as Major's Leap, and the place is now said to be haunted by the ghosts of both Smallman and his poor horse – spectres who have also said to have been seen at Wilderhope Manor, too.*

The Old Mill at Longnor is Grade II listed and dates from the early 17th century.

Also at Longnor is Cobbler's Cottage (nearside) which dates from the mid-17th century with 18th century additions.

kicked off. The Newports were prominent Royalists and, having been raised to the peerage in 1643, Lord Newport garrisoned the "new" hall for the King with 200 troops, while he also constructed a large earthen bank over the north and north-west curtain walls to provide a defence against cannon and musket fire. It was as well that he did, as the house was besieged *three* times by Parliamentary forces between 1644 and 1646. The first siege resulted in the loss of the drawbridge, but ended with a Parliamentarian withdrawal. A reinforced garrison then saw off the second siege, but it was the third (and lengthy) siege which proved decisive. It commenced in July 1645, with Parliamentary troops now able to bombard the buildings with artillery, meaning that the 1608 mansion was irreparably damaged. The garrison still held out for nine months though, but was forced to surrender on 28th March 1646. Under the terms of surrender the 212 surviving members of the garrison, were allowed to leave for the Royalist city of Worcester, and 40 cavalry were allowed to keep their arms – a far cry from Hopton Castle two years earlier, when the roles had been reversed. As for the "new" hall, the Parliamentary forces made sure that the fortifications were demolished. Fortunately for the Newports, the original medieval manor house and associated buildings were still habitable. Today, only a fragment of the 1608 house remains as a short row of arches in the garden of the older house, which although around 300 years older, has outlived its younger sibling by an additional four centuries.

Elsewhere in 1646, Bridgnorth Castle surrendered to the Parliamentarians after a one-month siege, while the final Royalist garrison to fall was at Ludlow Castle on 9th July. By this stage, Charles was on the run having put himself into the hands of the Scots – who eventually handed him over to Parliament in January 1647. Meanwhile, back in Shropshire, fear of Royalist uprisings led to Parliament ordering Shrewsbury to be re-garrisoned.

Of course, Charles escaped in 1647, was re-captured and executed on 30th January, 1649 – after which, the Royalists accepted Charles II as their king although his demise came at the Battle of Worcester on 3rd September 1651. However, he escaped northwards, and at 3 o'clock in the morning of 4th September 1651, Charles II and the Earl of Derby arrived at White Ladies Priory in east Shropshire, finding sanctuary on the estate of the Roman Catholic Giffard family. It was here that Charles had his famous hair cut off, and was disguised in the clothes of the resident Penderels, before he made his way to Boscobel House, where he was concealed during the night. The following day, he set out for Wales, accompanied by Richard Penderel, hoping to cross the Severn at Ironbridge Gorge. However, they were challenged by the miller at Evelith, and hence spent the night in the barn of Francis Wolfe, master of the Coalbrookdale ironworks, at Upper House, Madeley. With the Severn crossings all guarded, they had to return to Boscobel on the 6th September, and it was here

Boscobel House began its transformation from a small farmhouse in the 1630s, thanks to John Giffard – the original farmhouse being the wing on the left-hand side of the photograph. The house and its grounds were destined to play a remarkable role in the English Civil War, harbouring the future Charles II and preventing his discovery against all the odds.

View from the opposite side of Boscobel House. Much of the garden, farmyard and interior of the house dates from the 19th century when it was owned by Walter Evans (1764-1839), a cotton manufacturer from Derby.

that Charles had to hide in an oak tree on the Boscobel estate, where he remained for an entire wet evening, while soldiers searched the surrounding woodlands. Once again, he evaded capture, and from Boscobel he headed eastwards into Staffordshire, ending up at

The view from the top of the cliff at Bridgnorth, looking eastwards over the River Severn. King Charles I once referred to his walks in Bridgnorth as "the finest in his dominion".

LEFT: This plaque at Boscobel House depicts the Parliamentarian soldiers searching for the future Charles II in the grounds of the house; Charles is hiding in the oak tree above. CENTRE: Here is a cutting from that same oak tree, thriving in the grounds of Boscobel House where its predecessor was one of many more oaks than we see today. By the late 18th century, the original had been destroyed by souvenir hunters! RIGHT: This is the opening to the priest hole in Boscobel House in which Charles had hidden two days previously.

Rose Cottage on Dale Road between Ironbridge and Coalbrookdale. The Grade II listed building dates from 1642 – so was built on the eve of the English Civil War.

At Boscobel House is this copy of an original 1651 account of "The History of His Sacred Majesty's Most Miraculous Preservation After the Battle of Worcester, 3 Sept. 1651."

A rare example of a Commonwealth era church (1649-1660), this is St Bartholomew's in the grounds of Benthall Hall.

Bentley Hall on 10th September where the Lane family disguised him as a servant. From there, despite further close calls, he made it to Bristol and then France – although the escape took around six weeks in total.

It is hard to imagine how terrifying this entire escapade must have been, for had he been captured, both Charles and his helpers would have suffered the most hideous of executions; probably hung, drawn and quartered as traitors. It is therefore no surprise that when he returned as king in 1660, Charles II rewarded the Penderels with a pension which is still paid to their descendants today!

Following the demise of Charles I, the now Colonel John Benbow, had been so appalled by the treatment of the King that he re-joined the Royalist party. His reward was to be executed on Shrewsbury Castle's green, on 15th October 1651, as an example to other potential deserters. Meanwhile, further attempts to capture Shrewsbury Castle for the exiled Charles II failed, such as that made by Sir Thomas Harries in 1654 and another in 1659.

One interesting observation on the English familiarity with war is made in Barrie Trinder's *A History of Shropshire*. He refers to some building work carried out in 1969, which uncovered varying ages of Shrewsbury's defensive walls. This revealed a marked contrast between the superb masonry of the 13th century and the "clumsy" work of the 1640s, thus

The gatehouse at Stokesay Castle was built in 1640-41 by Earl Craven. It survived an English Civil War siege in 1645, but afterwards, most of the wall around the castle was almost entirely destroyed.

St Oswald's in Oswestry is a medieval church, but was largely re-modelled in the late 17th century after extensive Civil War damage.

suggesting how unused Englishmen had become to military defence. As for the common man, there was little to commend the Civil War. Many thousands died in battle, with Richard Gough stating that 20 men from the small village of Myddle went to fight for the King and only 7 returned alive, one of whom was crippled for life thanks to a musket bullet which had passed right through his leg. Meanwhile those trapped in besieged Shropshire towns, suffered from shortage, and the demand of hundreds of troops, while the blockade of the Severn led to shortages everywhere else. Many houses in the suburbs of Ludlow, particularly in Corve Street and Galdeford, were burned down, probably by Royalist defenders wanting to clear their lines of fire! Out in the countryside, farms were also wide open to the pillage of marauding soldiers.

One of the lasting effects of the English Civil War, was that many castles and strongholds were scuttled, lest they provide a foothold for Royalist garrisons again. The castle walls of Oswestry and Bridgnorth were totally destroyed, leaving an interesting geometric survivor at Bridgnorth, and next to nothing at Oswestry, while the castles at Caus, Dawley and Shrawardine became quarries for hardcore!

During the 17th and 18th centuries, Shropshire mercers had large ranges of woollen and linen fabrics, made in both Britain and imported from abroad. They also sold hosiery and haberdashery, and imported groceries like sugar, spices and dried fruit. As well as the standard trades found in most towns, inventories for pewterers have been found in Ludlow and Newport, and for glaziers in Bridgnorth. Elsewhere, Joseph Wayman of Ludlow, had razors, periwig ribbons and curling pipes, while Thomas Holland, sword cutler of Shrewsbury made swords with silver hilts and boxes with fish-skin decorations, as well as shoemakers' knives and scissors. Meanwhile, Whitchurch began to forge a reputation for clockmaking, particularly tower clocks, following the founding of JB Joyce & Co in 1690, who still survive today and are the oldest tower clock manufacturers in the world. Many of their timepieces can be seen around Whitchurch and beyond, including Australia, China and India.

On 16th May 1665, 162 houses were destroyed in Newport due to a devastating fire, with High Street being almost totally wiped out – hence only a few medieval structures survive in the town. However, this paved the way for many fine Regency and Georgian frontages, thus allowing the main streets of Newport

Quirk Alert: *New Invention*

The hamlet of New Invention on the A488 between Knighton and Clun, comprises just four houses at a crossroads, one of which is a former Methodist chapel dating from 1874, and another the former Stag's Head. Its name origin, however, remains a mystery – but there are theories and legends, of course. One theory suggests the place was the first in the district where water-powered cotton-spinning was deployed – but this is unlikely as the earliest known reference to New Invention dates from 1677 – long before the process was invented. That said, fulling mills were water-powered in medieval times, with at least two at nearby Clun, so they could have been pre-dated by one at New Invention. Another theory suggests there was a New Inn here at some stage, although that doesn't explain the "vention" suffix – unless you consider that to be a derivative from the Anglo-Saxon words fenn and tūn, meaning "farmstead in a marshy place". Put that together, and you might have "new inn in a marshy place" – and the hamlet is low-lying between hills with a river running through it.

As for the legends, one suggests that the name derives from a local farrier who decided on the idea of fitting horseshoes backwards to confuse the enemy in times of war! A variation of this story is that the farrier reversed the shoes on the horse belonging to Charles I to help him evade capture!

Quirk Alert: *Mind Your Scolding!*

Shown below are the remains of a former ducking stool which can be found in St Peter's church at Myddle. It dates from 1660 to 1685, but is missing its former pole and wheels. When intact, the latter was a medieval form of punishment for witches, prostitutes, disorderly women...and even scolding wives! They would be strapped to the chair and then wheeled, in this case, to nearby Marton Pool where they would be unceremoniously ducked into the water. Elsewhere, some ducking stools were simply a chair into which the offender could be tied and exposed at her door or the site of her offence!

The ducking stool inside St Peter's church at Myddle.

Ducking stools were eventually phased out at Myddle in favour of a new pratice, which was used particularly for suspected witches. Apparently, the suspect's right thumb was bound to her left big toe, a rope was attached to her waist and the accused was thrown into Marton Pool. If the suspect floated it was deemed that she was in league with the devil, as she was deemed to have rejected the baptismal water. If she sank, she was graciously retrieved before drowning!

to be wider and less cluttered than those of the other towns of this age. Meanwhile, in the late 17th century, Wem became home to George Jeffreys (1645-1689), 1st Baron Jeffreys of Wem. Known more infamously as "Judge Jeffreys", he rose to fame during the reign of James II for his services as a ruthless judge, eventually rising to the position of Lord Chancellor, and occasionally serving as Lord High Steward. Jeffreys also became known as the "hanging judge", particularly due to his propensity to pass a sentence of capital punishment on supporters of the Duke of Monmouth, following the Monmouth Rebellion of 1685 – an attempt to overthrow James II.

During the 18th century, members of the Whig gentry families almost exclusively held the Lieutenancy of the county, while they also monopolised the ten borough seats. Conversely, Quarter Sessions and the two prestigious parliamentary seats for Shropshire were largely controlled by Tory squires. Prominent among the latter was Sir John Astley (1687-1772), who sat in the House of Commons for almost 45 years from 1727 to his death in 1772, first as MP for Shrewsbury (1727-1734) and then as MP for Shropshire (1734-1772). Richard Lyster (1691-1766) of Rowton Castle, who had been MP for Shrewsbury from 1722-1723, shared the MP for Shrewsbury role with Astley between 1727 and 1734, and was MP for Shropshire between 1740 and his death in 1766. Lyster was actually unseated as MP for Shrewsbury in 1723, at which point he marched out of the House with his back to the Speaker and was called to order for discourtesy! His response was to state: "When you learn justice, I will learn manners". He lost his Shrewsbury seat for a second time in 1734 when it was ruled that residents in Abbey Foregate were not entitled to vote in Shrewsbury elections – which presumably tested his acceptance of justice to the limit!

Another powerful politician in 18th century Shropshire was Henry Newport, 3rd Earl of Bradford (1683-1734), a Whig politician who sat in the House of Commons between 1706 and 1722, at varying times as MP for Bishop's Castle and MP for Shropshire. He also held

This 17th century house on High Street in Much Wenlock has the words "John and Mary Raynalds 1682" engraved above the right-hand, second floor windows and is known locally as Raynalds Mansion.

Close-up of the detail of Raynalds Mansion on the second floor.

the post of Lord Lieutenant and *Custos Rotulorum* of Staffordshire between 1715 and 1725 and Lord Lieutenant of Shropshire and *Custos Rotulorum* of Montgomeryshire between 1724 up to his death in 1734. He was succeeded by H.A. Herbert, who held the posts until 1761 having gained the lapsed titles of Lord Herbert of Chirbury in 1743 and 1st Earl of Powis in 1748. Herbert was also the acknowledged leader of the "Shropshire Whigs" in the 1750s, a group of gentry MPs who met in London before each parliamentary session. On his death in 1772, he was succeeded as Lord Lieutenant by one of Shropshire's most famous sons, Robert Clive.

Born at Styche Hall, Moreton Say on 29th September 1725, Robert Clive was a troublemaker at the various schools he was sent to, and when he was older, he and a gang of teenagers established a protection racket that vandalised the shops of uncooperative merchants in Market Drayton! He is also reputed to have climbed the tower of St Mary's church in Market Drayton and perched on a gargoyle, terrifying those down below – but also demonstrating his characteristic fearlessness. In 1744 Clive's father found a position for him as a clerk in the service of the East India Company, and young Robert arrived in Fort St George near Madras (modern-day Chennai).

The Grade I listed St Alkmund's church at Whitchurch, was built 1712-13 by John Barker of Rowsley.

Shortly afterwards, the French took Madras from the British, but Robert Clive escaped to Fort St David where he helped defend it against further French attacks. Recognised for his bravery, he was given a commission as an ensign, and went on to distinguish himself against the French before the war (known as the War of the Austrian Succession) ended in 1748, with Madras being returned to the British.

Robert Clive then distinguished himself further in local hostilities in India, including the stout defence of Arcot in 1751 – actions which made him famous back in Europe. Clive returned home in 1753, but returned to India in 1755 to act as deputy governor of Fort St David at Cuddalore. Now promoted to lieutenant-colonel in the British Army, Clive took part in the capture of the fortress of Gheriah, a stronghold of the Maratha Admiral Tuloji Angre. However, in June 1756, the Nawab of Bengal took the British fort at Calcutta, with the losses to the East India Company estimated at £2,000,000, while those British who were captured were placed in a punishment cell which became infamous as the Black Hole of Calcutta. In stifling summer heat, it was alleged that 123 of the 146 prisoners died as a result of suffocation or heat stroke. Admiral Charles Watson and Robert Clive were therefore dispatched to attack the Nawab's army and remove him from Calcutta by force. Their first target was the fortress of Baj-Baj which was quickly taken with minimal British casualties, and then, on 2nd January 1757, Calcutta itself was re-taken. However, a month later, the Nawab's army took up a position to the east of Calcutta, estimated to be around 40,000 cavalry, 60,000 infantry and thirty cannon; Clive's force was around 540 British infantry, 600 Royal Navy sailors, 800 local sepoys, fourteen field guns… and no cavalry! Nevertheless, during the early hours of February 5th, in a battle unofficially called the Calcutta Gauntlet, Clive marched his small force right through the Nawab's camp, despite being under heavy fire from all sides. By noon, his force broke through the besieging camp and arrived safely at Fort William. The British lost around a tenth of their force, and while technically not a victory, the sudden British assault intimidated the Nawab into making terms with Clive, and surrendering control of Calcutta on 9th February, while also promising to com-

Statue of Major-General Robert Clive (1725-1785), in Shrewsbury Square.

Laura's Tower at Shrewsbury Castle was built in 1790 as a folly.

pensate the East India Company for damages suffered and to restore its privileges.

Thereafter, Clive continued to serve with distinction in India. In 1757, he won the Battle of Plassey, which finally established British military supremacy in Bengal, while he also repelled the aggression of the Dutch. Elsewhere, he improved the organisation of the sepoy army, based on a European model, and enlisted into it many Muslims from the Mughal Empire, while he also re-fortified Calcutta. However, in 1760, he returned to England in poor health, albeit with a personal fortune of around £300,000, and he remained in Shropshire until 1765. Here, he sought political position, mainly to influence the course of events in India. He became the Whig MP for Shrewsbury from 1761 until his death in 1774, while he also became Baron Clive of Plassey, County Clare. Furthermore, he was elected Mayor of Shrewsbury for 1762–63 and received an honorary degree as DCL from Oxford University in 1760, while in 1764 he was appointed Knight of the Order of the Bath. Other gains included purchasing the Walcot estate in 1763, and with it, electoral influence at Bishop's Castle.

Meanwhile, in Clive's absence, the East India Company's service had become riddled with corruption, while the resident Indians were pauperised. The now Lord Clive therefore returned to Bengal with the double powers of Governor and Commander-in-Chief. During

> ### Quirk Alert: *The Sleep Rouser*
>
> *Having already written* Staffordshire Unusual & Quirky, *I immediately recognised a tale in Arthur Mee's* Shropshire *volume of* The King's England, *relating to Claverley, that had already been told about neighbouring Trysull. The Trysull tale is dated as 1725, while the Claverley tale is "time was when…". Both stories commence with a man (named as John Rudge for Trysull; unnamed for Claverley), who left eight shillings (one pound in Trysull) a year, to be paid to somebody who would drive dogs out of the church and rouse people who were sleeping. The Sleep Rouser would be armed with a long rod (a staff for Trysull) that had a fox's tail at one end – for tickling the faces of sleeping ladies – and a knob at the other end – for whacking men on the head!*

his final two years in India (1765-67), Clive secured from the emperor one of the most important documents in British history in India. It appears in the records as "firman from the King Shah Aalum, granting the diwani rights of Bengal, Bihar and Odisha to the Company 1765." By this deed, the company therefore became the real sovereign rulers of thirty million inhabitants, yielding revenue of £4,000,000.

Robert Clive was undoubtedly one of the most controversial figures in British military history. He established the military and political supremacy of the East India Company in Bengal and is credited with securing a large swathe of South Asia and the wealth that followed, for the British East India Company. Of course, in the process, he also turned *himself* into a multi-millionaire, too! More recent accounts have likened him and his achievements to Napoleon Bonaparte. He was certainly one of the key early figures who paved the way for what would later become British India, and he also enabled the East India Company to adopt the French strategy of indirect rule via a puppet government. But for his methods and his self-aggrandisement he was also vilified by contemporaries in Britain, and put on trial before Parliament, while modern historians have criticised him for atrocities, for high taxes, and for the forced cultivation of crops which exacerbated famines. Robert Clive died on 22nd November 1774, aged only forty-nine, after taking his own life; he had been suffering from poor health for a number of years and it is thought that this was his way out – brave to the last.

The second Lord Clive married the sister of the second Earl of Powis in 1784, and when the Earl died unmarried in 1801, his estates passed to his brother-in-law, for whom the title Earl of Powis was re-created in 1804. The Lieutenancy remained in the family until 1839, and through the control of Ludlow and Bishop's Castle, the Herbert-Clives remained a powerful force in Shropshire politics. Meanwhile, the borough of Bridgnorth was largely under the influence of the Whitmores of Apley Park, at least one of whom was returned for the town at every election between the Restoration and 1870, with the exception of 1810. Indeed, there was a local saying during these times: "All on one side like a Bridgnorth election!"

High Street, Whitchurch. The building in the centre is the former Town Hall and Market House, built in 1718 – and now masquerading as a bank!

Next door, further down High Street, is Liverpool House which dates from the mid-18th century.

The Lion Hotel in Shrewsbury was built by lawyer John Ashby, an influential figure in mid-18th century Shropshire society and known as "the guardian of many secrets". He provided magnificent assembly rooms here "to promote the general good of this town and county."

The Grade I listed Attingham Park was built between 1783 and 1785 for Noel Hill, 1st Baron Berwick from May 1784. Hill was the Whig MP for Shrewsbury between 1768 and 1774 and for Shropshire between 1774 and 1784. He also served as Mayor of Shrewsbury in 1778–79 and of Oswestry in 1779–80.

> **Quirk Alert:** *Icarus of the Rope*
>
> On 2nd February 1739, a rope was attached to the top of the 222ft (68m) spire of St Mary's church in Shrewsbury, with the other end anchored in Gay Meadow on the other side of the River Severn. It was from here that a young steeplejack, professional ropewalker and showman called Robert Cadman, walked up the 800-foot (243m) rope span, firing off pistols and performing tricks during his ascent. His nickname was "Icarus of the Rope", and he had performed his party-piece many times before, including from the cupola of St Paul's Cathedral in London, sliding face-first down a rope while blowing a trumpet.
>
> At the top of St Mary's, on 2nd February 1739, Cadman strapped on a grooved wooden breastplate, and launched himself into his flight. Alas, with his wife collecting coppers from the watching crowd below, the rope snapped when he was half way across and Cadman fell to his death, aged just twenty-eight. There is a commemorative plaque in his memory in St Mary's which contains a poignant verse.

> **Quirk Alert:** *Namby-pamby Fire Fodder*
>
> Bishop Thomas Percy was the author of Reliques of Ancient English Poetry, published in 1765, and which was the first great collection of English poetry, including works dating back to the 12th century. However, a significant part of the volume is comprised of poetry rescued from Humphrey Pitt's house at Shifnal. The story goes, that Percy caught Pitt's housemaid lighting the lounge fire with leaves from one of Pitt's old folios – and hence rescued much of the volume in the nick of time! Meanwhile, 18th century poet, Ambrose Philips (1674-1749), was the unwitting source of the phrase "namby-pamby", coined by fellow poets Henry Carey and Alexander Pope in an attack on Philips' sentimentalist works!

It was a similar scenario in the borough of Wenlock, where the Forester family dominated during this period, but in Shrewsbury, there was a bit more competition. Here, the Whig dominance was challenged by the Bath family, including William Pulteney, Earl of Bath, described as "a brilliant, eloquent, vindictive, mean man". He became Lord Lieutenant in 1760, while one of his successors, also a William Pulteney, gained one of the seats after Robert Clive's death via the by-election of 1775. Meanwhile, there was much competition for the other Shrewsbury seat which reached its height in 1796 when there was an ongoing contest between the Hawkstone and Attingham branches of the Hill family.

Prior to the 18th century, the responsibility for maintaining roads rested with the manorial lord during the medieval period and, after that, with under-funded local parishes – although religious institutions or guilds were responsible for the maintenance of some bridges and causeways. Following an Act of 1555, a surveyor of highways was chosen annually in every parish, who called out able-bodied men to work on the roads for four, and later for six days per year. This system was fine for parishes without main routes (such as those in Corvedale or the Shropshire Hills), but for those that were traversed by busy routes, like Newport on the great road from London to Chester, it was hugely unfair. To add insult to injury, these parishioners were also repairing roads used principally by others! Of course, as the number of carts, pack-horses, coaches and riders ramped up throughout the 17th century, many of Shropshire's roads were in a dreadful condition, and totally impassable in winter; local labour was no longer enough.

The solution was the introduction of turnpike trusts – bodies set up by Acts of Parliament with powers to collect tolls in order to maintain principal highways, and which were generally run by groups of local trustees or county justices. The first turnpike trust in Shropshire appeared in 1726 – this being a stretch of Watling Street, the London to Holyhead route that passed through Shropshire from the mid-east to the

LEFT: The Grade II listed English Bridge, Shrewsbury, was originally built 1769-1774 to John Gwynne's design. It was 400ft (120m) long and comprised seven semi-circular arches, with the 55ft (17m) span central arch built high, to provide headroom to watercraft – making the road approach very steep. For this reason, the bridge was partly rebuilt and widened in 1926 to lower all the arches, converting the central one into a segmental arch, and reducing the height of the roadway by 5ft (1.5m). RIGHT: The Grade II listed Old Atcham Bridge, built 1769-1771. Thomas Farnolls Pritchard (1723-1777), the son of a Shrewsbury joiner, was a surveyor on both bridges. He also designed the Foundling Hospital in Shrewsbury, Swan Hill Court and Hatton Grange, Shifnal, and refurbished older houses such as the 16th century Shipton Hall; it was also Pritchard who first suggested the building of an iron bridge across the Severn near Coalbrookedale.

north-west, taking in Wellington, Shrewsbury and Oswestry. The table below lists all of the turnpike roads that were built in Shropshire, with the glut of roads turnpiked in the 1750s mostly networks radiating from market towns. It wasn't until the early 1770s that more remote areas were connected, with the two routes from Wem to Bron y Garth (1771) and Burlton to Llanymynech (1772) enabling lime from the kilns and quarries in the county's north-west to be transported eastwards.

Of course, many of these roads received subsequent overhauls, but the most notable were actioned by Thomas Telford (1757-1834). For nearly two decades after 1815, Telford undertook a major reorganisation of the existing trusts along the London to Holyhead Road and the construction of large sections of new road, until it was the best road in Europe. In 1808 the journey took 38 hours. Following Telford's improvements, the journey time was reduced to 26 hours, with the best mail coach speeds increasing from 5 mph to 10 mph across the new surface. Elsewhere, a new road avoiding the congestion in Shifnal market place was built between 1828 and 1830, and the route over Snedshill (regarded by Telford as "one of the worst I ever saw a mail coach travel over") was bypassed between 1822 and 1824. Other new routes completed were Gobowen to Chirk in 1825, round Oveley Hill in 1835, and Shrewsbury to Montford Bridge in 1838. Elsewhere, a new road from Coalbrookdale to Wellington was completed in 1817, while south of Ludlow, the roads leading to Tenbury and Leominster were completely re-routed in the 1830s. Similarly, the road from Bridgnorth to Ludlow was re-routed in 1843 via Morville and Shipton, to avoid the Clee Hills.

The better roads resulting from turnpike trusts meant that coaching became a growth industry in the 18th century. By 1753, it took about 3½ days to make the trip by coach from Shrewsbury to London, but thanks to improvements made, by 1772 the time had been cut to 1½ days. One person who operated coaches on the route in 1774 was Robert Lawrence of the Raven and Bell, and by 1779 he had introduced a thrice-weekly service to Holyhead through Ellesmere, and the following year added a second coach through Oswestry, thus being able to offer his services six days a week. In 1781, he moved to the Lion, the great Shrewsbury inn built a few years previously by lawyer, John Ashby. Passengers had previously journeyed to Holyhead via Chester, but Lawrence succeeded in creating a new route through Shrewsbury and, by 1808, the Royal Mail, carrying letters for Ireland was also calling at the Lion.

Turnpike Trusts of Shropshire

Name of Trust	Act	Length (miles)
Shifnal District of Holyhead Road	1726	18
Shrewsbury to Oswestry	1726	18
Watling Street, Shrewsbury District	1726	7
Watling Street, Wellington District	1726	22
Ludlow to Monk's Bridge	1750	1
Ludlow (2nd district)	1751	83
Overton District of Shrewsbury Road	1751	23
Bridgnorth Black Brook	1752	8
Bridgnorth Morvill	1752	8
Bridgnorth Smithy Brook	1752	4
Ellesmere District of Shrewsbury & Wrexham	1752	22
Shrewsbury to Wrexham	1752	9
Wall upon Eyewood to Blackwood	1752	1
Ludlow (1st district)	1756	14
Much Wenlock to Church Stretton	1756	12
Preston Brockhurst (Shrewsbury to Shawbury)	1756	60
Shrewsbury to Church Stretton and Condover	1756	14
Shrewsbury to Longden and Castle Pulverbach	1756	8
Shrewsbury to Welshpool	1758	5
Shrewsbury to Westbury	1758	9
Shrewsbury to Baschurch	1758	7
Welch Gate and Cotton Hill to Shrewsbury	1758	1
Shrewsbury to Minsterley	1759	9
Newport and Ternhill	1760	12
Whitchurch to Ternhill	1760	9
Cleobury Mortimer District (Bridgnorth)	1762	37
Kelsall to Whiston Cross	1762	8
Cleobury North & Ditton Priors	1763	15
Honington and Hilton	1763	3
Bridgnorth and Shifnal	1764	8
Madeley	1764	19
Uckington to Longnor Green	1764	7
Shrewsbury to Bridgnorth	1765	11
Whitchurch & Marchwiel	1767	27
Whitchurch to Nantwich	1767	38
Whitchurch to Madeley	1767	9
Bishop's Castle, First Division	1768	93
Shawbury to Newcastle	1769	18
Wem to Bron y Garth	1771	25
Burlton and Llanymynech	1772	18
Ellesmere to Oswestry	1772	9
Meadowgate Shrewsbury	1772	1
Oswestry	1772	56
Cleobury Mortimer District (Bewdley)	1774	4
Ironbridge (Buildwas to Tern Bridges)	1778	7
Wenlock	1778	25
Atcham to Dorrington	1797	10
King-Street	1797	6
Wem to Sandford	1811	4
Coalbrookdale & Wellington	1817	5
Minsterley to Churchstoke	1834	11

The Grade I listed Butter Cross in Ludlow, built by William Baker of Audlem in 1746. The building to the left is the Grade II listed Tamberlane House which dates from the early 17th century, while the red-brick house to the right is 1 King Street, also Grade II listed and dating from 1829. The 15th century Grade I listed St Laurence's church is in the background.

A surviving turnpike tollhouse at Minsterley. In the 18th century, turnpike trusts applied funds to erecting tollhouses that accommodated the pike-man or toll-collector beside the turnpike gate. In Shropshire there were around 300 tollhouses built, of which 100 are still in existence.

The Wynnstay Hotel in Oswestry dates from the late 18th century. It was built for Sir Watkin Williams Wynn as a coaching inn on the routes from London to Holyhead and Cardiff to Liverpool.

Around a century earlier, The Castle was built at Wem. This 17th century inn was also a popular coaching inn during the 18th century.

Looking up Cartway in Bridgnorth. The pub on the right dates from the early 18th century and is named after Charles II.

Another 17th century coaching inn, this time the Grade II listed Six Bells at Bishop's Castle. There are still stables around the back.

Apart from the Lion and the adjacent Raven and Bell, the other main coaching inns in Shrewsbury were the Britannia, which had stabling for 150 horses, and the Talbot built in 1775 on land owned by the Ottleys of Pitchford Hall. Coaching in Shropshire reached its pinnacle in the mid-1830s, but the railways then took most of their passengers away when they arrived in the 1840s – although coaches in Shropshire still served as feeders to the railways until the Shrewsbury to Wolverhampton railway arrived in the county in 1849. Within a few months, the former best coaching route in Europe was almost deserted.

The second half of the 17th century saw the birth of a number of non-conformist religions, and when the Declaration of Indulgence of 1672 allowed the registration of dissenting places of worship, 57 were duly recorded in Shropshire, including seven in Shrewsbury. By the mid-18th century, dissenting chapels existed in all Shropshire towns, although there were occasional public backlashes, such as that in 1715 which saw meeting houses destroyed in Shrewsbury, Wem and Whitchurch. In 1742, a chapel was established in Broseley which eventually developed into a Baptist society, while there was a congregation of Methodists in Shrewsbury from around 1744 – although it was another seventeen years before John Wesley (the founder of Methodism) visited the town. Meanwhile, John Fletcher, vicar of Madeley from 1760 to 1785, was located at the core of the burgeoning Industrial Revolution, and his sermons and publications became increasingly concerned with the brutal impact upon workers in the expanding forges, ironworks and on the canals. Although ordained as a priest of the Church of England, John Wesley visited him in 1764 and several times afterwards, and saw Fletcher as his successor as leader of the connexion which he had built up. However, Fletcher preferred to avoid involvement in national affairs, while ill-health forced him to spend increasing time abroad. He died in 1785, but his wife, Mary, continued his work until her death in 1815, collaborating with both the church authorities and Wesleyan ministers. Her daughter, also Mary, continued the work, culminating in a Wesleyan chapel being built in Madeley in 1833.

> **Quirk Alert:** *The Hurricane Gravestone*
>
> *Wentnor churchyard is home to the Hurricane Gravestone. Its inscription tells of a terrible storm which lashed the village in 1772. Tragically, it caused a wall in the church to collapse, crushing the villagers sheltering in the church's sanctuary. Meanwhile, at nearby Asterton, a house was said to have been swept clean away, killing the seven people within.*

Wesleyan Methodism was particularly strong in the coalfields, and in most towns but was relatively weak in the countryside. Primitive Methodist preachers from Tunstall in Staffordshire (where the movement was born) then arrived in Wrockwardine Wood in 1821 where they built the first Primitive chapel in the county. From here, they moved to Shrewsbury and then on to Bishop's Castle and Clun, while a circuit was set up in 1822 at Prees Green in the north of the county. Then, in 1823, missionaries from Darlaston established the Hopton Bank circuit in one of the remotest parts of the county on Clee Hill, thereafter taking the movement to Ludlow and Leintwardine. Revivalists also arrived in Dawley in 1821.

Shropshire's industry from the 16th century to the 1770s, was largely based on its mineral resources. There is some evidence of medieval coal working but the first significant industrial development was the rapid growth of coal mining in the parishes of Benthall, Broseley and Moseley in the second half of the 16th century. Indeed, between the 1570s and the 1670s, the population of Broseley increased tenfold! There were also two important innovations in the Severn Gorge during the 17th century. The first was the development of the longwall system of mining – which also became known as the Shropshire method. This involved mining a long wall of coal in a single slice. Miners would undercut the coal along the width of the coal face, removing coal as it fell, and then use wooden props to control the fall of the roof behind the face. This method enabled the recovery of a far larger proportion of coal in a seam compared to previous methods. The second innovation occurred in 1605, when two wooden railways had been built in Broseley parish on land belonging to James Clifford.

As for the product, coal was being deployed for a number of industrial purposes by 1700; for smelting lead ore, for boiling brine to make salt, for the extraction of tar, for firing tobacco pipes, for the making of bricks,

Shrewsbury St Chad's was built between 1790 and 1792 by George Steuert of London, and has the country's largest circular nave.

Ludlow market place. In the background are largely 18th century buildings, including on the far left, the Grade II* listed Ludlow College High Hall.

tiles and pottery, and for the manufacture of glass. Elsewhere in Shropshire, the coal mining community on the slopes of Titterstone Clee grew substantially in the late 16th and early 17th century, the coal being used in the creation of pottery here known as Clee Hill ware, and possibly also in local glass-making. Most of these miners occupied cottages of which there were 49 on the wastes of Snitton township alone in 1745, growing to 68 by 1778.

Alongside coal, Shropshire's ironworks were important long before the Industrial Revolution. As early as the 1530s there were three bloomery furnaces in Coalbrookdale making small quantities of wrought iron. Meanwhile the first blast furnace in Shropshire was built somewhere on Shirlett Common in the 1540s, with another following at Shifnal in 1564. Many ironworks followed between 1600 and 1750, all using charcoal as their fuel and water as their source of power – although supplies of charcoal were scarce and therefore limited the growth of ironmaking at this time.

There were two groups of blast furnaces in Shropshire, one using ore from the Coalbrookdale coalfield, and the other from the coal measures on the Clee Hills, while the majority of the forges stood on the Cound Brook, the Rea, the Tern and the Worfe. There were also several ironworks in the Oswestry area. As for the iron trade, this was focused on Bridgnorth at this time, receiving the iron from the Clee Hills to be despatched to forges in other counties, and inbound pig iron from the Forest of Dean and America to be despatched to Shropshire forges. However, the most significant development occurred in 1708 when the blast furnace at Coalbrookdale, which had stood derelict after an explosion, was leased by Abraham Darby (1678-1717) – he being the first of four famous men to bear that name. Darby rebuilt the furnace, but when he began to smelt iron in January 1709, he used coke made from local coal and not charcoal for his fuel – thus taking a major step forward in the production of iron as a raw material. That said, the iron produced wasn't suitable for being forged into good wrought iron – possibly due to the presence of silicon as an impurity – but it was perfectly good for making castings, which was Darby's principal interest. Darby's accounts from 20th October 1708 to 4th January 1710 still survive, showing the production of "charked" coal in January 1709, and the sale of 81 tons of iron goods during the period.

A second blast furnace followed in Coalbrookdale around the time of Darby's death in 1717. By the early 1720s, his successors were producing cast-iron cylinders for the Newcomen steam engines invented in 1712 by Thomas Newcomen; the business also made and sold pots and pans throughout the region. As for Abraham Darby I, his method of casting pots in sand provided

GEORGIAN SHREWSBURY BUILDINGS

The former Bowdlers School, founded by Thomas Bowdler, 1724.

Houses in St John's Hill were built in around 1750.

This set of houses on Town Walls is known as The Crescent. They were designed in 1793 by architect Joseph Bromfield.

Quarry Place. The large building in the centre is the former coach house and dates from the early 19th century.

Wem Grammar School (now Adams House), in Wem, was founded by Sir Thomas Adams in 1650, but was rebuilt in 1776 and enlarged in 1930.

This 18th century house on Noble Street, Wem, is Grade II listed, as are the gate piers. Today, the building is home to Wem Conservative Club.

Company played an important role in using iron to replace the more expensive brass for cylinders for Thomas Newcomen's steam engines. In the early 1740s, he began to employ a steam engine to return the water which had flowed over the water wheels of the blast furnaces back to the pool above the upper furnace, thus setting up a circulation system which made the ironworks independent of rainfall. In the early 1750s, he discovered that iron of good quality for forging could be made using coke as his fuel. In 1755 he and his partner, Thomas Goldney, opened a new blast furnace at Horsehay, 2 miles north of Coalbrookdale, with another following at nearby Ketley. Within four years, another eight furnaces had been built in the area. Unsurprisingly, therefore, Shropshire had become the leading iron-producing area of Great Britain. The scene was set for one of the original hotbeds of the Industrial Revolution.

Shropshire's Industrial Revolution

The Industrial Revolution began in England in the late 18th century, with the arrival of water-powered cotton mills, the birth of factories and mass production of goods, along with an increase in heavy industries such as coal mining. During the second half of the 18th century, Shropshire was the leading iron-producer in Britain and the home of many innovations, with the Ironbridge Gorge area attracting engineers, writers and artists from all over the western world. Early innovations included the first iron railway wheels and track, John Wilkinson's (world's first) iron boat, the *Trial*, launched in 1787, and the steam railway locomotive built by Richard Trevithick at Coalbrookdale in 1802.

However, the most lasting late 18th century innovation in the area, is the famous Iron Bridge over the River Severn at Ironbridge. Opened in 1781, it was the first major bridge in the world to be made of cast iron, and was rightly celebrated wide and far. It was built due to the area being a recognised centre for the iron industry, and the fact that the wide River Severn was a massive barrier to travel in the area, particularly the need to travel between the important industrial parishes of Broseley to the south and Madeley and Coalbrookdale to the north. Prior to the

his successors with a viable business that operated for over two centuries. Iron smelting with coke released the iron industry from the limitations of cutting and burning trees to make charcoal, and coke-smelted cast iron eventually enabled the production of the huge quantities of iron used to drive the Industrial Revolution – with it being used extensively in 19th century steam engines, bridges, and many other products.

Abraham Darby II (1711-1763) entered the business in 1728, aged seventeen. Under him, the Coalbrookdale

LEFT: The ruins of the Bedlam Furnaces, just east of Ironbridge. They were built between 1757 and 1759 by the Madeley Wood Furnace Company, and are the most complete set of mid-18th century ironworking furnaces in the country, hence designation as a Scheduled Monument. These furnaces transformed iron ore into molten ore and were among the first to be specifically designed to use coke as fuel instead of charcoal. CENTRE: The furnaces were famously captured by painter Philip James de Loutherbourg in 1801 known as "Coalbrookdale by Night", in one of the most iconic images of the Industrial Revolution. This photo is a shot of the information panel at the site. RIGHT: Remains of mine workings on Titterstone Clee Hill.

Iron Bridge being erected, the nearest crossing was at Buildwas, 3 miles away.

The use of the Severn by boat traffic and the steep sides of the gorge meant that the bridge had to be of a single span, and high enough to allow tall ships to pass underneath. Those steep sides also made life difficult for the builders, plus there was no obvious point where to build as none of the roads on opposite sides of the river faced each other. The Iron Bridge was first proposed in 1773, by architect Thomas Farnolls Pritchard and local ironmaster, John Wilkinson of Broseley. In 1775, a subscription of around £4,000 was raised, and Abraham Darby III (1750-1789), the ironmaster at Coalbrookdale, was appointed treasurer to the project. In March 1776, the Act to build a bridge was passed, and Abraham Darby III was commissioned to cast and build it.

Interestingly, things could have turned out very different, for in May 1776, the trustees withdrew Darby's commission, and advertised for alternative plans for a single arch bridge to be built in "stone, brick or timber". Thankfully, no satisfactory proposal was made, and the trustees reverted to Pritchard's design. Work began in November 1777, with the bridge sited adjacent to where a ferry had run between Madeley and Benthall,

The famous Iron Bridge over the River Severn at Ironbridge Gorge looking from east to west – seen in spring (left) and summer (right). Opened in 1781, it was the first major bridge in the world to be made of cast iron.

LEFT: View from the other side, looking west to east. The bridge is engraved on both sides with: "THIS BRIDGE WAS CAST AT COALBROOKDALE AND ERECTED IN THE YEAR MDCCIXXIX". RIGHT: View over the bridge towards the town of Ironbridge on the northern shore of the Severn.

LEFT: The tollhouse at the south end of the Iron Bridge. RIGHT: The 18th century Swan Hotel claims to be the oldest public house in Ironbridge. It is said that bridge construction site meetings were sometimes held here.

> ### Quirk Alert: *Hi Ho Tontine*
>
> *The Tontine Hotel was built between 1780 and 1784, and was intended to accommodate the many tourists who flocked to view the new Iron Bridge, completed in 1779. A tontine was a private club to which members contributed. The unusual name derives from a 17th century Neapolitan banker, Lorenzo di Tonti, and relates to a popular investment scheme at that time, devised in Italy, and used for raising capital. Its popularity grew in the 18th and 19th centuries, and combines features of a group annuity and a lottery wherein each subscriber pays an agreed sum into the fund and thereafter receives an annuity. As members die their shares devolve to the other participants and so the value of each annuity increases. The principle was that the last surviving member would inherit all of the funds, which could be considerable, while on the death of the last member the scheme is wound up. Unfortunately, statistics showed that members were prone to suffering premature deaths…and as a result, tontines were eventually outlawed!*
>
>
>
> The Tontine Hotel is shown here on Ironbridge's High Street. It wasn't always healthy to be a member of the Tontine Club, though.

and was chosen for its high approaches on each side. The masonry and abutments were constructed between 1777 and 1778, and the ribs were lifted into place in the summer of 1779 by the use of wooden derricks and cranes. The 100ft (30m) bridge was opened to traffic on 1st January 1781. Exactly 847,800 lb (384,556 kg or 385 tonnes) of iron was used in the construction of the bridge, and there are almost 1,700 individual components, the heaviest weighing 5.6 tonnes. Meanwhile, the original budget for the bridge was £3,250, money raised mostly by Broseley subscribers – but although the final cost is unknown, contemporary records suggest it was as high as £6,000, with the excess being borne by Darby. However, by the mid-1790s the bridge was highly profitable, and tolls were giving the shareholders an annual dividend of 8 per cent. Unsurprisingly, the opening of the bridge changed the immediate area, with the town of Ironbridge developing at the northern end – with the trustees, as well as local hotel keepers and coach operators, promoting interest in the bridge among members of high society.

Elsewhere in the area, the first porcelain manufactory in Shropshire was set up in 1772 by Thomas Turner, at Caughley, Broseley, while two of Turner's former apprentices, brothers John and Thomas Rose, set up two more factories at Coalport in the 1790s. Meanwhile, in 1784, Archibald Cochrane, 9th Earl of Dundonald began to make coke in closed ovens, condensing the gasses given off to produce tar and varnishes. By 1800, William Reynolds, who ran the ironworks at Ketley, had begun experimenting with some of these oils to drive an engine, in his laboratory at his home at Ketley Bank. Together, Dundonald and Reynolds planned an alkali works at Coalport where by using coal, limestone and common salt to make soda, they proposed to manufacture glass, fertilisers, dyestuffs and soap. Reynolds also had interests in another alkali works at Wombridge and a glassworks at Wrockwardine Wood.

William Reynolds was born in 1758, the son of the ironmaster and philanthropist Richard Reynolds. His father managed the works at Coalbrookdale from 1763 to 1768, but it was William who became the most innovative of the various Shropshire ironmasters, meeting regularly with Coalbrookdale visitors such as Matthew Boulton, James Watt, John Wilkinson, Lord Dundonald and Thomas Telford. Working with Abraham Darby, Reynolds built several Boulton and Watt steam engines for his Ketley ironworks while between 1787 and 1788, he constructed three tub boat canals, which brought coal and iron ore a short distance from local mines to his ironworks.

This leads us nicely into the canal revolution, which exploded all over England in the late 18th century. The transport of the bulk product being manufactured in Shropshire's industrial heartlands would not have been possible without the development of the canals which had two objectives: firstly to provide cheap transport for heavy goods such as coal, clay, iron, limestone and manufactured goods, and secondly, to connect the manufacturing districts of the area with deep-water ports and hence with national and international markets for their produce.

In the early 18th century, Shropshire's principal link with the outside word was the River Severn. Barges exported wool, cheese, leather, coal and lead ore, and imported the cloth, tobacco, spirits, spices and groceries subsequently sold in the county's market towns. In the second half of the 18th century, passenger wherries operated time-tabled services from Shrewsbury to Worcester and Gloucester. However, barges only sailed when the water was deep enough to accommodate them, and it wasn't unusual for them to be moored for up to nine months of the year during periods of low rainfall; alternatively, inbound cargos could be transhipped from large to small vessels at Bewdley.

All of this changed in the late 18th century when Shropshire became served by four canal systems. The first, the Donnington Wood Canal, was built between 1765 and 1767 as a private venture by Earl Gower &

Co., and ran for 5.5 miles (8.9km) from Earl Gower's mines at Donnington Wood to a wharf on Pave Lane on the Wolverhampton to Newport turnpike road. Earl Gower was the brother-in-law of the Duke of Bridgewater, who had pioneered the canal age with his Bridgewater Canal, opened in 1761. As the owner of limestone quarries and coal mines in Shropshire, Gower recognised the potential of canals to ship his product. He therefore formed Earl Gower & Company in 1764, joining forces with two land agents, John and Thomas Gilbert before building the canal. His limestone quarries at Lilleshall were served by the Lilleshall Branch line, but where it met the main canal at Hugh's Bridge, the branch was 42.7ft (13.0m) lower, and so a tunnel was built into the hill, with vertical shafts up to the main line. A pulley system enabled coal to be sent down to the lower level, for use in the production of agricultural lime, and limestone to be raised up to the top level, for use in the production of iron. This system was eventually replaced in 1797 by an inclined plane which was 123 yards (112m) long and powered by a steam engine – although the inclined plane was used to transfer tramway waggons loaded with cargo between the two levels, and was never used to carry boats. The Lilleshall Branch also ran further north to the limeworks at Pitchcroft, via a junction at Willmore Bridge. Again, the Pitchcroft limeworks were 35ft (11m) lower than the junction, and so seven locks were constructed to reach them.

New furnaces were built at Donnington Wood in 1785, after which much of the limestone was transported to them, rather than transporting coal to Lilleshall. At Old Yard Junction, connections were made to the Wombridge Canal in 1788, and to the Shropshire Canal in 1790 (more on those shortly). Later, in 1825, a new set of furnaces were built at Old Lodge, Donnington Wood, and a new arm was built to connect them to the main line of the canal. Then, between 1818 and 1835, 74 shafts were sunk in the area around the Donnington Wood Canal and, enterprisingly, the majority of the water supply for the Donnington Wood Canal was pumped out of these surrounding coal mines. The Lilleshall Company recorded 15 operational pumping engines in 1870, raising water from depths of 150ft (46m) to 600ft (180m), and producing 20,000 tons of water per month. Some of these engines remained in use until the late 1920s, but once pumping ceased, the western end of the canal dried out.

As for Lord Gower, he became the first Marquis of Stafford in 1786 and his son, George Leveson-Gower, became the Duke of Sutherland in 1833.

The next Shropshire canals to be built were William Reynolds' private canals at Ketley and Wombridge, both of which were opened in 1788 to service his ironworks, while a third – the Shropshire Canal – was opened in 1792, linking the Wombridge and Ketley Canals to Coalport and Coalbrookdale. All three were tub-boat canals on which tub boats – box-like, rectangular vessels measuring 20ft by 6ft 4in (6.1m by 1.9m) – were deployed to transport coal, limestone and ironstone from the locations where they were mined to furnaces where the iron ore was processed.

The Ketley Canal ran for 1.5 miles (2.4 km) from Oakengates to Ketley and was built to transport ironstone and coal to Reynolds' foundries at Ketley. The canal terminated to the south of Ketley Hall, but at this point there was a 73ft (22.3m) drop to his works. A lock system was out of the question due to an insufficient water supply, so Reynolds constructed the first inclined plane in Britain which involved the raising and lowering of the tub boats from one level to another in caissons. A boat would enter one of two locks at the top of the incline, which had two tracks, so that a loaded boat descending on one track was counterbalanced by an empty or lightly loaded boat ascending on the other. Then, from the foot of the incline, the canal continued through a 60-yard (55m) tunnel to reach the Warehouse Pool, where the works was situated. Construction of the inclined plane required over 200 men. In a letter to James Watt in 1789, Reynolds wrote that: "We have let down in average about thirty boats daily and have not yet had an accident." The inclined plane continued to work for twenty-eight years, until the Ketley ironworks closed in 1816, although the upper canal remained in use until the 1880s.

The Wombridge Canal also opened in 1788, this time to transport the iron ore and coal mined at Wombridge along its 1.75m (2.82km) length, to the furnaces at Donnington Wood, where it also joined the Donnington Wood Canal. Five years later, a 1793 Act of Parliament created the Shrewsbury Canal Company to build a canal from Wombridge to Shrewsbury. To do this, the new company bought 1,848 yards (1.690 km) of the Wombridge Canal at a cost of £840. Despite its short lifespan, the Wombridge Canal saw a glass house erected alongside it in the early 1790s by William Reynolds' sons, William and Joseph, where they made a variety of objects from dark green glass, including door-stops, rolling pins, jugs and bottles for French wine manufacturers. Less than 300 yards (270m) to the west, John Bullock erected a corn mill by the side of the canal in 1818, which produced flour – a business that survived until the 1970s. Also built in 1818 were two furnaces owned by James Foster, with a third added a few years later, with these surviving until the early 20th century.

The third and final of Reynolds' early Shropshire tub boat canals was the Shropshire Canal, completed in 1792, this time to supply coal, ore and limestone to the industrial region that adjoined the River Severn below Coalbrookdale and at Coalport, by linking them to the Donnington Wood Canal. An Act of Parliament was obtained on 11th June 1788, and the first section was completed in early 1789. This required a new 360-yard long (330m) incline plane to be built at Wrockwardine Wood, which lifted the canal by 120ft (37m) and from the top of that, a canal section was built to link with the Ketley Canal at Oakengates, including the 279 yard (255m) long Snedshill Tunnel. At the connection between the Shropshire and Ketley Canals, the water level on the former was 1ft (0.3m) higher than that of the latter, and so a lock was constructed near the junction. The Donnington Wood Canal then built a short extension to link to the bottom of the Wrockwardine Wood plane at the northern end, and by 1790, the Shropshire Canal had been built as far south as Southall Bank. By 1791, most of the main line was serviceable, although piling for the wharves on the River Severn at Coalport wasn't completed until 1792.

The stretch from Southall Bank to Coalport on the River Severn also included two new inclined planes, descending along the 600-yard long Windmill Farm Inclined Plane at the northern point of this stretch, and the 350-yard long Hay Inclined Plane at Coalport. At the bottom of the Hay Inclined Plane, a level section of canal then ran alongside the river, heading eastwards, and which is sometimes referred to as the Coalport Canal, while a number of warehouses were built between the canal and the river, with small inclined planes leading from the warehouses to wharfs on the river.

Also completed in 1792 was the Horsehay branch line which headed off west from Southall Bank to Horsehay, Brierly Hill and terminated on the hill about 120ft (37m) above the Coalbrookdale works. A tramway from the works tunnelled into the hill, ending in a cavern below the terminus of the canal. From here two vertical shafts were constructed, with coal and iron ore descending and limestone ascending in crates. The shafts and tunnel belonged to the Dale Company, who charged tolls for their use, but the system was not a success, and was replaced by a tramway inclined plane in 1794. The tramway was soon extended along the length of the Horsehay branch, making the canal redundant.

On completion, the Shropshire Canal main line was about 7.75 miles (12.5km) long, while the Horsehay branch was about 2.75 miles (4.4km) long. As for the new inclined planes, the design was modified from that used on the Ketley Canal, where there was a lock at the top, which resulted in a loss of water each time the plane was used. Instead Reynolds used a steam-powered system that eliminated water loss, whereby the boats would pass over a hump, after which a short downward-sloping section took the boats into the canal. On the Wrockwardine Wood inclined plane, most of the traffic was uphill, and so the steam engine was used to raise the boats up the incline. On the other inclines, the traffic was downhill, and so they were counterbalanced, with the descending load raising the empty boats on the other track. The engine was only required to assist the boat over the hump at the top.

The terminus at Coalport soon developed into a village with two potteries, a factory making ropes, and a works manufacturing chains. In 1810, a new basin

TOP LEFT: Coalport on the part of the Shropshire Canal that was also known as the Coalport Canal. The Shropshire Canal was built between 1788 and 1793 to transport goods between the east Shropshire coalfield and the River Severn. In order to lift and lower boats up and down the 207ft (63m) steep-sided gorge, using a combination of steam power and gravity, the Hay Inclined Plane was built – thus negating the need for locks, which were slow and expensive to run. The Coalport section of the canal ran parallel to the river from the bottom of the Hay Inclined Plane to the terminal near Coalport Bridge half a mile downstream. The Hay Inclined Plane was in operation from 1793 to 1894 and was formally closed in 1907. TOP RIGHT is the bottom of the Hay Inclined Plane BELOW LEFT, a section in the centre, and BELOW RIGHT, the top.

with capacity for 60 tub boats was constructed, while the wharfs were also extended. It has been estimated that some 100,000 tons of cargo passed through the warehouses each year during the canal's peak years, most of it coal and iron.

The Shropshire Canal operated successfully until the 1830s. It was then leased by the Shropshire Union Canal in the 1840s, but was suffering from subsidence by the 1850s, and most of it was closed in 1858. A railway was laid along parts of it, but a small section at the southern end remained in operation until 1912, and was not formally abandoned until 1944.

We've already mentioned the Shrewsbury Canal, and its buy-up of part of the Wombridge Canal to provide access to the tub boat canal network to the industrial east. The Shrewsbury Canal opened in 1797 and was used mainly to ship coal to Shrewsbury. The original Chief Engineer was Josiah Clowes, but when he died in 1795, he was succeeded by Thomas Telford, who had just been appointed Shropshire's County Surveyor.

One of Telford's first tasks was to rebuild Longdon-on-Tern Aqueduct over the River Tern, as the previous stone bridge built by Clowes had been swept away by floods in February 1795. The replacement used a 62-yard (57m) cast-iron trough, cast in sections at William Reynolds' Ketley ironworks and bolted together in 1796. The main trough was 7.5ft (2.3m) wide and 4.5 ft (1.4m) deep, with a narrower trough to one side which formed the towpath – and the aqueduct became the world's first large-scale iron navigable aqueduct, and served as a prototype for Telford's much longer Pontcysyllte Aqueduct on the Llangollen Canal, where he mounted the iron trough on high masonry arches.

When completed in 1797, the Shrewsbury Canal was 17 miles (27km) long. It descended through 11 guillotine locks to Eyton, crossed the rivers Tern and Roden via aqueducts, through a 970-yard (890m) tunnel at Berwick which was 10ft (3m) wide, before entering Shrewsbury from the north. Yet another inclined plane was built at the other end, this time at Trench. At 223 yards (204m) long, it raised boats 75ft (23m) up to the Wombridge Canal, from where they could travel via the Shropshire Canal southwards to the River Severn at Coalport. The inclined plane's engine was replaced

The Coalport China Works were established alongside the Shropshire Canal at Coalport in 1796 by John Rose. Coal to fire the kilns was transported along the canal from the coalfields and the china was shipped down the River Severn. Rose's brother, Thomas, along with William Reynolds set up a separate china works on the opposite side of the canal in 1800.

by a high-pressure Cornish engine in 1842, supplied by the Coalbrookdale Company, and the plane and engine remained in use until 1921, making it the last operational canal plane in Britain.

The Shrewsbury Canal was finally linked to the national canal network in 1835, when the Birmingham and Liverpool Junction Canal built the Newport Branch from Norbury Junction to a new junction with the Shrewsbury Canal at Wappenshall, with the branch including 23 locks. Then in 1844, the Humber Arm branch was constructed to Lubstree Wharf, owned by the Duke of Sutherland. Tramways ran from the end of the branch to various works owned by the Lilleshall Company, who shipped cargoes of pig iron, coal and limestone. Much of this trade had previously used the Donnington Wood Canal, but the new arm provided a more direct connection to the canal network, and the transfer of trade was a factor in the closure of the Donnington Wood Canal. The latter's eventual demise followed the closing of the Lilleshall limeworks in the 1870s, which led to the closure of the section to Pave Lane in 1882; the whole canal was finally abandoned by 1904. Meanwhile, the Shrewsbury Canal's ownership passed to a series of railway companies from the mid-19th century and the

The cast-ron acqueduct at Longdon-on-Tern. It was built in 1796 by William Reynolds for Thomas Telford, and carried the Shrewsbury Canal across the River Tern.

canal was officially abandoned in 1944 by the London, Midland and Scottish Railway (LMS) who were the last railway company to own the canal.

The Ellesmere Canal was also authorised by an Act of Parliament in 1793. It was planned to carry boat traffic between the rivers Mersey, Dee and Severn, thus creating a link between Liverpool and the mineral industries in north-east Wales and the manufacturing centres in the West Midlands. It was originally intended to run from Ellesmere Port on the Mersey to the River Dee at Chester, then head south to the River Severn at Shrewsbury. A branch line extension was opened in 1796, running from the main line at Frankton Junction, to the copper mines at Llanymynech, where it met the Montgomeryshire Canal at Carreghofa Locks. However, the planned route from Frankton Junction to Shrewsbury was abandoned in the early 19th century, when they had got as far as Weston Lullingfields – 9 miles (15km) short of Shrewsbury. It was abandoned because the Shrewsbury Canal was already serving the town, and the poor navigational state of the Severn meant that additional traffic no longer justified the cost. Instead, a 29-mile (47km) link was built between 1797 and 1806, from Frankton, via Ellesmere, to the Chester Canal at Hurleston Junction. This extension included an arm to Whitchurch, and another branch to Quina Brook – although the original intention was for the branch line to reach Prees, but it fell short by 1-mile (1.5km).

In 1813, the Ellesmere Canal company merged with the Chester Canal to form the Ellesmere and Chester Canal Company, and then in 1845, merged with the Birmingham and Liverpool Junction Canal. A year later the canal was taken over again by the formation of the

> ### Quirk Alert: *"Mad Jack" Mytton*
>
> *John Mytton (1796-1834) was born in Halston Hall, near Whittington. He was an eccentric and rake of the Regency period who was briefly a Tory Member of Parliament for Shrewsbury in 1819, a position acquired by bribery, and in which he spent the sum total of just 30 minutes in the House of Commons! Expelled from two public schools, he graduated as a hopeless gambler, mainly on horses, but then made his name following a series of outrageous capers. In 1826, in order to win a bet, he rode a horse into the Bedford Hotel opposite the Town Hall in Leamington Spa, up the grand staircase and onto the balcony, from which he jumped, still seated on his horse, over the diners in the restaurant below, and out through the window onto the Parade!*
>
> *Mytton also had a penchant for hunting naked, even through snow-drifts and rivers in full flow – and continued to do so despite multiple falls and broken bones. He also had a wardrobe containing 150 pairs of hunting breeches, 700 pairs of handmade hunting boots, 1,000 hats and some 3,000 shirts. Meanwhile, he also kept up to 2,000 dogs, with his favourites fed on steak and champagne. As for his favourite horse, Baronet, he had free range inside Halston Hall and often lay in front of the fire with Mytton.*
>
> *Elsewhere, Mytton once drove a horse and carriage at high speed to see if they could both clear a tollgate. Unsurprisingly, they couldn't. And on another occasion, on learning that his fellow passenger had never experienced a coaching accident, he promptly drove the gig up a sloping bank at full speed, tipping himself and his passenger out!*
>
> *Unsurprisingly, Mytton wasted his inheritance and was eventually declared bankrupt, fleeing to Calais in 1831 to avoid his creditors. It was here that – in order to cure a bout of hiccups – he allegedly set fire to his nightshirt! According to an eye-witness, a fellow guest and Mytton's servant helped to beat out the flames, after which Mytton stated: "The hiccup is gone, by God!", and then reeled, naked, into bed!*
>
> *Returning to England in 1831, he was jailed for his debts, and died in 1834 of delirium tremens, where he was described as: "a round-shouldered, tottering, old-young man bloated by drink, worn out by too much foolishness, too much wretchedness and too much brandy."*
>
> *Married twice, his first wife died in 1820, and in 1830, the second wife ran away!*

The wharf at Ellesmere on the Shropshire Union Canal (Llangollen Branch). The early 19th century warehouse has "Shropshire Union Railways and Canal Company" emblazoned across the end.

The Montgomery Canal (formerly the Montgomeryshire Canal) at Llanymynech, which connected to the Llanymynech Branch of the Ellesmere Canal here. The link was opened in July 1797.

Tyrley Locks, just south of Market Drayton, on what is now the Shropshire Union Canal. It was built by the Birmingham & Liverpool Junction Canal Company, engineered by Thomas Telford, and completed in 1835. The flight of five locks at Tyrley lowers the canal by 33 feet (10.06m).

The screen wall and pier adjoining Attingham Park entrance is Grade II listed and dates from 1805-07.

Shropshire Union Railways and Canal Company. By 1917 the Weston Branch had closed following a breach near Hordley Wharf and all remaining Shropshire elements were closed to navigation by an Act of Parliament in 1944. However, today, the Ellesmere Canal south of Frankton Junction (the Llanymynech Branch) forms part of the Montgomery Canal, which is now considered part of the main line of the Shropshire Union Canal.

As for the Birmingham and Liverpool Junction Canal, this was authorised in 1826, and was built to link the West Midlands with Merseyside, running for 40 miles from Autherley near Wolverhampton to the Ellesmere and Chester Canal at Nantwich. In May 1845, it then merged with the Ellesmere and Chester Canal, as schemes to build railways in the area gathered pace. Then, in 1846, a company calling itself the Shropshire Union Railways and Canal Company incorporated those two canals along with the Montgomeryshire Canal, the Shrewsbury Canal and the Shropshire Canal. Three Acts of Parliament were obtained in 1846, to enable railway construction, and extra clauses enabled the name change to the Shropshire Union to be made. Alongside this, on 1st January 1846, various realignments of railway companies saw the formation of the London and North Western Railway Company (LNWR), who saw the Shropshire Union as a threat. However, an arrangement was made whereby the Shropshire Union dropped all plans for further railway expansion, but they were given full control over the

Both of these Ellesmere inns date from the early 19th century. On the left is the Black Lion and on the right is the Red Lion.

Quirk Alert: *Heber's Hoard*

In the 19th century, Richard Heber, of Hodnet, was a collector of books on a massive scale. Furthermore, not only did he have thousands of books, but he kept three copies of most: one to use, one to lend, and one in reserve. It is therefore no surprise to find that when he passed away, he left behind three libraries!

Quirk Alert: *Returns Policy*

After the Reformation, the Tudor chalice of beaten silver at St Andrew's church at Shifnal disappeared. It remained lost for centuries, until it showed up at a curio shop in Yorkshire in the 19th century. And as it had the words engraved on it: "Return Mee to Sheafnall in Shropshire", someone sent it home again!

LEFT: The cast-iron Cantlop Bride, built in 1813 to an innovative design by Thomas Telford – innovative as it one of the first to not follow the design of a wooden bridge, with the structure strong enough to support a flat deck without a central pier that could hinder navigation. It was part of an expanding network of bridges built to improve communication and trade in Shropshire. Telford worked as the County Surveyor of Shropshire from 1787 until 1834 and was responsible for 42 bridges in the county, seven of which were made of cast-iron. RIGHT: The Grade II listed Acton Burnell Hall was originally a country house built in 1814 by John Tasker for Sir Joseph Edward Smythe. However, today it belongs to the private Concord College.

running of the canals – although by this stage, the tub-boat network was in a poor state of health.

The first recorded railway line in Shropshire dates from 1605 – which ran for just over a mile from the Birch Leasows near Broseley church to the Calcutts. Iron railway wheels were also being cast at Coalbrookdale as early as 1729, probably for use on Richard Hartshorne's railway from Little Wenlock to Strethill wharf, while the Coalbrookdale Company were casting the first iron rails in England by 1767. January 1802 then saw Richard Trevithick arrive at Coalbrookdale, where boiler plates for steam engines had been made for some time. He built and tested a stationary engine which operated with an unprecedented high boiler pressure of 145 psi. Trevithick, who had built a road locomotive in Cornwall (the Puffing Devil), then built a locomotive at Coalbrookdale that ran on rails. Few details are known about this experiment, but it is likely to have been the first occasion of a locomotive running on rails.

Mainline railways arrived in Shropshire a little later than elsewhere in the Midlands. The first was the line from Shrewsbury to Chester, via Whitchurch, which was opened in 1848 by the London and North Western Railway (LNWR). The following year, the joint Shrewsbury & Birmingham and Shropshire Union line from Shrewsbury to Wellington was opened, with the former then extending to Wolverhampton via Oakengates, and the latter to Stafford via Newport. The Shropshire-based companies then faced a period of intense defence as the big railway companies sought mergers. Eventually, they came to an agreement in 1854 with the Great Western Railway (GWR) and created a junction at Wolverhampton with the GWR's West Midlands to London line, thus creating a through-route from London Paddington to Merseyside. Shrewsbury was then linked to Ludlow in 1852 with the section from Ludlow to Hereford completed the following year. This line prospered as a route between the north of England and South Wales, particularly after the LNWR opened its section from Shrewsbury to Crewe in 1858. Elsewhere, between 1851 and 1855, the Lilleshall Company began to replace its extensive tramway system with a private standard-gauge railway network, linking Priorslee and Snedshill furnaces.

The Buttercross Market at Market Drayton dates from 1824. It is located on the spot where a buttercross has stood since the 16th century, from where farmers' wives sold their dairy produce.

The former infirmary at Shrewsbury, built 1826-30 by Edward Haycock.

LEFT: This building in The Square, Shrewsbury, was built in 1839 and was formerly known as The Music Hall and Civic Hall, while today, it is a museum and art gallery. CENTRE: Wrockwardine Wood Methodist church founded in 1863. Four decades earlier, in 1821, Primitive Methodism first arrived in the county at Wrockwardine Wood. RIGHT: The Grade II listed Shrewsbury railway station was built in 1849, and extended in 1900. Its initial build displaced several hundred people as houses on both Howard Street and Castle Hill were demolished to make way for the station.

In the north-west of the county the Oswestry and Newtown Railway was completed in 1860, with the Shropshire section running from Oswestry to Llanymynech before heading south-west to Newtown in Powys. This linked Llanymynech's limestone quarries and Hoffman kilns into the railway network for the first time. The LNWR-sponsored Oswestry, Ellesmere and Whitchurch Railway (OEWR) opened in 1864, thus linking Oswestry and Llanymynech with the Midlands and the North West. On completion, the OEWR was promptly merged with its neighbouring railway companies, including the Oswestry and Newtown Railway, to form Cambrian Railways (CR), which installed its headquarters at Oswestry. Cambrian Railways then survived until 1923 before becoming part of the Great Western Railway.

In the opposite south-eastern quadrant of Shropshire, the Severn Valley Railway (SVR) was built between 1858 and 1862, and linked Hartlebury, near Droitwich Spa, with Shrewsbury, including Shropshire stations at Highley, Hampton Loade, Bridgnorth, Coalport, Ironbridge and Broseley, Buildwas, Cressage and Berrington, before arriving at Shrewsbury. However, although the railway was built by the SVR, it was operated from opening on 1st February 1862 by the West Midland Railway which was then absorbed into the Great Western Railway on 1st August 1863.

During the 1850s and 1860s, the railways spread through Shropshire to serve most of the county's main settlements, the exceptions being Ruyton XI Towns in the north-west and Clun in the south-west. In addition to these local lines, the Snailbeach District Railways was opened in 1877, linking Pontesbury on the Minsterley branch line with the lead mines on the Stiperstones. Also opened in 1865 was the Bishop's Castle Railway, running from the Shrewsbury to Ludlow mainline section, just north of Craven Arms to Lydham Heath; from there, trains reversed to Bishop's Castle. Meanwhile, the Glyn Valley Tramway was completed in 1874, serving the slate quarries of Glyn Ceriog, with its eastern terminus on the Ellesmere Canal at Gledrid – although the company abandoned the Shropshire

The Grade II listed Oswestry Railway Station, former headquarters of the Cambrian Railway Company, and now the Cambrian Visitor Centre. The station building dates from 1865 with later additions and alterations.

The Grade II listed former railway works at Oswestry, with attached footbridge of 1865/6, attributed to Sharp, Stewart & Company, Thomas Savin and John Robinson.

> **Quirk Alert:** *Pedlar's Parish*
>
> Bettws-y-Crwyn churchyard is home to the Cantlin Stone, engraved "W. C. Decsd. here. Buried 1691 at Betws." It is in memory of a pedlar who died on his rounds here, and in so doing, granted a future favour to the parish. This occurred following the Clun Forest Enclosure Act of 1875 – for on proof of Bettws having given burial to the pedlar 184 years earlier, the parish was granted several hundred additional acres that aligned to the pedlar's rounds!

> **Quirk Alert:** *Matthew Webb*
>
> In 1875, Matthew Webb (1848-1883), of Dawley, became the first person to swim the English Channel, achieving this in less than twenty-two hours. Prior to this, he had rescued his twelve-year-old brother from drowning in the Severn near Ironbridge in 1863. Then, when in the merchant navy, he had attempted to rescue a man overboard in the mid-Atlantic – for which he received an award of £100 and the first Stanhope Medal, whilst also making him a hero of the British press. By 1883, he was a well-known celebrity, and therefore attempted to swim through the Whirlpool Rapids below Niagara Falls – a feat deemed by most to be impossible. Apparently, he thrilled the gathered crowd for ten minutes, but then "threw up his arms, sank, and was seen alive no more". His body was recovered some days later 7 miles down the river.

LEFT: Statue of Charles Darwin (1809-1882) outside Shrewsbury library. Darwin was born at The Mount in Shrewsbury in 1809 and baptised the same year at St Chad's church. From September 1818, he joined his older brother Erasmus attending the nearby Anglican Shrewsbury School. CENTRE: Lord Hill's Column, outside the Shirehall in Shrewsbury was built 1814-16. It is the tallest Doric column in England, standing at 133ft 6in (40.7m), and commemorates Rowland Hill, 1st Viscount Hill, with a 17ft (5.2 m) statue standing on top. The column's diameter of 2ft (0.6m) is actually wider than Nelson's Column, and, not including the pedestal, is 15ft (4.6m) higher. RIGHT: The Grade II listed Ellesmere town hall dates from the early 1830s.

portion of its system in 1888 when it changed from horse to steam traction, and built a new route to Chirk.

A second railway station was opened in Shrewsbury in 1866 when a line from the Potteries to North Wales via Llanymynech was opened as part of a trunk route from London to Dublin. It only lasted for fourteen years, though, before being closed in 1880 – but was twice revived, once in the 1920s and '30s and again by the War Department between 1941 and 1960. As for Shrewsbury's main station, this was one of the most important junctions in the late 19th and early 20th centuries, with important routes radiating out to the north, east, south and west.

The Coalbrookdale coalfield remained one of the most intensive industrial areas in the country during the Industrial Revolution. Workers came from all over Shropshire and from the neighbouring Welsh districts, to earn comparatively high wages – although until the 1840s, blast furnacemen worked seven twelve-hour shifts a week – and under the most hazardous of conditions. The most dangerous occupation, though, belonged to the coal miners, with several fatal accidents a month – ranging from falling down shafts to roof falls to major gas explosions. One particular accident in 1864 at Crawstone Pit, elicits some terrible images, as it was here that nine males, the youngest being only twelve years of age, fell to their deaths when a rope lowered to haul them out, snapped.

The importance of the Coalbrookdale coalfield did decline throughout the 19th century, though, relative to the rest of the country. In 1805, the area was producing around 50,000 tons of iron a year, about a fifth of the national output, but by 1869, despite producing a

LLANYMYNECH LIMEWORKS

When limestone is burnt it turns into a chalky substance known as quicklime (calcium oxide). Traditionally, limestone was used as a building material as well as a "flux" for making iron and steel. Farmers also used quicklime to make their land more fertile, and builders used it to make lime mortar and plaster. The downside, was that lime burning was an uncomfortably hot and disfiguring occupation and serious accidents were never far away in quarries. In 1860, Thomas Savin, a Victorian railway entrepreneur persuaded investors to speculate in limestone and quicklime production on Llanymynech Hill. Apparently, the initial blasts were so titanic that they damged houses in the village below. The following sequence of photographs takes you through the process. The works were closed in 1914 when the process became uneconomic.

LEFT: Once an Iron Age hillfort, the top of Llanymynech Hill is now unrecognisable following the contant blasting for limestone between the 1860s and 1914. RIGHT: This is the brake drum house at the top of an incline known as the English Inclined Plane – one of a pair with the Welsh Inclined Plane – a few yards apart but in different countries! There were two because before 1867, the extraction rights to the Welsh (Powis and Chirk estates) and English (Bradford estates) were held by different companies. And as well as two inclines, there were also two tunnels and, lower down, two canal wharves! As for operation, a cable ran around the drum, helping to transport stone quarried at the top of the hill down to the limeworks below, and to haul the empty trucks back up ready for another consignment. At either end, horses, mules and donkeys would toil, on the hilltop bringing stone to the top of the incline, and at the foot, transporting the stone to the limekilns.

LEFT: The stables, where recent excavations revealed piles of worn-out horse-shoes discarded by blacksmiths. In 1902, Egyptian donkeys from the Boer War were purchased to add extra pulling power. RIGHT: A draw kiln, built at Llanymynech in the 1870s. From the top, enveloped by smoke, men tipped in layers of limestone and coal. At the arched access point, a kiln worker would rake out the burnt lime from the "draw hole" and load it straight on to waiting railway trucks. Unsurprisingly, this was unpleasant and sweaty work which damaged the skin. Meanwhile, alongside the draw kiln was a cupola kiln which was used to burn limestone with a high magnesium content, with compressed air providing the necessary blast to increase the heat within the kiln. However, these kilns were abandoned in 1900 when they were…

…replaced by this Hoffman kiln – one of only three survivors in the country, and shown above from the outside and inside. This type of continuous burning ring kiln was invented by a German called Friedrich Hoffman in 1858, initially for brick-making, but in 1867, the design was adapted for burning lime. A Hoffmann kiln consists of a main fire passage surrounded on each side by several small rooms. In the main fire passage, there is a fire wagon, that holds a fire that burns continuously. Each room is fired for a specific time, and thereafter the fire wagon is rolled to the next room to be fired. At Llanymynech, a 139ft chimney (42.5m) also survives, which helped to draw the heat and smoke through the kiln. Coal was brought to the site by mainline steam engines that ran right alongside the Hoffman kiln. The Llanymynech Hoffman kiln measures 147ft by 57ft (44.8m by 17.5m), and has two tunnel vaults entered through 14 round-headed arches.

> **Quirk Alert:** *General Backacher*
>
> *Claverley is home to the grave of General Gatacre, who fell during World War I. In the late 19th century, he earned a reputation of getting his men in such fine condition that they could march 140 miles a week. Not sure he was appreciated by his men though – who nicknamed him General Backacher!*

peak output of 200,000 tons, by this stage, this only represented around two percent of national output.

Meanwhile, down in the Titterstone Clee area, coal was still being mined and had been joined by two coke-fired ironworks on Clee Hill which were built in 1778, with the Cornbrook Furnace following in 1794 – although it was only producing 292 tons of iron a year in 1805 and was out of blast by the 1820s. The Knowbury Works was constructed in 1804-05, and by 1851, it included a forge, a rolling mill and a slitting mill as well as its blast furnace. Coal mining on Clee Hill continued to survive into the 20th century, but its importance declined as the neighbouring quarrying of Dhustone for road metal expanded.

Coal was also mined in the far north-west of the county, as the demand for lime from local farmers and builders, and the build of the Ellesmere Canal, resulted in pits being sunk in the St Martin's and Weston Rhyn area. And in the opposite corner of the county, the outskirts of the Wyre Forest coalfield resulted in a blast furnace being built at Billingsley, using coal and ore from the local mines, and which operated between 1801 and 1812. By 1928, the Ifton colliery in St Martin's parish employed 1,357 men, making it the largest ever to operate in Shropshire. Meanwhile, at Highley, the mining company had been formed much later, in 1870. By the 1930s, though, the colliery had incorporated buildings on the other side of the Severn, and employed around 1,250 men in the 1950s. Ifton colliery eventually closed in 1968, with the Highley colliery having closed a year earlier.

As for the Coalbrookdale works, it also started producing art castings in iron from around 1838, for which it gained an international reputation after mounting a display at the Great Exhibition of 1851. Meanwhile, in the 1860s, the Lilleshall company built an engineering works in the growing settlement of St George's, and its stationary engines, pumps and locomotives were sold in many other countries. And in the Severn Gorge, the decorative tile factories built by Maw and Co. and Messrs. Craven Dunhill made ceramic products for public buildings in all parts of the world towards the end of the 19th century. However, from the 1870s, the iron industry began to decline and the population of mining villages began to decline with them. At Dawley, for example, there were 9,200 people in 1881, but only 6,996 by 1891.

Newport's former Town Hall was built in 1869, having been designed by architect J. Cobb.

Holy Trinity church, Coalbrookdale, dates from 1850-54. The architects were Reeves and Voysey and the church was built with money provided by the Darby family and furnished by them for their workers.

The Corn Market & Agricultural Library at Much Wenlock, built in 1852.

Grade II listed Georgian buildings in Broad Street, Ludlow.

Shropshire was also home to lead mining in the west, and had been since Roman times. Mining ramped up here in the late 18th century, with Boulton and Watt steam pumping engines being deployed at The Bog mine in 1777 and 1789, and at Old Grit in 1783. Snailbeach mine was then leased in 1782 by Thomas Lovett of Chirk, who proceeded to develop a coal mine at nearby Pontesford. More mines were sunk in the area during the 19th century, with output hitting optimum levels in the 1870s when ten mines were producing more than 7,000 tons of lead ore per year – a remarkable ten per cent of the nation's output. The Snailbeach mine was closed for good in 1911, bringing an end to Shropshire's lead mining industry.

Shropshire's textile industry wasn't particularly large, but there were carpet mills established at Bridgnorth in the late 1790s, and a flax and hemp-spinning mill built at Eardington in 1794, while in 1790, a woollen factory was built in Shrewsbury and was acquired by Charles Hulbert of Manchester in 1803, who used it for weaving cotton. Another cotton mill existed at Broseley in 1792, while a further mill was built on the River Rea at Stottesden in around 1794 for carding and spinning cotton.

John Marshall, a Leeds linen merchant, built a flax spinning mill in Ditherington between 1796 and 1797, in partnership with Thomas and Benjamin Benyon. The new mill was built to a revolutionary fire-proof design by Charles Bage, consisting of brick walls, an internal iron frame of cruciform section uprights, and beams supporting brick arches which formed the floors of the storeys above. It thus became the world's first iron-framed building, and is seen as the world's first skyscraper, also known as "the grandfather of

Ditherington Flax Mill was completed in 1797 and was the world's first iron-framed building, also known as "the grandfather of skyscrapers."

skyscrapers" – hence its Grade I listing. The partnership was dissolved in 1804, with Ditherington Mill being retained by John Marshall, having paid off the Benyons – who promptly went and built nearby Castlefields. By 1851, these two flax mills provided the "chief manufacture" of Shrewsbury. However, Ditherington Mill closed in 1886, before its conversion to a maltings – which lasted 101 years until 1987. It is currently undergoing extensive renovation and redevelopment.

Throughout the 19th century, industrialisation and the general migration of people from villages to towns brought about huge population increases in England's towns, and one of the effects of this was that people lived in squalor, with disease and epidemics rife. This wasn't so acutely felt in Shropshire, though, and despite its significant industrial areas already discussed, it largely retained its rural identity. However, in Shrewsbury, there were still 158 deaths from cholera in 1832 and 75 in 1849. Measures were taken to counter these conditions, such as an Improvement Commission in Shrewsbury in the 1820s, which removed from the streets, encroachments such as flights of steps and bootscrapers, rounded many corners, and began a street-cleaning service. Following the Public Health Act of 1848, local boards of health were established in both Shrewsbury and Bridgnorth to maintain sewers, clean the streets, regulate environmental health risks (including slaughterhouses), and ensure their towns received a supply of water. These local boards were eventually merged with the corporations of municipal boroughs in 1873, or became urban districts in 1894. Also, by the middle of the 19th century, most Shropshire towns were lit by gas, too – with the maintenance of sewers and piped water supplies following in the 1860s.

Also different in Shropshire, was the rate of population increase – much lower than in most other English counties. In fact, in the 1830s, the population of Shrewsbury actually declined as a result of the closure of the Benyons flax mill and a steep falling off

Wem Mill is located on the River Roden and dates from the early 19th century.

INDUSTRIAL REVOLUTION POPULATION INCREASES IN SHROPSHIRE TOWNS
Population increases in Shropshire Towns

Town (Alpha)	Population 1801	Population 1871	%inc
Bishop's Castle	1,076	1,805	67.8%
Bridgnorth	4,408	5,876	33.3%
Cleobury Mortimer	1,368	1,708	24.9%
Clun	794	1,029	29.6%
Ellesmere	5,553	5,913	6.5%
Ludlow	3,897	5,087	30.5%
Market Drayton	3,162	4,844	53.2%
Newport	2,307	3,202	38.8%
Oswestry	2,672	7,306	173.4%
Shifnal	3,642	6,681	83.4%
Shrewsbury	14,739	23,406	58.8%
Stretton	924	1,756	90.0%
Wem	3,087	3,880	25.7%
Wenlock	1,981	2,531	27.8%
Whitchurch	4,515	6,264	38.7%
Shropshire	170,000	248,000	45.9%
England & Wales	8,893,000	22,712,000	155.4%

Town (% inc.)	Population 1801	Population 1871	%inc.
Oswestry	2,672	7,306	173.4%
Stretton	924	1,756	90.0%
Shifnal	3,642	6,681	83.4%
Bishop's Castle	1,076	1,805	67.8%
Shrewsbury	14,739	23,406	58.8%
Market Drayton	3,162	4,844	53.2%
Newport	2,307	3,202	38.8%
Whitchurch	4,515	6,264	38.7%
Bridgnorth	4,408	5,876	33.3%
Ludlow	3,897	5,087	30.5%
Clun	794	1,029	29.6%
Wenlock	1,981	2,531	27.8%
Wem	3,087	3,880	25.7%
Cleobury Mortimer	1,368	1,708	24.9%
Ellesmere	5,553	5,913	6.5%
Shropshire	170,000	248,000	45.9%
England & Wales	8,893,000	22,712,000	155.4%

of thoroughfare trade. Nevertheless, populations did increase, as the above table demonstrates.

So, the average increase in population throughout England and Wales between 1801 and 1871 was 155.4%, but other than Oswestry (173.4%), none of Shropshire's towns come remotely close to the national average. Oswestry's population surge was caused by the arrival of the Cambrian Railway, who promptly installed their headquarters there, along with their centre for the construction and repair of the company's rolling stock. One town not listed in the table is Craven Arms – which grew into a small town in the 19th century thanks to the arrival of the railway, while it took its name from an 18th century crossroads inn. Meanwhile, Bishop's Castle saw rapid population growth due to the clearance of cottages in the surrounding parishes.

Additional 19th century industry in Shropshire saw iron foundries producing agricultural implements in Bridgnorth, Ludlow, Market Drayton, Newport, Oswestry, Shrewsbury and Wellington. Carpets were made in Bridgnorth, gloves in Ludlow, bedding in Oswestry, and horsehair in Market Drayton, while the manufacture of linen thread and yarn in Shrewsbury provided work for several hundred people until 1886. The clockmaker, J.B. Joyce & Co. continued to make clocks in Whitchurch, creating all of those Victorian clocks that appeared in every station on the London & North Western Railway.

During the 19th century, the outskirts of most Shropshire towns contained brickyards and gravel pits – such as those at Belle Vue in Shrewsbury and New Road at Ludlow. Many suburban houses were built from this locally quarried material, although suburban

Quirk Alert: *Tight Squeeze and the Tracts of Life*

The census of 1851 reveals that one of the tiny houses in Bellman's Yard, Newport, was home to 23 Irish, while another housed 25! These figures were topped, though, by the 28 Irish who lived in a house on St Michael's Street, Shrewsbury, and the 30 who lived in a house on Cartway, Bridgnorth! However, the most diverse lodging house has to be on Hills Lane, Shrewsbury, in 1861 – for it was home to two pedlars, a hawker, a Welsh tailor, a drover from Somerset, an Irish army pensioner, two carpet weavers, a plate engraver… and Asam Ali, a forty-four-year-old vendor of tracts born in the city of Mecca in Arabia – and married to a woman from Cork!

The Craven Arms Inn after which the small town of Craven Arms is named.

Grade II listed mill cottages on Wharf Road, Ellesmere, dating from around 1890.

St Mary's church at Ellesmere is of Norman origin, but was rebuilt and restored in Perpendicular Gothic style by Sir George Gilbert Scott in 1849.

growth in Shropshire was on a much smaller scale compared to other English counties. The first freehold estate in Shrewsbury was built in the early 1850s in the north-east of the town – now Albert Street, Victoria Street and the south side of Severn Street. Later estates included further parts of Castlefields, Bradford Street (originally Union Street) in Cherry Orchard on the other side of the river, and Oak Street and Oakley Street in Belle Vue, south of the river, while again to the east of the river, non-freehold estates were built at Holywell Terrace in 1830 and Tankerville Street and Cleveland Street in the 1880s. The 1880s also saw large-scale development of villas in Kingsland, to the south-west of the town centre, all built with locally-sourced building material.

Victorian Shropshire, however, remained overwhelmingly agricultural, with the 1881 census revealing 5,566 farmers and 21,142 other agricultural workers. Other rural industries included quarrying, limeworks, brickyards, a few country tanneries and paper mills, and many water corn-mills. As for agricultural improvements, a radical rationalisation of farming was achieved in the early 19th century on the Lilleshall estates of the Duke of Sutherland. The steward of the estates, James Loch, altered road and field boundaries, new cottages were built for labourers, and logically-planned groups of barns, cow stalls and waggon sheds were designed. Elsewhere, Lord Hill of Hawkstone kept celebrated shorthorn cattle and Southdown sheep, Lord Berwick at Attingham bred Alderney, Hereford and West Highland cattle, and at Dudmaston, William Wolryche Whitmore specialised in pigs. Farming mechanisation advanced in the second half of the 19th century, too, with widespread use of threshing machines, and by the 1870s, William Elcock of Alveley made his living as a threshing machine proprietor.

Shropshire was less affected by the agricultural depression of the late 19th century, thanks to its numerous dairy and sheep farms. However, it did suffer from the succession of wet seasons, outbreaks of foot and mouth and other disasters of the late 1870s and early 1880s. The emphasis moved away from grain, and new implements and new crops were adopted, while creameries – such as that at Minsterley – were built, supplying milk to the Birmingham market. The agricultural community was also becoming more united towards the end of the century. The Shropshire Chamber of Agriculture was formed in 1866, providing a county-wide forum for farming interests, and the Shropshire branch of

This is St Agatha's church at Llanymynech. Grade II listed, it was built in a striking Neo-Norman style between 1844 and 1845 by Thomas Pearson on the site of a former medieval church.

Inside St Michael's church at Llanyblodwel. It was largely rebuilt by Revd John Parker between 1847 and 1853 incorporating substantial parts of the former medieval church, dating principally from the 12th and 15th centuries.

The Talbot Hotel at Cleobury Mortimer is a 19th century remodelling of a 17th century core.

> ### Quirk Alert: *School's Out!*
> In 1868, a large crop of acorns coincided with a shortage of feeding grains in Shropshire. As a result, all over the county, children were kept away from school to collect acorns for feeding to pigs! And in most years, school holidays began in the Stiperstones and Long Mynd areas when the whimberries were ripe, and the children didn't return to school until they were all picked!

This signal box at Bromfield was built in 1873 on the Shrewsbury and Hereford Railway, which had opened in 1853.

the National Farmers' Union was founded in 1908. Meanwhile, in 1892, Thomas Harper Adams, a farmer from Edgmond, died leaving £37,000 with 178 acres of land as an endowment for an agricultural college, which opened with the support of the Shropshire and Staffordshire county councils in 1901.

The enclosure of land continued throughout the 19th century with 35 enclosure Acts passed between 1815 and 1891, mostly in upland areas, with extensive land enclosed at Church Stretton in 1822, Clun Forest in 1845 and 1847, and Bettwys-y-Crwyn in 1865. Landowners in closed villages typically demolished cottages when they were vacated to limit their overhead of maintaining the poor in the estate or parish – examples between 1831 and 1871 include Diddlebury, Ditton Priors, Eaton-under-Heywood, Hopton Castle, Lee Brockhurst, Moreton Say, Munslow, Neen Sollars, Pitchford, Stoke-on-Tern and Upton Magna. Conversely, some landowners built model dwellings in closed villages, such as those on the Alberbury and Dudmaston estates, and at Caynham Court – with dwellings typically comprising a living room, scullery and pantry, three bedrooms, an entrance porch, a piggery, privy and fuel store.

Modern local government was introduced following the Local Government Act 1888. This was the Act which introduced county councils and county boroughs in England and Wales, alongside administrative counties based on the boundaries of their historic county counterparts. Just to be clear, though, the Local Government Act 1888 did *not* abolish or alter the historic counties and went to great lengths to distinguish between historic and administrative counties. In terms of impact upon Shropshire, the Act introduced the democratically elected Salop County Council, superseding the previous system of administration by the county justices and Quarter Sessions. However, Shropshire was one of only a handful of English counties that didn't have any county boroughs, as none of the urban areas in the county were deemed large enough to require independence from the county council.

The reforms of the 1890s also introduced a second layer of local government which consisted of 17 rural district councils, nine urban district councils and six municipal boroughs. The latter included the borough of Wenlock which comprised large tracts of entirely agricultural countryside and the southern portion of the Coalbrookdale coalfield, and Bishop's Castle

Shewsbury's Roman Catholic Cathedral of Our Lady Help of Christians and St Peter. It was built in 1856 by Edward Welby Pugin possibly to designs initially prepared by his father, Augustus Welby Northmore Pugin.

Built 1879-81 by Ellison of Liverpool, this fine Victorian building was Shrewsbury's eye, ear and throat hospital.

Dinham Bridge over the River Teme at Ludlow dates from the 19th century. The 11th century Ludlow Castle is in the background.

Oswestry Guild Hall, built in 1893. On the left side of the middle floor is a statue of King Oswald after whom the town is named.

Coleham Pumping Station in Shrewsbury is Grade II listed and dates from 1901.

which, with a population of under 2,000 prided itself on being the smallest borough in England. So rural was Shropshire, that Whitchurch and Chirbury Rural Districts, consisted of only two and three parishes, respectively, and hence struggled to pull in enough rate income to carry out their duties efficiently.

By the end of the 19th century, Shropshire's boundaries had barely changed for a thousand years. There were a couple of tweaks following an Act of 1844, when exclaves – areas belonging to a county that were completely surrounded by another county – were annexed by that surrounding county. Hence, the chapelry of Farlow (in the parish of Stottesdon) was

The rocketesque tower of Llanyblodwel St Michael's church was built in 1855-56.

A Grade II listed Victorian cast-iron post box in Abbey Foregate, Shrewsbury.

> **Quirk Alert:** *The Wenlock Olympian Games*
>
> *Much Wenlock is home to the Wenlock Olympian Games, founded by local resident, William Penny Brookes, who settled in the town in 1831 having qualified as a doctor. Dr Brookes founded the Wenlock Olympian Class (later called the Wenlock Olympian Society) in 1850, and it held its first games in October later that year. The aim of the games was to "promote the moral, physical, and intellectual improvement of the inhabitants of the town and neighbourhood of Much Wenlock." This statement reflected Dr Brookes' beliefs, which were that exercise was beneficial for everyone and he wanted to inspire people to participate and enjoy sport.*
>
> *In terms of content, traditional sports, such as football, cricket and athletics were showcased, along with other more-quirky competitions, such as a blindfold wheelbarrow race, and another race between old women racing for pounds of tea! The first games in 1850 were also accompanied by much pomp and pageantry as a procession of flag bearers, officials, and competitors followed a band through the streets of Much Wenlock to the sports field which was later named as Windmill Hill.*

The athletics events consisted of running, jumping, and throwing, but in 1858, it was a new event called Tilting at the Ring which drew the biggest crowds. Dr Brookes had intended that the event should capture the chivalry of the medieval knight and his lady, and the strength and skill of good horsemanship. The aim, therefore, was to lance a ring hanging from a supported beam whilst charging past on a horse – akin to non-contact medieval jousting.

Another of Brookes' aims was to revive the Greek Olympics in Greece. He was therefore delighted when, in 1859, he heard that the first Athens modern Olympian Games were to take place, and he hence donated £10 on behalf of the Wenlock Olympic Society. As a result, the winner of the "long" or "sevenfold" race was awarded the "Wenlock Prize".

By 1861, the Wenlock Olympian Games had been joined by the Shropshire Olympian Games – which were then held in different towns each year – thus providing the format for the modern Olympic games being hosted in different cities. In the meantime, Brookes, along with John Hulley of Liverpool and Ernst Ravenstein of the German Gymnasium in London, set about founding the National Olympian Association. This held its first festival in 1866 at the Crystal Palace, and was a huge success, attracting 10,000 spectators and competitors, including W.G Grace who won the 440-yard hurdles!

By 1870, the Games were attracting some of the most notable athletes in Britain, with winners presented with olive crowns and medals, and odes were declaimed in their honour. Meanwhile, in Queen Victoria's Ruby jubilee year of 1877, Brookes used his Greek connections to request an Olympian prize from Greece – and the Greek King, George I, duly donated an engraved silver trophy. It was also through this contact with King George, that Brooks was introduced to His Excellency J Gennadias, the Greek Charge d'Affaire in London. It is therefore thought that this contact triggered the reality of reviving the Greek Olympic Games. Indeed, in June 1881 the Greek newspaper, Clio, stated: "Dr Brookes, this enthusiastic philhellene is endeavouring to organise an International Olympian Festival, to be held in Athens ....".

Memorial at Windmill Hill sports ground to Dr William Penny Brookes, founder of the Wenlock Olympian Games in 1850.

The Wenlock Olympian Games eventually attracted many competitors from all around England. However, Brookes insisted that the games would not exclude any able bodied man, so when the railways arrived in Much Wenlock in 1862, the first train was timed to arrive in the town on the day of the games – with Brookes insisting that all working-class men be allowed to travel free. Of course, it helped that Dr Brookes was also the Director of the Wenlock Railway Company!

The most significant event occurred in 1890, though, when Baron Pierre de Coubertin – a fellow-believer in physical education – accepted Brookes' invitation to attend the Wenlock Olympian Games, where it is thought the two discussed their similar ambitions for an International Olympic Games. Coubertin liked what Brookes had established in Much Wenlock, and wrote the following in a review, later that year: "…and of the Olympic Games which modern Greece has not yet revived, it is not a Greek to whom one is indebted, but to Dr W. P. Brookes…now aged 82…still active and vigorous, organising and animating them…Athletics does not count many partisans as convinced as W.P. Brookes."

Four years later, Coubertin arranged a meeting for 79 like-minded delegates from twelve countries to discuss a potential Olympic Games – and the first International Olympic Committee was created. Alas, Brookes was unable to attend due to poor health. However, his dream was taking off, for the new committee went on to organise the first modern day Olympic Games during April 1896 – and which naturally took place in Athens. Sadly, the event took place four months after the death of Dr William Penny Brookes and he never saw his dream come true.

The Wenlock Olympian Games are still held today and take place annually in July.

transferred from Herefordshire to Shropshire, while Shropshire lost previously affiliated exclaves to other counties. This included the townships of Cakemore, Halesowen, Hasbury, Hawne, Hill, Hunnington, Illey, Lapal, Oldbury, Ridgacre, and Romsley (all in the parish of Halesowen), which were transferred to Worcestershire.

From the Late Victorians to Present Day

The early 20th century saw a revolution on the roads, which started with motor buses, trolley buses and trams, and then later with motor cars. In 1903, there were a mere 125 cars in Shropshire, but as they rose in popularity, the county eventually began a large-scale programme of reconstruction and re-surfacing of roads in 1925-26. In 1929, a new concrete bridge over the Severn was opened at Atcham, and in 1933, the first part of the Shrewsbury bypass was opened. Bypasses were also constructed at Church Stretton and St George's. Then in 1937, the Ministry of Transport took over the administration of 118 miles of Shropshire trunk roads from the County Council. Meanwhile, the 1920s had seen omnibuses appear in the larger Shropshire towns, with most of the county shared between the Midland Red company based in Shrewsbury, Wellington and

Two views of the Bridgnorth Cliff Railway, England's oldest and steepest inland electric funicular railway, opened on 7th July 1892 by The Bridgnorth Castle Hill Railway Company Ltd. Each car was mounted on a triangular frame of steel girders which housed a 2,000-gallon water tank. The tank on the car at the top was filled with water from a 30,000-gallon tank mounted on the roof of the top station. When the tank was full, the total weight of the car was more than 9 tons, easily enough to counterbalance the bottom car with its 18 passengers. As the top car was being filled, the tank on the bottom car was being emptied, and the water pumped directly up to the top station tank by means of a pair of pumps driven by gas engines.

> **Quirk Alert:** *Race to The Line*
>
> *In 1904, a white line was painted in the middle of the Berwick tunnel on the Shrewsbury Canal. If boats travelling in opposite directions met in the tunnel, the one which had passed the mark had right of way!*

Ludlow, and the Crossville group based in Oswestry. That said, in the coalfield area, the Mid-Shropshire Omnibus Operators Association was formed in 1930 to compete with the Midland Red's routes from Wellington to Donnington and St George's.

During World War I, the county regiment was the King's Shropshire Light Infantry, formed under Edward Cardwell's army reforms in 1881, and they were joined by many other civilian Salopians at recruiting offices following the declaration of war on 4th August 1914. The regiment's first battalion (the former 53rd regiment of foot) crossed to France on 10th September 1914 but soon suffered heavy casualties, including 200 dead in the First Battle of Ypres on 19th October 1914. The battalion remained in the trenches around Ypres until August 1916, when it moved to the Somme, where it took part in the tank-led assault on Cambrai, and bore much of the brunt of the Ludendorff offensive in early 2018. Meanwhile, the second battalion (the former 85th regiment of foot) found themselves in India at the start of the war, but were soon redeployed to Europe and the horrors of Ypres and the Somme, before being sent to Salonika in December 1915, remaining there until the end of the war.

The fourth battalion of the King's Shropshire Light Infantry was sent to the Far East in December 1914 and remained there until 1917 when it returned to fight at Passchendaele. The fifth battalion was comprised of early volunteers to Lord Kitchener's initial 1914 appeal, while the sixth was a "pals" battalion, consisting entirely of men from Shrewsbury. Their "reward" was to spend most of the war on the Western Front, while the Shropshire Yeomanry spent the first 15 months of the war on the east coast before being converted to an infantry regiment. They then sailed to Alexandria in the spring of 1916, serving in Palestine before returning to the final stages of the war on the Western Front.

Back home, the latter stages of the conflict saw troops from the United States and Canada stationed

The former Nurses' Home, St Mary's Place, Shrewsbury, was built in 1910.

Also built in Shrewsbury in 1910 was Shrewsbury Sixth Form College, built by Frank Shayler for Shropshire County Council.

in Shropshire, while a German prisoner-of-war camp was established at Abbey Foregate in Shrewsbury. The Royal Flying Corps also flew Sopwith Camels from a newly-established airfield at Tern Hill in 1916, while the flying field at Shawbury was established in 1917. Then in 1918, a flying field was laid out at Monkmoor in Shrewsbury, where it was used as an aircraft acceptance park, an aircraft repair depot and a school of reconnaissance and aerial photography.

The most famous Salopian associated with World War I is the soldier and poet, Wilfred Owen (1893-1918). Owen was born on 18th March 1893 in Oswestry, and grew up in first Birkenhead and then Shrewsbury. In 1913, young Wilfred began work as a private tutor teaching English and French at the Berlitz School of Languages in Bordeaux. When war broke out, Owen eventually returned to England and, in October 1915, he enlisted in the Artists Rifles Officers' Training Corps. He was then commissioned in June 1916 as a second lieutenant in the Manchester Regiment, and thus began his experience of war: he fell into a shell hole and suffered concussion, and was then blown up by a trench mortar and spent several days unconscious on an embankment lying amongst the remains of one of his fellow officers. Suffering from shell-shock, he was sent for recuperation to Craiglockhart War Hospital in Edinburgh – which is where he met fellow poet Siegfried Sassoon. He was then discharged in November 1917 to home duty, but returned to active service in France in July 1918. It is likely that he decided to return following Sassoon being sent back to England, after being shot in the head; Owen feeling it was his duty to maintain a commentary on the horrors of war. He went on to lead with distinction, earning the Military Cross for his courage and leadership in the storming of the enemy at Joncourt. Alas, Wilfred Owen died on 4th November 1918, exactly one week before the armistice, killed in action during the crossing of the Sambre–Oise Canal. He was promoted to the rank of Lieutenant the day after his death, while his poor mother received the telegram informing her of his death on Armistice Day, as the church bells in Shrewsbury were ringing out in celebration.

Wilfred Owen's war poetry on the horrors of trenches and gas warfare – most of which were published posthumously – stood in stark contrast to the public perception of war at the time and to the patriotic verse written by earlier war poets. He is buried at Ors Communal Cemetery in northern France, and the inscription on his gravestone is a quote of his own: "SHALL LIFE RENEW THESE BODIES? OF A TRUTH ALL DEATH WILL HE ANNUL".

It was during World War I that the Glasgow company, Alley & MacLellan, moved its steam wagon production to Shrewsbury. Founded in 1875, the firm initially made valves and compressors for steam engines, and later whole steamships. In 1903, they acquired Simpson and Bibby, a firm based at Horsehay, who made steam-powered road vehicles. With the move to Shrewsbury in 1915, the steam wagon business was given a new name, Sentinel Waggon Works Ltd. Based in the north of Shrewsbury, the company built a hundred houses for their workforce on the opposite side of Whitchurch Road to the factory, each equipped with central heating, hot water and electric power supplied from the factory.

It was at the Shrewsbury site that the company launched their famous "Super" model in 1923, with assembly of the steam lorry based on Henry Ford's Model T factory in Michigan. The company also produced steam railway shunting locomotives and

Statue of The Borderland Farmer in Oswestry, by Ivor Roberts-Jones who was born in Oswestry in 1913.

Statue of Wilfred Owen MC (1893-1918), in Cae Glas Park, Oswestry.

The war memorial in Bridgnorth Town Park was sculpted by Captain Adrian Jones, who took up art as a career after twenty-three years in the army.

LEFT: Shrewsbury's war memorial was built 1922-23. CENTRE: War memorial in Alberbury. RIGHT: This 19th century malthouse in Atcham was presented by Thomas Henry, 8th Lord Berwick, to the parish of Atcham to be converted into a war memorial hall in commemoration of the men of Atcham who fell in the Great War, 1914-18. It was opened on 31st December 1925.

railcars, but in the 1930s, the success of the steam wagon range fell into decline as new legislation forced the development of lighter lorries. Sentinel therefore launched a new and advanced steamer in 1934, and 3,750 Sentinel "Standards" followed in the next seventeen years; the biggest selling steam lorry ever. It was lighter and featured a modernised driver's cab with a set-back boiler and was available in four, six and eight-wheel form, designated S4, S6 and S8.

The company eventually ceased lorry production in 1956, after which, the factory was acquired by Rolls-Royce for diesel engine production. By 1959, the prototype Sentinel diesel locomotive was being trialled on the former Shropshire & Montgomeryshire Railway, while by 1963, four different Sentinel diesel models were being produced, with the Sentinel Steelman following shortly afterwards. Rolls-Royce continued to build diesel engines and diesel-powered railway locomotives at the plant until 1971.

Elsewhere, the Castle Works at Hadley began manufacturing tramcars at the beginning of the 20th century. However, in 1910, it was taken over by John Sankey of Bilston to make pressed steel wheels, and the following year began to make steel bodies for road vehicles. Following World War I, the company expanded and began specialising in making chassis for the growing motor car industry. Meanwhile, the Coalbrookdale Company was still going strong, but had to reorganise after becoming a subsidiary of Allied Ironfounders Ltd in 1929, installing the first completely mechanical moulding and sand conditioning plant in a British foundry. In contrast, the Lilleshall Company went backwards, and by the 1930s, three major collieries had been closed along with the Bessemer steel plant at Priorslee, Snedshill Forge, and the heavy engineering works at the New Yard, St George's.

Shrewsbury and Oswestry had been the first two Shropshire towns to get electric power in 1895, and further power stations were built at Market Drayton in 1902, Church Stretton in 1905, Ludlow in 1906, and Bishop's Castle in 1914. A new coal-fired station was then built at Ironbridge in 1932 which powered large parts of the county. Meanwhile, many new houses were built during the inter-war period, with one of the first council house schemes taking place in Shrewsbury in Longden Green and Hill Crescent, with the latter fully built up by 1927. At Wellington, 50 houses were built in Hadley with a further 222 provided under the Housing Provisions Act of 1924. Alongside this, private houses were also being built in Shrewsbury, in the Woodfield Road area by 1927, while 130 houses were built on the site of a disused RAF mechanical transport depot at Harlescott by the builders A. & G. R. Fletcher. During the 1930s, the same company built 450 houses in Shrewsbury, 200 in Wellington, 80 in Whitchurch, and 14 in Dawley. This building contributed to a county population increase of 18.7 percent between 1931 and 1951, with Shrewsbury

Porthill Bridge over the Severn was built in 1922 by David Rowell & Co. It connects Porthill with The Quarry, Shrewsbury's main recreation park.

The Castle Grounds were donated to Bridgnorth by Major Foster in 1956.

> **Quirk Alert:** *Brick or Trick?*
>
> *Arthur Mee's 1930's volume of* The King's England *claims that the doorstep of Munslow St Michael's church is actually "a brick from the Great Wall of China". I can't find anything to corroborate that, though, so perhaps someone was pulling Arthur's leg all those years ago!*

growing by 38 per cent, Ludlow by 14 percent and the coalfield area by 36 per cent.

On the outbreak of World War II on 1st September 1939, mechanical excavators dug trenches in The Quarry in Shrewsbury as a precaution against air raids, while Ludlow town hall was converted into a casualty clearing station. The evacuation of children from urban areas also commenced, with Shropshire taking most of its children from Merseyside, although Dawley, Newport and Oakengates took in children from Smethwick. Remarkably, the evacuation programme, which commenced on 1st September, was complete by the 4th. This included 1,550 children moving to the Atcham district, arriving at Pontesbury station, while four trains delivered 2,000 evacuees from Liverpool to Bridgnorth. Elsewhere, Oswestry hosted more children from Liverpool and Birkenhead, while the Convent of Our Lady of Sion at Acton Burnell, received no less than the daughter of Colonel (later General) Charles de Gaulle, while de Gaulle's wife rented Gadlas Hall near Ellesmere.

In the first month of the war, the first battalion of the King's Shropshire Light Infantry were already in France, only to be pushed back to Dunkirk in May 1940. They were later deployed in North Africa, arriving there in March 1943, crossing to Italy in December 1943, and entered Rome on 4th June 1944 before being stationed in the Middle East in February 1945. Meanwhile, the second battalion trained in Scotland in 1944 for the D-Day landings, after which they pushed into Belgium fought in the Battle of Overloon, and crossed the Rhine on 29th March 1945, reaching Minden by VE Day. Elsewhere, the fourth (territorial) battalion landed in Normandy on 14th June 1944, were involved in the battle for Caen, and achieved distinction in the fighting to dislodge the Germans from Antwerp. They then crossed the Rhine and captured Osnabruck on 3rd April 1945, ending the war at Bad Oldesloe, east of the Elbe.

Back home, the Woolwich Arsenal had been re-located to Donnington just before the outbreak of war, and between 1941 and 1943, 844 new houses were built for the employees of the Ordnance Depot. Meanwhile, the training camps around Oswestry were used for thousands of new recruits, as was the former flax mill at Ditherington. Elsewhere, the Shropshire and Montgomeryshire Railway was resurrected when the War Department took it over in 1941, the objective being to use it as a communications lifeline for the Central Ammunition Storage Depot at Nesscliffe. Ammunition of 1,502 different types arrived in wagons

This memorial and garden marks the site of the former RAF Bridgnorth station and commemorates those members of the RAF and WAAF Commonwealth and allied forces who served here between 1939 and 1963.

and was stored in buildings protected by large earthen banks. Elsewhere, the RAF had a huge training base at Bridgnorth, while two World War I bases, at Shawbury and Tern Hill, were re-opened in 1939. New bases were also built at High Ercall and Cosford, the former having the only concrete runway in the county at the time, while the new base that saw the most action was Peplow with Wellington bombers stationed there.

Even the Royal Navy had a presence in Shropshire with the Fleet Air Arm locating its instrument flying school at Hinstock, while the Admiralty began storing ammunition at Ditton Priors. The Blind Veterans UK, formerly known as St Dunstan's, also moved their patients to Church Stretton, who would guide themselves along a system of wires between the town centre and the hospital's headquarters at the Long Mynd Hotel.

Of course, alongside this, Shropshire's manufacturing giants were aiding the war effort. The Lilleshall Company made 1.25 million bullet-proof rivets per month between 1940 and 1943, while the Horsehay Company manufactured steel landing craft. And in agriculture, the first year of the war saw 47,000 extra acres of Shropshire land ploughed up, while members of the Women's Land Army worked on many

Shropshire farms and hundreds of Shropshire children spent several autumn weeks picking potatoes.

In stark contrast to other areas of Britain, only eight lives were lost to air raids in Shropshire. Two people were killed in Bridgnorth and three in Ellesmere Road, Shrewsbury, in late August 1940. Elsewhere, many bombs fell relatively harmlessly in rural areas, leaving great craters – such as those between Caer Caradoc and Little Caradoc and another on Lilleshall golf course,

> **Quirk Alert:** *Jam Today and Wartime Ghosts*
>
> In 1943, the combined force of Shropshire's Women's Institutes, made 92,642 lbs of jam, putting them top of the national jam-making leaderboard for that year!
>
> Meanwhile, James Lees-Milne's in People and Places, recalls that Lord Berwick of Attingham Hall, and his neighbour, Lady Sybil Grant of Pitchford Hall, regularly toasted the survival of their historic houses with champagne. Perhaps too much of that refreshment accounts for the diary's other claim, that Lord Berwick became convinced that a ghost had invaded his vacuum cleaner! Meanwhile, the apparently orange-haired Lady Sybil, had already moved out of Pitchford Hall into a nearby tree-house, again due to hauntings. However, check out the Quirk Alert, Perfect Pitchford, on page 61. Lady Sybil was probably very wise!

> **Quirk Alert:** *Fond of Barbirolli*
>
> In January 1944, Sir John Barbirolli – the well-known conductor and cellist – delivered a series of concerts at the Grenada cinema in Shrewsbury, covering works such as Mozart's 40th Symphony, Beethoven's 5th and Tchaikovsky's 4th. In order for the concerts to go ahead, though, inhabitants of the town gladly made room in their homes for Barbirolli and his orchestra!

while some windows were shattered in Tugford and a haystack destroyed at Woore!

Following World War II, the National Health Service took over the running of the county's hospitals, while Shropshire's coal mines and railways, along with the gas and electricity services, were all nationalised. In 1950, Shrewsbury Town were elected into the Football League, bringing the county its first taste of professional football, while in 1951, Lilleshall Hall became a residential sports centre. Over the next three decades, Lilleshall became famously used by the English governing bodies of cricket, Rugby League and Rugby Union, lawn tennis, badminton, hockey, lacrosse, netball, the Professional Golfing Association, while the Football Association selected Lilleshall for its facilities and convenience for players meeting up from around the country to train. Indeed, the 1966 England

Ironbridge B power station was built in the late 1960s, including its 670ft chimney and four gigantic cooling towers.

World Cup-winning team trained at Lilleshall for two weeks prior to the start of the tournament.

Alongside this, traditional industries began their decline. At the time of nationalisation in 1947, there were 16 mines in the Coalbrookdale coalfield, but by 1963, only three remained, while iron smelting in Shropshire came to an end when the Lilleshall Company closed its remaining blast furnaces at Priorslee in 1959. Conversely, new industries were born in the county such as diesel engine manufacture in Shrewsbury, while the Ironbridge B power station of two 500 MW turbine generators, costing £50,000,000 and employing 540 staff, began to operate in 1969.

It was in the mid-1960s that an area of east Shropshire was designated for a new town. It was originally named as Dawley New Town and was planned to cover much of the land laid waste by the Industrial Revolution. Under the Dawley New Town Development Corporation, who set up their headquarters at Priorslee Hall, the first homes were built on the new Sutton Hill housing estate built and were occupied by March 1967. Interestingly,

This radar station on top of Titterstone Clee Hill belongs to the National Air Traffic Services (NATS), the main air navigation service provider in the UK. It monitors all aircraft within a 100-mile radius. There is also a Met Office weather radar station at the summit, which is part of a network of 16 radars across the country used to detect cloud precipitation.

plans were laid in 1968 to extend the town by another 12,000 acres (49 km^2) to the south, which would have also included the historic area of Ironbridge Gorge, including a strip on the south side of the Severn, but this never came to fruition due to local objections. However, the "Dawley New Town (Designation) Amendment (Telford) Order" was passed in November 1968, extending the new town area by 10,143 acres (41.05 km^2) which included land within the urban and rural districts of Oakengates, Shifnal and Wellington. It was also at this point that the new town was named as Telford, beating competition from Wrekin Forest City! The new town was, of course, named after the Scottish-born civil engineer Thomas Telford who had contributed much engineering excellence in the county, including his time as Surveyor of Public Works for Shropshire.

Many of Telford's early inhabitants came from Birmingham or Wolverhampton. The new town grew rapidly in size throughout the late 1960s and the 1970s, with a modern shopping mall constructed at the town's geographical centre along with the extensive Town Park, while a bypass around the centre of Madeley was constructed in 1969. Housing expanded rapidly throughout the 1970s, particularly between the A5 and the Severn, with housing developments including Brookside and Hollinswood. Alongside this, industrial estates appeared at Halesfield and Stafford Park. The M54 was also completed in 1983, linking Birmingham and Wolverhampton with the new town, and therefore also linking Telford with the M6, and hence to the rest of the UK's motorway network.

Back in 1965, the population of Telford had been predicted to rise to over 220,000 by 1990. However, the population at the 2011 census was only 142,723. One of the reasons for the slower growth was the disappearance of basic industries, with the last of the collieries having closed by 1979 – with the loss of over a thousand jobs. Several brick and tile works' and much of the railway system also closed during this period, while GKN Sankey, which was employing around 7,500 people in 1965, was employing fewer than 3,000 by the mid-1980s.

In 1966, the Royal Commission on Local Government was commenced. This culminated in the Redcliffe-Maud Report in 1969 which would have decimated a number of historic counties and actually removed several others – although its effect on Shropshire would have been negligible. However, in 1970, the incoming Conservatives rejected the Redcliffe-Maud Report and its subsequent Labour-issued White Paper, and created their own White Paper instead. The subsequent Local Government Act 1972 also had little territory impact on Shropshire. At the same time, the *administrative* county of Shropshire was abolished and the new non-metropolitan county of Salop took its place – although the name proved to be unpopular and was reverted to Shropshire again in 1980. It is also worth noting that although the administrative county of Shropshire was abolished in 1974, the county still retains the offices of Lord Lieutenant and High Sheriff for ceremonial purposes under the Lieutenancies Act 1997, and thus Shropshire is still an English ceremonial county.

In 1974, the new county was comprised of six non-metropolitan districts: North Shropshire, Oswestry, Shrewsbury and Atcham, The Wrekin, Bridgnorth and South Shropshire. Shropshire therefore remained a "shire county" with the standard two-tier layers of local government. From 1974 to 1998, the top layer county council was run from the new Shirehall in Abbey Foregate, and the six non-metropolitan districts were run by their own district councils.

The next development was that The Wrekin district was given unitary authority status in 1998, making it independent from Shropshire County Council and it was re-named as Telford and Wrekin. The two-tier structure remained in the rest of the county and hence became the least populated two-tier area in England. Next, further proposals for unitary authorities throughout England were tabled in 2006. Uppermost, were non-metropolitan counties with small populations, such as Cornwall, Northumberland and Shropshire, while existing unitary authorities within the counties' ceremonial boundaries (such as Telford and Wrekin) were not to be affected and no boundary changes were planned. Shropshire County Council, supported by South Shropshire District Council and Oswestry Borough Council, proposed to the government that the non-metropolitan county of Shropshire become a single unitary authority, but this was opposed by the other three non-metropolitan districts, with Shrewsbury and Atcham Borough Council taking their objection to the High Court in a judicial review. It came to nought, though, and a new Shropshire unitary authority, covering the area of the existing non-metropolitan county, was created in 2009, with the former Shropshire County Council being the continuing authority, having the powers of a non-metropolitan county and district council combined.

Finally, part of these proposals included parishing and establishing a town council for Shrewsbury. The parish was created on 13th May 2008 and Shrewsbury became the second most populous civil parish in England, with a population of over 70,000 (only Weston-super-Mare parish has a greater population).

Hopping back to the 1960s, the Beeching Axe cut deeply in Shropshire. The Severn Valley Railway was closed, as was the Much Wenlock branch, the Wellington to Crewe line, and the whole of the Cambrian Railways mainline from Buttington to Whitchurch. At the same time, the goods yards and locomotive works at Oswestry were closed, leading to local unemployment problems. Then, a little later in 1969, trains from Lancashire to South Wales ceased to run through Shrewsbury and Ludlow.

In terms of leisure, Offa's Dyke Path was opened in 1971, winding in and out of the county's western boundary with Wales, and the Llangollen line of

Surrounding Counties: Pre-1974

Surrounding Counties: Redcliffe-Maud Proposals, 1969

Surrounding Counties: 1974-1996

Surrounding Counties: 1996-2019

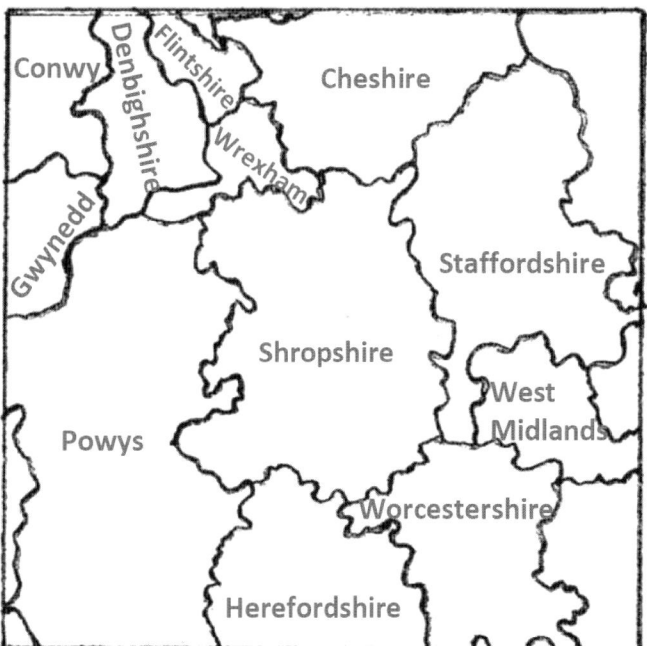

the Ellesmere Canal, along with the main line of the Shropshire Union Canal, became one of the most popular stretches for canal holidays in the country. The highlight of Shropshire tourist areas, though, is Ironbridge Gorge. In 1959, in commemoration of the 250th anniversary of the invention of coke smelting, Allied Ironfounders Ltd uncovered the Old Furnace at Coalbrookdale, and set up a small museum alongside it. The Ironbridge Gorge Museum Trust was founded in 1967, absorbing the Coalbrookdale Museum in 1970. The Blists Hill Open Air Museum followed in 1973, while work also began on the restoration of the Iron Bridge, which was completed in 1980. A new museum followed at the Coalport China Works in 1976 and the following year, a visitor centre was opened in the Gothic warehouse which the Coalbrookdale

Engines at Bridgnorth (left) and Highley (right) stations on the Severn Valley Railway – a heritage railway running for 16 miles from Bridgnorth to Kidderminster. Following the demise of the line in 1963, the Severn Valley Railway Society was formed in 1965 and is still going strong today.

Ironbridge Gorge seen from the other side of the Severn Gorge, and a hotspot for tourism in Shropshire today.

Two of many steam engines celebrating Bishop's Castle's annual Michaelmas Fair, which has been held every year since 1995. This one took place on Saturday 21st September 2019.

> ### Quirk Alert: *Undefeated*
>
> Oswestry-born cricketer, Andy Lloyd, played in one Test and three One Day Internationals for England in 1984. The Test Match came against the West Indies in June 1984. Alas, after making 10 runs, and batting for 33 minutes, opener Lloyd was hit on the head by a bouncer from lethal West Indian fast bowler, Malcolm Marshall. Despite wearing a helmet, Lloyd spent several days in hospital and didn't play again in 1984. Moreover, he never played for England again either – and is therefore the only Test Match opening batsman never to have been dismissed from the national team!

Company had built beside the Severn – with the Ironbridge Gorge Museum winning Museum of the Year for 1977 and the European Museum of the Year in 1978.

Today, the open-air museum is known as Blists Hill Victorian Town and has grown to include buildings that were already part of the industrial site, such as the brickworks and blast furnaces. Elsewhere there are Victorian buildings such as the sweet shop, which are replicas of those still standing in other towns, while

> ### Quirk Alert: *The Break*
>
> Arthur Mee writes of a "seasonal algae" that appears on The Mere at Ellesmere every summer, clogging the waters like a thick soup for two or three weeks. He also mentions that it is called "The Break". Fast forward to the 21st century, and you won't find any reference of "The Break" on Google. What you will find, though, are accounts of the algae now appearing as early as February, thanks to our unseasonably warm winters. An account from 2019 talks of "algae growing and blooming, turning the water an almost florescent blue green", and also warns that it is poisonous to dogs.
>
> However, one local angler helps tie the story back to Arthur Mee's account from the 1930s, stating that: "As a child, the lakes always had an algae bloom in June or July. We used to say the water had 'broken' and this would last a couple of weeks then the water would clear. Seeing this so early is very worrying." Alas, it is unlikely that world-leader knowledge of this story would provide "the break" that we desperately need to properly tackle climate change.

original buildings have also been relocated to the museum site, such as The New Inn public house, which originally stood between Green Lane and Hospital Street in Walsall. The site also includes the famous Hay Inclined Plane.

Shropshire in the 21st century is consistent with most other counties: a move away from traditional industries to the service industry, and growing populations in all towns and cities, all of which have seen significant regeneration of town and city centres. Despite this, the Shropshire of today remains one of England's most agricultural counties.

It is also a total delight to visit, with innumerable beautiful villages and historic buildings and vast stretches of stunning landscape, particularly the stretch running up the centre of the county through the Shropshire Hills.

Stiperstones viewed from the west.

View south-westwards from the top of Stiperstones.

The motte of Ellesmere Castle survives today, but if you walk up the pathway that spirals around it, this is what you will find at the top – a lovely bowling club and bowling green!

And these are the lovely views looking towards St Mary's church and The Mere.

Another bowling green at the top of a town hill and former castle site, this one in Bishop's Castle. A Shropshire quirk, perhaps?

Introducing the Shire-Ode

Time for a bit of fun with Shropshire place-names now! Readers of other books in this series will be familiar with the Shire-Ode – a tale, told in rhyming verse, about fictitious characters from the subject county – and seamlessly incorporating as many county place-names into the flow of the poem as possible. These places then go on to form a county almanac, of sorts. Each place appears in roughly alphabetical order, although some of the smaller places are batched up into trios known as a "Three's Up" or appear in the final "Best of the Rest" section. The location of all of the places is pinpointed on the map following the Shire-Ode.

For Shropshire, I was drawn to a strangely-named area to the east of Bridgnorth called The Hobbins – a name that conjured up a hobbit-goblin hybrid – so when I spotted another place called The Bog (in West Shropshire), the Hobbins had their home…or do I mean their Myddle Earth…

Shropshire Shire-Ode: The Hobbins From Beyond The Bog

The clan called **The Green** was a peaceful tribe
Hoo would **Greete** Salop folk with a smile
They'd not had a **Woore** for ten decades or **More**
They had **Hope**; as a **Rhewl** lived in style.

Their pleasant land, in the **Myddle** of their Earth
Was bordered to east by **The Grove**
To the north was **The Wood**, where many **Oaks** stood
And **Round Oak**, stoat and **Badger** would rove.

Then to south was **The Down** – it was pleasant all around
'Cept to west where there's mist on **The Marsh**
And beyond this **Lowe** fog, is a land called **The Bog**
Where **The Hobbins** are rumoured at large.

Now, **Stanley Green** and **Tilley Green**
Scared their kids with **The Gore** from folklore
"A **Cross** between hobbit and goblin, they say"
"Who at night comes a-**Knockin** at your door."

"They're **Burley** with **Hornspike**," **Lyde Stanley**, one day
"They **Howle** and they **Pant**," **Tilley** said
"**Tong** and teeth **Nash**, with their clubs they **Bache**;
"With **Great Bolas** they'll take off your head."

"Yes, they've **Forton** many-a **Battlefield**
"Caused **Bedlam** on **Hillside** and **Trench**,
"Wear **Harton** their sleeve, they will grant no reprieve,
"Not to child, nor indeed **Comley** wench."

So young **Abbey Green**, with the **Willey**'s put up
Saw **Folley** to head to the west
So when she left home, to **Northwood** she'd roam;
Amid **Long Oak** she began her life's quest.

She shared a log **Cabin** with **Leigh**, **Lynn** and **Bryn**
In **The Nook**, by **Cherry Orchard** trails
But she still wasn't right; couldn't **Sleap** well at night:
Grimmer nightmares **Broughton** by those tales.

And whether she should, she still feared **Bagginswood**
For that name **Hints** at Hobbins, you see
Did these beasts from the west, **Stowe** away in **Crowsnest**,
In **The Foxholes** or round **Broad Oak** tree?

So her worst fears remained, making **Woodside** life strained
Fearing **Lightwood** and **Foxwood** at night
And in **Myddlewood** glade, were **Six Ashes** in shade
Of which **Three Ashes** filled her with fright.

Now the winters, I'm told, can be **Bitterley** cold
So **Coton** and **Mytton**s are key
But when **Bluebell** arrives, and then **Somerwood** thrives
Inwood is the best place to be.

Here Abbey played cricket – bowled **Overs** galore
Plus **Bouldon** the **Bowling Green**, too
Her **Anchor** was fixed, though her thoughts were still mixed
Couldn't **Shelve** that old Hobbins taboo.

Though these **Nox** were still rife, she just **Preston** with life
Tried to **Steeraway** thoughts from her fear
But her friends knew the score, she did **Twitchen** galore
Was on **Edge**, and turned **Mardy** with beer.

But when the **Fitz** came, twas a terrible shame
For they'd leave her as white as a **Sheet**
But then what could she do, with this harsh **Waterloo**
There was no **New Invention** to treat.

She was thus **Highley** strung – so strange when so young
But then **Clive** arrived – **Ryton** cue
The future looked bright, their **Chemistry** right
Plus she'd now turned **The** fear **Corner**, too.

Come their big wedding day, Stanley gave her away
Whilst her Mum held **The Hem** of her dress
They then hired **Sutton Hall**, for their plush wedding **Ball**
Where you'd **Betton** egg sandwich with cress.

Having **Eaton** his food, and in jovial mood
Stan gave Clive a **Patton** the back
"It's **The Hope** of us two, that life's good to you,"
"Why thank you," said Clive, as they sat.

"So, where are you from?" asked Stanley of Clive
"From the west," he replied, "'yond that fog,"
"Oh, didn't I say," Abbey said, in sly way,
"He's a Hobbin! He comes from The Bog!"

Place-Name Table for The Hobbins From Beyond The Bog

1	Abbey Green	2	Anchor	3	Bache	4	Badger	5	Bagginswood
6	Ball	7	Battlefield	8	Bedlam	9	Betton[1]	10	Bitterley
11	Bluebell	12	Bouldon	13	Bowling Green	14	Broad Oak[1]	15	Broughton
16	Bryn	17	Burley	18	Cabin	19	Chemistry	20	Cherry Orchard
21	Clive	22	Comley	23	Coton[1]	24	Cross	25	Crowsnest
26	Eaton[1]	27	Edge	28	Fitz	29	Folley	30	Forton
31	Foxwood	32	Great Bolas	33	Grimmer	34	Greete	35	Harton
36	Highley	37	Hillside	38	Hints	39	Hoo	40	Hope
41	Hornspike	42	Howle	43	Inwood	44	Knockin	45	Leigh
46	Lightwood	47	Long Oak	48	Lowe	49	Lyde	50	Lynn
51	Mardy	52	More	53	Myddle	54	Myddlewood	55	Mytton
56	Nash	57	New Invention	58	Northwood	59	Nox	60	Oaks
61	Overs	62	Pant	63	Patton	64	Preston[3]	65	Rhewl
66	Round Oak	67	Ryton	68	Sheet	69	Shelve	70	Six Ashes
71	Sleap	72	Somerwood	73	Stanley[1]	74	Stanley Green	75	Steeraway
76	Stowe	77	Sutton Hall	78	The Bog	79	The Corner	80	The Down
81	The Foxholes	82	The Gore	83	The Green[1]	84	The Grove[1]	85	The Hem
86	The Hobbins	87	The Hope	88	The Marsh[2]	89	The Nook[1]	90	The Wood[1]
91	Three Ashes	92	Tilley	93	Tilley Green	94	Tong	95	Trench
96	Twitchen	97	Waterloo	98	Willey	99	Woodside[1]	100	Woore

[1]Appears twice in Shropshire; [2]Appears three times in Shropshire; [3]Appears four times in Shropshire

Shropshire Location Map for The Hobbins from beyond The Bog

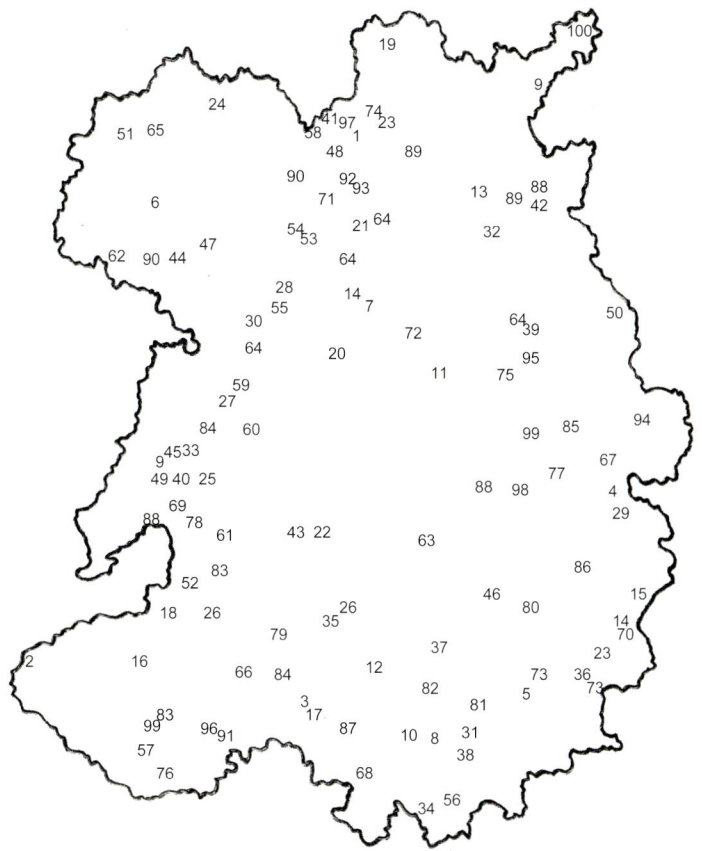

The Hobbins From Beyond The Bog – A Shropshire Shire-Ode Almanac

Three's-Up!

	ANCHOR	BACHE	BALL
STATUS:	Hamlet	Hamlet	Hamlet
DISTRICT:	South Shropshire (1974-2009); Shropshire (post-2009)	South Shropshire (1974-2009); Shropshire (post-2009)	Oswestry (1974-2009); Shropshire (post-2009)
EARLIEST RECORD:	19th century	19th century	19th century
MEANING AND DERIVATION:	Probably named after the Anchor Inn which dates from at least 1830.	Probably derives from the de la Bache family who owned land in the area in the 13th century.	Named after the Ball Inn.

Three's Up Trivia!

The remote hamlet of **Anchor** is located in south-west Shropshire, in the civil parish of Bettws-y-Crwyn, and is the most westerly place in the county, with the Welsh border lying 400 metres further west. The point where England and Wales meet is known as Anchor Bridge – this being a bridge over the watercourse known as Nant Rhuddwr (in Welsh) and Rhuddwr Brook (in English). This point is also the pass between the Vale of Kerry and the Clun Valley, making Anchor the most westerly settlement in England on the Welsh border. There is also an annual Anchor Horse Fair held in the area.

Meanwhile, **Bache** is a tiny hamlet in south Shropshire, where you will find Bache Pool and Bache Tower. The former is a 1.5-acre pool dating back to the 17th century, when it was used by monks as a stock pool for carp – which it still stocks today, along with other fish, and is a popular location for anglers. As for the three-storey crenelated Tower House on the Colwinston Estate, this was apparently built for the shepherds to look out from to watch their flocks, while today, the 2-acre garden occasionally holds events for the National Gardens Scheme. There is also a nearby village of Seifton Bache, where you will find Bache Primitive Methodist Church. Built in 1862, it remained in use until 1952. Thereafter, it fell into disrepair until it was renovated and is now a private home. There was also a Wesleyan chapel at Bache Mill, half a mile to the north-east – this one built in 1879, closed in 1964, and also since converted to residential use.

Finally, **Ball** is a hamlet in north-west Shropshire between Maesbury and Oswestry. It includes the original Ball public house (shown top right), and a number of houses along Ball Lane, amongst which are farm buildings and Maesbury Primitive Methodist Church, founded in 1834. The Primitive Methodist website states that one of the wall plaques is in memory of a poor chap who died close to this spot when transporting stones from Sweeney Mountain on his horse and cart – possibly for the build of the chapel. Apparently, the cart overturned and crushed the man to death. According to one comment, the man was buried in a lead coffin under the church, while the same reference also mentions the graves of "several children who died during the construction". Elsewhere, another account states that by 1851, there was "free seating for 84 people and rented spaces for 48". Sadly, this chapel has been derelict since 2002.

LEFT: The Anchor Inn at Anchor is the second highest pub in Shropshire at 1,266ft (386m), the highest being the Kremlin Inn above Cleehill village on Titterstone Clee. The Anchor may well once have been called the Mermaid's Rest, another nautical reference for an inn that is a considerable distance from the sea, this also being its name as it appears in Mary Webb's 1922 novel, Seven For A Secret. *CENTRE: The Tower House at Bache is part of the Colwinston Estate. RIGHT: Stream running alongside Ball Lane.*

NAME (STATUS):	**BADGER** (Village)
POPULATION:	126
DISTRICT:	Bridgnorth (1974-2009); Shropshire (post-2009)
EARLIEST RECORD:	*Beghesovre*, 1086 (Domesday Book); *Bagsore*, 1870
MEANING:	Hill spur of a man called Bæcg.
DERIVATION:	From the Old English personal name, *Bæcg*, plus the Old English word *ofer* (flat-topped ridge, hill spur or promontory); there is indeed a hill spur rising up behind Badger Farm, with a slope to the south-east enfolding the village.

Badger Church: St Giles

The majority of St Giles' church was rebuilt from 1833 onwards, to a design by Francis Halley of Shifnal, with both nave and chancel built, without division, under a single pitched roof. It was built in the same place as its predecessor and used as much of the original sandstone masonry as possible – although more sandstone was quarried on the estate to complete the work. Arthur Mee dates the base of the tower to Norman times while the first known rector dates from 1174.

St Giles' church had its own rector until 1952, at which point it became part of a united benefice with Ryton and Beckbury, with one rector for all three parishes – and indeed, this was one of the first three-parish united benefices in the country. In 1989, a further three parishes were added to the benefice.

Interestingly, Badger and the neighbouring parish of Beckbury belonged to the Diocese of Hereford in medieval times, as an exclave, and they weren't moved to the Diocese of Lichfield until 1905. This was probably due to the parish being aligned to Wenlock Priory, which was a Cluniac house and was thus viewed as an alien priory – as it was the daughter house of an abbey in France, and England was constantly at war with France throughout the 14th century.

Badger Historical Trivia: Kynnersleys, Brownes and Badger Dingle

Badger was held by an Anglo-Saxon landlord, Bruning, prior to the Norman Conquest, but by 1086 and Domesday Book, it was held for Roger de Montgomerie,

St Giles' church at Badger. It was largely rebuilt in the 19th century from Triassic sandstone found to the north of the village.

1st Earl of Shrewsbury, by Osbern fitz Richard; both of whom were of Norman descent! By the end of the 12th century, though, the landlord was the Prior of Wenlock Priory, while the occupiers of the parish were the de Badger family – a typical case of the Lord of the Manor taking on the place-name as his own name. The manor remained under the control of the de Badger family until 1402 when Alice, widow of John de Badger, died without an heir, while by 1560, the manor was owned by Thomas Kynnersley. The Kynnersleys then controlled the manor for more than two hundred years, with a number of them serving as High Sheriff of both Shropshire and Staffordshire. In around 1719, John Kynnersley demolished the medieval manor house

LEFT: Badger Lower Pool, also known as the Town Pool. The pool was formed many centuries ago following the damming of a small stream running down to the Snowden Brook in Badger Dingle. The earliest reference comes from 1614 when Francis Kynnersley threatened to throw the rector's head into the pool – this due to a dispute as to who had named the latest rector! A few yards further north is Badger Upper Pool, also known as the Church Pool. The pools were further landscaped in the 18th century by William Emes on behalf of Isaac Hawkins Browne. RIGHT: Badger Dingle, also created by William Emes. This delightfully secluded path weaves through woods and sandstone outcrops above a gently burbling stream.

LEFT: The Birdhouse, originally built in 1783 as an architectural ornament, but which became the site of an annual tea party in the early 20th century, where the Capel Cure family waited on the servants! CENTRE: This headless cross stands in St Giles' churchyard and probably dates from the 14th or 15th century. RIGHT: This lovely thatched cottage sits alongside the Town Pool in Badger.

and built a new stone-fronted hall around 150 yards to the north. John died without an heir though, and the manor eventually passed – in 1774 – to Isaac Hawkins Browne, an industrialist and Tory MP for Bridgnorth between 1784 and 1812.

Between 1779 and 1783, Browne greatly extended the hall, to a design by James Wyatt. It included a museum, library, and conservatory, elaborate plasterwork by Joseph Rose, and paintings by Robert Smirke. Next, Browne had the gardens landscaped, and it was at this point that that Badger Dingle was shaped to designs by William Emes, a pupil of Capability Brown. It had 2 miles of walks, cascades created by damming the brook, a Doric temple and other architectural features. The village pools, which drain into the Dingle, were also enlarged and reshaped at this time. Further improvements were made to the dingle in the early 19th century by John Webb, including a network of paths and several architectural features were added, such as the boathouse, Rotunda, an icehouse and caves. However, the dam burst after a storm in 1828, and it took nine weeks to reconstruct the Dingle.

Elsewhere, James Chelsum was the rector of Badger from 1780, but he combined his benefice at Badger with the rectory of Droxford in Hampshire from 1782, and a chaplaincy at Lathbury in Buckinghamshire! Browne therefore replaced Chelsum in 1795 with William Smith, who was never absent from the parish for more than two weeks. As for Browne, he died in 1818, but his wife, Elizabeth, lived for another twenty-one years and contributed significantly to the cost of rebuilding the parish church.

The estate passed to Robert Henry Cheney in 1839, an architectural and landscape painter. It was also Cheney who opened Badger Dingle to visitors for the first time in 1849. Four years later (1953), much of Badger Hall was demolished, although a utility building and the gatehouse survive to this day and thanks to their grandness, were re-christened as Badger Hall a few decades ago!

In 1952, the long-serving Reverend Archibald Dix retired and this was the point that the parish was amalgamated with Beckbury. His daughter, Margaret Dix, lived at the rectory until her death in 1992. She was a distinguished surgeon at the National Hospital for Neurology and Neurosurgery, and the Dix–Hallpike test for a benign paroxysmal positional vertigo is half-named after her.

Badger Quirk Alert: Going Out With A Bang!
In 1884, Badger Hall passed to Alfred Capel Cure of Blake Hall, Ongar. A hero of the Crimean War, Capel Cure was also an early photographer, while he was the owner responsible for the addition of the private family chapel to the north side of St Giles' church. Alas, he died a bizarre death, after he blew himself up whilst attempting to dynamite tree stumps on one of his other estates!

In the early 20th century, the Capel Cure family introduced an annual tea party, in which they waited on the servants – this taking place in the building in Badger Dingle known as The Birdhouse. Originally built of sandstone in 1783 as an architectural ornament, the building had a basement containing a service area and a main salon above with views out over the pool. The salon was heated like a Roman hypocaust, with flues in the rear apsidal wall conducting heat from fires in the basement.

SHROPSHIRE: UNUSUAL & QUIRKY

NAME (STATUS):	**BEDLAM** (Hamlet)
POPULATION:	c.50
DISTRICT:	South Shropshire (1974-2009); Shropshire (post-2009)
EARLIEST RECORD:	19th century
MEANING:	A corruption of the word Bethlehem.
DERIVATION:	Explained below in the Historical Trivia.

LEFT: Titterstone Clee Hill. Bedlam is located on the southern slopes, while quarries are located across all faces of the hill. CENTRE: Trig point at the summit of Titterstone Clee Hill (1,749ft/533m), with the National Air Traffic Services (NATS) radar station behind. RIGHT: Remains of mine workings on Titterstone Clee Hill.

Bedlam Geographical Trivia: 360 Degrees

Bedlam is located on the southern slope of Titterstone Clee Hill (1,749ft; 533m), the third highest hill in Shropshire. The summit is said to have one of the best views in England, for on a clear day, you can see west to Snowdonia, north-east to the Peak District, east to the Black Country, south-east to the Cotswolds, south to the Malvern Hills, and south-west to the Black Mountains and Brecon Beacons.

Bedlam Historical Trivia: Asylums and Quarries

The name "Bedlam" is a compression of the word "Bethlehem" which originated from a priory in Bishopsgate in London dedicated to St Mary of Bethlehem in 1247. A century or so later, the priory was used as an asylum for the insane and hence the name "Bedlam" became associated with asylums – and as there was a medieval lunatic asylum just above the current Shropshire Bedlam, this is almost certainly how it came to be so-named. The foundations of the medieval asylum are still visible today.

However, the *village* of Bedlam was founded in the 19th century to house workers for the quarries on Titterstone Clee Hill which over the centuries have been quarried for basalt and other igneous rocks which are known locally as Dhustone (Welsh for black rock). The latter is an olivine basalt, sometimes coarse enough to be a dolerite, and the product is used mostly in road-building. Meanwhile, in medieval times and particularly in the mid-18th century, both ironstone and coal were mined from bell pits – these being localised mine shafts, one of which has now flooded to form a lake. At other times, both fireclay and limestone has been quarried here as well. The largest quarries have sheer drops of up to 100 feet (30m).

As for Titterstone Clee Hill, its history goes way back beyond the quarrying, as it was also an ancient 70-acre hillfort dating back to both the Bronze Age and Iron Age. The remains of a 4,000-year-old Bronze Age cairn are still visible at the summit, indicating that this was a likely ceremonial site, while parts of the Iron Age earthworks still survive despite the subsequent extensive quarrying.

Row of cottages at Bedlam. Over the decades, many of these cottages were occupied by quarrymen and their families who worked in the quarries on Titterstone Clee Hill.

The war memorial at Bedlam which reveals the terrible truth of World Wars I and II; 17 men from Bedlam went to fight, and none came back – including four members of the Millichamp family.

NAME (STATUS):	**BATTLEFIELD** (Village)
POPULATION:	126
DISTRICT:	Shrewsbury & Atcham (1974-2009); Shropshire (post-2009)
EARLIEST RECORD:	*Batelfeld*, 1415
MEANING:	The field of battle.
DERIVATION:	Derived from the Old French word *bataille* (battle) and the Old English word *feld* (field); the battle in question is, of course, the Battle of Shrewsbury which took place in 1403.

The church of St Mary Magdalene at Battlefield.

Looking from the chancel to the nave of Battlefield's church.

Battlefield Church: St Mary Magdalene

St Mary Magdalene church was originally built as a chantry in memory of the thousands who died at the Battle of Shrewsbury on this site on 21st July 1403 – and is therefore almost certainly built over a mass burial pit. The church is generally thought to have been founded by the local parish priest, Roger Ive, but it also received considerable support and endowment from Henry IV, and was so-named because the Battle of Shrewsbury had been fought on St Mary Magdalene's Eve. Its initial purpose was to provide a site for a chantry chapel to sing masses for the souls of the King himself, his ancestors, and those killed in the battle. Papal confirmation was sought in 1410, and the resulting papal bull was the first document which explicitly described St Mary Magdalene's at Battlefield as a collegiate church.

The college and chantry were both dissolved in 1548 by Edward VI, and it is thought that the college buildings became disused and were probably soon demolished. However, the church survived as the parish church of Albright Hussey, but its condition deteriorated over the next three centuries. The roof was repaired in 1749, but the nave roof collapsed at a later date and was abandoned by the late 18th century. Oddly, the chancel was restored in the late 18th century in neoclassical style, with four Doric columns forming a square, and hence the building continued as a parish church, albeit with an open-roofed nave! Much of what we see today, therefore, dates from the extensive restoration work carried out in the early 1860s, and most of the old church has now gone – although traces of the priests' dwelling have been found in the churchyard. Today's magnificent chancel has twelve pinnacles linked by a parapet, while over one of the windows is a figure of Henry IV with his dagger at his hip. Alas, after more than a century of further use as a parish church, the building was declared redundant in 1982 and is now owned by the Churches Conservation Trust, while the church remains a memorial chapel to the battle-dead, with an annual service of commemoration.

LEFT: *The nave roof of St Mary's church.*

CENTRE: *The west door of St Mary's church.*

RIGHT: *The main entrance to St Mary's churchyard.*

NAME (STATUS):	**BITTERLEY** (Village and Civil Parish)
POPULATION:	902 (parish of Bitterley at 2011 census); c.50 for village
DISTRICT:	South Shropshire (1974-2009); Shropshire (post-2009)
EARLIEST RECORD:	*Buterlie*, 1086 (Domesday Book)
MEANING:	Rich pasture which produces good butter.
DERIVATION:	From the Old English words *butere* (butter) and *lēah* (woodland clearing or glade; pasture or meadow).

Bitterley Geographical Trivia

The civil parish of Bitterley is quite extensive at 6,592 acres and, as well as covering the village of Bitterley, it also includes the settlements of Angel Bank, Angel Lane, Bedlam, Cleeton St Mary, Dhustone Lane, Farden, Henley, Lower Ledwyche, Middleton, Snitton, Squirrel Lane and Stoney Lane. The parish is actually divided into two wards, Bitterley and Cleeton St Mary, with the latter village effectively detached (by road) as it lies on the other (north-east) side of Titterstone Clee Hill.

Bitterley Church: St Mary's

The Grade II listed St Mary's church dates from the 12th and 13th centuries with 17th century additions, with the low-rise tower dating from that period when Norman architecture was merging into English; the font also dates from Norman times. Elsewhere, the church is home to a large wooden coffer which dates from the 13th century, while Arthur Mee writes in the 1930s that one of the bells still ringing in the tower was cast in time to ring for Agincourt (1415). He also waxes lyrical about the old chancel screen which separates the nave from the chancel. The church was restored in 1876 and 1880.

St Mary's church, Bitterley.

Bitterley Historical Trivia: Bitterley Court, Quarrying and Railways

Today, the church is located around half a mile east of the main core of Bitterley, and evidence of the medieval village that grew up around the church can still be seen in the parkland in front of Bitterley Court.

The Grade II listed Bitterley Court was built in the early 17th century, and by 1655, it had been jointly purchased by the Walcot and Littleton families. In around 1766, the house was sold to the senior branch of the Walcot family, who then sold what was then called Walcot Hall to Robert Clive (1725-1774), also known as Lord Clive of India. It was also at around this time that the house was extensively modernized by local architect, Thomas Farnolls Pritchard, with the orientation of the house also being turned by 90 degrees.

In 1899 Bitterley Court was purchased by James Volant Wheeler, younger son of Edward Vincent Wheeler of Newnham Court, Tenbury Wells. The house is still owned by the Wheelers to this day, having been restored in the 1960s in order to save it from demolition. Meanwhile, another Grade II listed building, Henley Hall, is located on the western outskirts of Bitterley. It was built by the Powys family in the 18th century, rebuilt again in 1772 by Thomas Knight, and has been extended several times since then.

In 1712, the school at Bitterley was endowed by John Newborough, a former headmaster of Eton, and

This medieval cross in St Mary's churchyard dates from the 14th century and is Grade I listed. It is considered the best surviving cross in Shropshire. One theory also suggests that the hole halfway up the shaft lines up along an ancient ley line!

retained its Grammar School status until as late as 1958. The original endowment was "for the instruction of the parish children, for which the master has a commodious house, with garden, play-ground, and also a weekly stipend from the parents of each child, according to the amount of their respective rents".

By the mid-19th century, the volume of coal and stone being quarried on Titterstone Clee Hill had grown to such an extent that a railway had to be constructed from Clee Hill via Bitterley to a junction with the mainline just north of Ludlow station, known as Clee Hill Junction. The first part of this branch line was opened in August 1864 and included the 4.5 miles from Ludlow to the sidings at Bitterley Wharf. The 1.5 mile extension to the quarries at Clee Hill was opened in June 1867, and included a cable-operated incline as far as the village of Dhustone. A little later, a rope-hauled incline was also constructed from the sidings in Bitterley, running via Bedlam up to the quarries on the top of Titterstone Clee Hill. Initially the line was used for coal and briefly for ironstone, but stone traffic soon became the main product. Wagons on the Titterstone incline were narrow gauge (3ft/914mm), and upon arrival on a raised siding at Bitterley Wharf, the stone would be tipped into standard gauge wagons located alongside in a lower siding. These wagons would then be steam hauled along the rest of the branch to the main line at Ludlow for onward transportation.

The stone mined on Titterstone Clee Hill is one of the hardest stones in the British Isles and was used to build Cardiff docks as well as being used extensively throughout the country for roadstone. Meanwhile, the branch line was also used for the delivery of general goods to Bitterley Wharf, and was so busy that a 13-lever signal box was built in 1907. Trains of 12 empty wagons would be hauled up the line from Ludlow, but because of the steep gradient when entering Bitterley Wharf the train had to be split into two trains of six wagons then shunted into the sidings. Despite being a goods-only line, it was occasionally used by locals for travelling between Bitterley and Ludlow in the guard's van – such as an occasion in 1865, when a special passenger train carried people from Ludlow to Bitterley Wharf to attend a celebration of the re-opening of St Mary's church following its restoration.

Bitterley Wharf was at its peak during the 1920s, and included a specially-constructed plant for the production of tarmac, while the Titterstone Clee Hill quarries employed more than 2,000 workers. However, thereafter railway traffic began to decline. The Clee Hill incline was the first section of the branch line to close in 1958, with the Titterstone incline closing in 1960; trains to Bitterley ceased in 1962. Nevertheless, remains of the old branch line and the two inclines up Titterstone Clee Hill still exist, as does a large concrete building under which the wagons were filled with stone.

Finally, in 1933, four lunettes were bequeathed to St Mary's church at Bitterley by Colonel Price Wood of nearby Henley Hall. They remained unidentified until 2003 when they were recognised as the work of Willes Maddox on behalf of 19th century MP William Beckford of Lansdown Tower in Bath. They were then purchased for £716,000 by the Beckford Tower Trust and returned to their original position in the tower sanctuary.

Bitterley Quirk Alert: Kings, Rooks and Cloaks

There is a stone in the floor of St Mary's church dedicated to Sir Thomas Walcot, on which are carved three chess-rooks, part of the arms given to John Walcot after he played chess with Henry V. The story goes that John played checkmate with the rook, whereupon the King gave him the rook for his coat-of-arms as a reward. Meanwhile, William Walcot was page to Charles I when the King was executed in January 1649. Immediately before his beheading, Charles gave half his cloak to each of his two pages on the scaffold. William Walcot's half was kept at Bitterley Court for many years, royal bloodstains and all! The cloak is still with the Walcot family today, but no longer at Bitterley Court.

View towards Titterstone Clee Hill from the eastern section of Bitterley village.

House in the centre of Bitterley village.

These unusual and quirky signposts can be found at Bitterley Primary School.

NAME (STATUS):	**BOULDON** (Hamlet)	
POPULATION:	c.40 (part of civil parish of Diddlebury, population 670)	
DISTRICT:	South Shropshire (1974-2009); Shropshire (post-2009)	
EARLIEST RECORD:	*Bolledone*, 1086 (Domesday Book); *Bullardone*, 1166	
MEANING:	A hill of some kind, although the meaning isn't clear.	
DERIVATION:	Part-derived from the Old English word *dūn* (hill).	

The Tally Ho Inn in the centre of Bouldon was first licensed in 1844.

Heath Chapel is located half a mile to the north-east of Bouldon.

The "main road" through Bouldon.

Bouldon Church: Heath Chapel and All Saints

Heath Chapel is located half a mile to the north-east of Bouldon, and dates from the mid-12th century. Much of its Norman architecture is still evident including the south doorway, while inside is a Norman chancel arch and a Norman font.

The roof of the two-bay nave was replaced in the 16th or 17th century, while a flat plaster ceiling was added to the two-bay chancel. The walls were also whitewashed during this period, thus covering the medieval wall paintings, and the pews were added along with a two-decker pulpit. The final restoration was in 1912 when the chancel ceiling was removed and a new roof built, while some of the medieval wall paintings were also restored, including one of St George on the south wall and the Last Judgement above the chancel arch. Unusually, the church does not possess a bellcote.

Interestingly, the hamlet of Bouldon was once home to an All Saints' church, built in 1873 by the rector of Holdgate parish, of which Bouldon was part until 1921. Built from corrugated iron, it survived until the 1980s by which stage it had become severely dilapidated and hence it was demolished.

Bouldon Historical Trivia: Through the Ages

At the time of Domesday Book (1086), Bouldon was part of the Anglo-Saxon hundred of Culvestan, although this was replaced by Munslow in the early 12th century. Bouldon was also part of the parish of Holdgate from the late 11th century until 1884, but it was located in a *detached* part of that parish for all of those centuries. In 1884, though, Bouldon was transferred to Diddlebury parish, but it wasn't transferred to the Church of England's *ecclesiastical parish* of Diddlebury (from Holdgate) until 1921.

In the 17th and 18th centuries, Bouldon was home to a charcoal-fuelled ironworks which produced pig iron. On 28th September 1643, Charles I authorised payment of £965 10s. to Bouldon's resident ironmaster, Francis Walker – this for manufacture of artillery and ammunition delivered to the Royalist forces at Shrewsbury, Bridgnorth and Worcester. The ironworks closed around 1795 and only a tree covered slag heap remains today.

Bouldon became more prominent in 1794 when it found itself on the turnpike route from Ludlow to Bridgnorth – a route which much later became the B4364, but which no longer includes Bouldon as it passes to the east of Brown Clee Hill. Meanwhile, Bouldon Mill was founded in 1790 on the Pye Brook, although it was located on the site of a former timber mill that was built in 1611. Bouldon Mill operated as a mill until the 1930s.

The centre of Bouldon where what was once Bouldon Mill survives (to the left of the photograph). The iron water wheel shown here was cast in Coalbrookdale.

	NAME (STATUS):	**CLIVE** (Village)
	POPULATION:	530
	DISTRICT:	North Shropshire (1974-2009); Shropshire (post-2009)
	EARLIEST RECORD:	*Clive*, 1255
	MEANING:	Place at the cliff or bank.
	DERIVATION:	From the Old English word *clif* (cliff or steep slope).

Clive Church: All Saints

The current All Saints' church originally dates from the 12th century, although much of it was rebuilt between 1885 and 1894. Only some Norman stonework survives, mainly in the north wall and nave doorways, with the north and south doorways being of Norman construction, but dating to around 1190. It is thought that the Norman church was comprised of just a basic nave, with no chancel or transepts.

All Saints' church was extensively restored between 1629 and 1654, which included replacing the roof (which required over 20,000 new slates), re-glazing the windows, installing more pews, adding new flagstones to the church floor, and constructing a bell-cote to house two bells. However, the major rebuilding took place in the 19th century. The first phase began in 1846 after William Jeudwine became rector, and he oversaw the transformation of the 14th century windows, creating a lighter nave and chancel. The roof was also heightened and the old wooden bell-cote was replaced by a stone turret containing two bells, while new pews and a new font were added, with the predecessor to the latter being buried beneath its successor! Finally, a small vestry was built on the north-eastern corner of the extended chancel.

Of course, the main transformation occurred in the late 19th century, as the church changed out of all recognition to become one of the finest village churches in England. The tale of how this came about is covered in the next section. But suffice to say that the only similarity is that both the old and the new church were built using local Grinshill sandstone!

Clive Historical Trivia: The Earliest Christian Church?

There are claims that the site of Clive's All Saints' church was home to one of the earliest Christian churches in the region. This is surmised because in 597, Pope Gregory the Great despatched St Augustine, a Roman Benedictine missionary, to Britain to convert the Anglo-Saxon population. Furthermore, the official Diocesan History of Lichfield, written in the 1880s by William Beresford, states that in 599 "it was thought probable that St Augustine of Canterbury made a tour up the Severn valley, only however, to find the district already Christian. At Cressage he preached under a tree, 'Christ's Oak,' from which some think the village took its name. At Clive, he found a little wooden church, which survived him to modern times." It certainly isn't an unreasonable theory, as many Christian Romans had dispersed into the local communities, and that journey of St Augustine to the monastery at Bangor-is-y-Coed may well have seen him spend his final night at a church at Clive before completing the last 16 miles of the journey.

During Anglo-Saxon times, the township of Clive belonged to the collegiate church of St Mary's at Shrewsbury, and continued to long after the Normans conquered England. Having such a powerful mother church came in handy in 1344 when a Whitchurch baron called John le Strange seized land in Clive – at which point St Mary's appealed directly to Edward III who

All Saints' church at Clive.

promptly returned the land to the Dean of St Mary's and fined le Strange £40. However, it hadn't been so straightforward a century earlier as the nearby Grinshill quarries were owned by the monastery at Haughmond, which resulted in a number of land disputes throughout the 13th century. Clive's relationship with St Mary's wasn't always smooth either, reaching a low point in 1580 when the inhabitants of Clive and Astley were expected to contribute to the cost of repairing the Trinity window in St Mary's church, despite receiving so little funding for their own Chapels of Ease.

The Grade II listed Old Manor House on Jubilee Street, Clive, dates from the late 16th and early 17th century, with 19th and 20th century alterations.

This Norman doorway at All Saints' church dates from around 1190, and is built into the north wall of the church. A Norman doorway also survives on the southern side of the church, but is now blocked up.

All Saints' church lych-gate.

The remarkable late 19th century transformation of St Mary's church can be largely attributed to three villagers. Firstly, James Jenkinson Bibby ran John Bibby & Co, a highly successful Liverpool-based shipping company, while he was also Chairman of the Liverpool Steamship Owners Association. J.J. Bibby transformed his business into a global concern before retiring to rural Shropshire. Besides creating three model farms and an extensive breeding stable, he made substantial contributions to the foundation of Clive School and the renovation of Hadnall Church. Secondly, Rev. John Cooper Wood was a graduate of St John's College, Cambridge, and he combined the roles of Headmaster of Halesowen Grammar School and Rector of the nearby St Kenelm-in-Romsley until he was appointed vicar of Clive in 1874. Finally, Thomas Meares was the son of a local farmer. Baptised in Clive Church in 1826, he was brought up in the village, but left penniless in 1844, and walked to Manchester where he was employed as a grocer's assistant. He subsequently became embroiled in the tea trade, eventually founding several retail companies and purchasing tea estates in Ceylon. He returned to Clive in 1873 and purchased Clive Hall, subsequently modernising the house and gardens over the next ten years before moving back to the village in 1884 upon his retirement.

Anyway, in 1883, J.J.Bibby bought the patronage of All Saints' church from the governors of Shrewsbury School for £700. The Carlisle architect, Charles John Ferguson, was immediately engaged to design a complete modernisation of the building, and his bold design proposed four new windows, an organ chamber and new vestry to the north aspect, with a doubling up of the south-facing windows to six lights. He also included a proposed tower to house the new font.

The masonry and roofing work were overseen by Treasure & Sons of Castle Foregate, Shrewsbury. They soon transformed the appearance of the church by using red and grey dressed ashlar to encase the existing stonework both inside and out; only a small section of original stonework in the south wall, incorporating the Norman doorway, was left exposed.

Inside, a major design feature was the chancel arch, as it heightened the oak roof, now supported on hammer beams, with an angel carved at the end of every collar truss. Two further arches framed the organ chamber and the vestry in the north wall of the chancel, while the surviving Norman south doorway was encased by a new porch. Elsewhere, the quality of the internal fittings, such as the font, pews, lectern, pulpit, choir stalls and screens are renowned for their beauty, thanks to the engagement of some of the finest Victorian carvers in England. All of the pews contain a unique end-panel, while the altar features a fine marble top surrounded by a carved wooden frame of exceptional quality. Finally, the reredos, which consists of an alabaster representation of the Last Supper, was crafted by the renowned London firm of Farmer and Brindley, sculptors and wood carvers who also completed the reredos for St Paul's Cathedral. As Arthur Mee states, "It forms a fitting centrepiece to reflect the craftsmanship of the very best English carvers of this period".

This work was then surpassed by the build of the tower and spire, both in memory of J.J. Bibby's beloved wife, Sarah, who died in 1892. C.J. Ferguson was again hired to design, which he did in the late-Decorated style. A new south entrance was added and a ringing chamber and belfry were built to house six bells, while above the belfry a viewing walkway with balustrading provided a panoramic view of the surrounding countryside. Finally, the broach spire was added, and in August 1894, a crowning finial cross was placed in position by Sarah Bibby, J.J.'s daughter, who agreed to be hauled up to the pinnacle of the spire in a wicker basket to complete the build.

When J.J. Bibby died in February 1897, his son Frank commissioned Clayton and Bell of Regent Street, London to install a further twelve windows in his father's memory.

Clive Quirk Alert: Embedded

In recognition of his major leadership in the All Saints' church re-building programme of the late 19th century, the Reverend John Cooper Wood was commemorated in the construction of both the lych-gate and Clive Village Hall. His wedding ring has also been embedded into the stem of the ancient 16th century chalice cup that is still used in communion services.

Three's-Up!

	COMLEY	**CROWSNEST**	**GREETE**
STATUS:	Hamlet	Hamlet at south end of Snailbeach	Hamlet
DISTRICT:	South Shropshire (1974-2009); Shropshire (post-2009)	Shrewsbury & Atcham (1974-2009); Shropshire (post-2009)	South Shropshire (1974-2009); Shropshire (post-2009)
EARLIEST RECORD:	*Comley*, 1766 (John Ellis map)	*Crowsnest*, 1850s	*Grete*, 1183
MEANING:	Woodland clearing in the valley.	Unknown	Gravelly place.
DERIVATION:	From the Old English words *cumb* (valley) and *lēah* (wood).	Unknown	From the Old English word *grēote* (gravel).

Comley Quarry, one of Britain's most important geological and palaeontological sites.

Entrance to Snailbeach mine. The plaque reads "SNAILBEACH MINE CO 1848".

St James' church at Greete.

Three's Up Trivia!

Comley is an isolated hamlet in central Shropshire. Its most notable feature is Comley Quarry, an SSSI site located on the north-east slope of Caer Caradoc, as this is where Britain's earliest trilobites were found. The fossils were discovered by Charles Lapworth in 1888, and they date from the Cambrian period some 550 million years ago, thus making Comley Quarry one of Britain's most important geological and palaeontological sites. The site includes rock strata from both the Lower and Middle Cambrian eras, and Lapworth's discovery was the first evidence that rocks of this age are present in Britain. Meanwhile, the faunas found here, such as Brachiopoda, Pteropoda, Gasteropoda, etc., provide a basis for correlating the British Lower and Middle Cambrian succession with North America, Scandinavia and Central Europe. Meanwhile, the most important *ecological* aspect of the site is the fact that dormice live here!

Next up, **Crowsnest** is a hamlet a mile north-east of Stiperstones and comprises the southern tip of the village of Snailbeach where you will find Crowsnest Dingle, a steep-sided valley. Crowsnest was originally a terminal on the Snailbeach District Railways, a narrow-gauge railway built in the 1870s to carry lead ore from mines in the Stiperstones area to Pontesbury where the ore was trans-shipped to the Great Western Railway's Minsterley branch line. As for Snailbeach mine, this was Shropshire's largest and richest lead mine, which is reputed to have yielded the greatest volume of lead per acre of any mine in Europe. Much later, barytes from Snailbeach Lead Mine were used to smother fuel cells after an accident at the Windscale nuclear reactor site in Cumbria.

Meanwhile, it is from these parts that an old legend comes about the Reynolds family. Apparently they were driven out of their farm by two bogies (think fairies) who had the appearance of an old man and woman. When the Reynolds' left, the bogies followed them to their new home and hid inside a salt cellar!

Finally, **Greete** is a hamlet close to the Herefordshire border. It is home to the Grade II listed St James' church, of which the nave dates from the 12th century and the chancel the 13th, with 14th century windows added on the south side of the nave. Further alterations were made in the 15th, 18th and 19th centuries.

A mile west of Greete is the 17th century Grade II listed Stoke Court. Meanwhile, on the western outskirts of Greete is the Grade II listed Lower Cottage, an attractive Tudor house with a staircase in a chimney! The core of the house dates from the late 15th century, while the rest is 17th century with 20th century alterations.

NAME (STATUS):	**COTON** (Village, Hamlet)
POPULATION:	Village: c.100; Hamlet: c.20
DISTRICT:	Village: North Shropshire (1974-2009); Hamlet: Bridgnorth (1974-2009); both Shropshire (post-2009)
EARLIEST RECORD:	*Cote*, 1086 (Domesday Book); Domesday Book also names *Ludecote*, aka Coton upon Tern, but which no longer exists.
MEANING:	Usually means "place at the cottages or huts".
DERIVATION:	From the Old English word *cot* (cottage, hut or shelter) in the dative plural form *cotum*.

Coton Geographical Trivia: Five Cotons

Today, the place-name "Coton" appears twice in Shropshire. The most northerly is located halfway between Wem and Whitchurch, and is known alternatively as Coton-near-Hollinwood. The linear village lies on a 2-mile stretch of the B5476, with the hamlet of Cotonwood lying half a mile to the west. The other Shropshire Coton is in the south-east of the county and is also known as Coton-near-Alveley. There is also a Coton Hill just north of the centre of Shrewsbury while a fifth Shropshire Coton (Coton upon Tern) is mentioned in Domesday Book (1086), but no longer exists.

The Dog and Bull is located in the more northerly Shropshire Coton.

Coton Church: Coton Methodist Chapel

Coton Methodist Chapel was built in 1888, and is located in the hamlet of Cotonwood. Prior to the chapel build, the Wem and Prees Green Circuit for 1874 refers to services at "Cotton" – this being a common spelling and pronunciation in early records of the place. Today, the chapel is part of the Northern Area of the Shropshire and Marches Methodist Circuit, holding around one service per month.

Coton Historic Trivia: Tale of Two Coton Halls

We will start with the more northerly Shropshire Coton Hall, which belonged to Admiral George Bowen in the early 19th century, but subsequently passed to the Honyman baronets, before eventually passing to the Viscounts Hill in 1924. The title had been created in 1842 for General Rowland Hill – who had also confusingly been the 4th Baronet Hill and the 1st Baron Hill at varying stages of his life.

Meanwhile, the more southerly Coton Hall has the longer history and is more celebrated. From around 1300, the manor of Coton belonged to the de la Lee family who would almost certainly have been of Norman descent. There was a medieval Coton Hall back then, and it was from this house that some of a certain General Robert E. Lee's ancestors left for America in the mid-17th century. The Lees originally went there to trade, but one branch of the family settled in America, acquiring land and power. Two of them, Richard Henry and Francis Lightfoot Lee, were the only brothers to sign the American Declaration of Independence, while Robert Lee's father was Henry "Light Horse Harry" Lee III, a famous soldier of the American War of Independence, where he was known for his courage in fighting the British. It is highly likely that Henry Lee III was responsible for the deaths of soldiers from Shropshire – as the 53rd Regiment (later the Shropshire Regiment), were all-but wiped out, with the remainder captured at the Battle of Saratoga in 1777. Henry Lee III resigned from the army as soon as the British were defeated, and settled down to raise a family.

That family included General Robert E. Lee (1807-1870), who was destined to become one of the most famous names in the American Civil War (1861-1865). He graduated from the West Point military school with not a single demerit point – the first and only time this has ever happened. However, he is best known as the finest commander of the Confederate States Army, where he commanded the Army of Northern Virginia in the American Civil War from 1862 until his surrender in 1865. As well as being a top graduate of the United States Military Academy, Lee was an exceptional officer and military engineer in the United States Army for thirty-two years. During this time, he served

Coton Methodist Church is located in the hamlet of Cotonwood.

These two stunning timber-framed cottages are located in the more northerly Shropshire Coton, and sit opposite each other on a quiet country lane.

throughout the United States, distinguished himself during the Mexican–American War, and served as Superintendent of the United States Military Academy.

Little remains today of the Coton Hall that Robert E. Lee's ancestors would have known, although there is the ruin of a 13th century chapel in the grounds. However, the best surviving remains are underground, where the former Coton Hall's cellar is two storeys deep and in the lower of the two levels there survives an entrance to a tunnel which runs all the way to Alveley village 2 miles away! That said, it has been blocked off beyond the chapel for safety reasons.

The previous Coton Hall was replaced by the present Georgian building in around 1800 for Harry Lancelot Lee on an estate of some 5,000 acres. However, Harry was the last in a long line of Lees to live at Coton Hall, and when he died in 1821 the house was immediately sold to James Foster (1786-1853), an ironmaster and coalmaster of Stourbridge. By 1851, the estate was owned by the Reverend Edward Ward Wakeman (1801-1855), but he died four years later with the estate passing to his eldest son, Offley Francis Drake Wakeman (1836-1865) when he came of age in 1857. Alas, Offley Wakeman suffered a tragically young death when he ruptured a blood vessel whilst playing cricket, and Coton Hall passed to his youngest brother, Edward Maltby Wakeman (1846-1926). Edward was succeeded by his daughter, Gladys Louisa, but by the 1940s, the hall had passed to the Thompson family.

In 1878 the chapel roof finally collapsed and all the Lee monuments were moved to Alveley church. The house itself was extended in about 1860, when a new wing and an Italianate tower were added, but apart from that the house has survived remarkably well, with all fireplaces and cornices being the originals.

The main road through Coton-near-Alveley.

NAME (STATUS):	**EATON** (Village; Hamlet)
POPULATION:	c.25 (Eaton-under-Heywood parish is 171); less than 10!
DISTRICT:	Both South Shropshire (1974-2009); Shropshire (post-2009)
EARLIEST RECORD:	*Eton*, 1227; *Eton*, 1252
MEANING:	Farmstead or estate on a river.
DERIVATION:	From the Old English words *ēa* (river) and *tūn* (farmstead); the Eaton hamlet is situated on the River Onny while Eaton village is on a tributary of the Onny.

Eaton Geographical Trivia

There are two Eatons in Shropshire, as well as Eaton Constantine. The smaller of the two Eatons (the hamlet) is on the A489, around 3 miles east of Bishop's Castle, while the larger (the village) is another 8 miles east again in Hopedale, and is also known as Eaton-under-Heywood, to distinguish it from the other Eaton. Eaton-under-Heywood is located alongside Wenlock Edge, and there is a path leading from the village to the top of the edge which is known as Jacobs Ladder. Finally, Eaton Constantine lies south-west of the Wrekin, and is part of the Leighton and Eaton Constantine civil parish which had a population of 467 at the 2011 census.

Eaton Church: St Edith's

St Edith's church at Eaton-under-Heywood is a major gem, and is Grade I listed. Before launching into its superlatives though, it is worth mentioning that there is some doubt as to which St Edith it is dedicated to. Some experts believe she was St Edith of Polesworth, the daughter of King Egbert of Wessex, who had founded a Benedictine nunnery in the Forest of Arden. Others believe the church is named after St Edith of Wilton, the daughter of Edgar the Peaceful, King of England from 959 to 975, and who also became a nun (that's Edith, not Edgar).

The current church was founded in the 12th century and the nave is still the original, while the tower and chancel date from the early part of the 13th century. Alterations were made in the 14th and 15th centuries, while the church underwent a major restoration in 1869 by W. J. Hopkins. The tub font is still the Norman original (see page 34 for photo) while, somewhat unusually, the whole church rests on a plinth!

The church is also unusual in that its tower is located at the mid-point of the south side of the church, as opposed to appearing at the standard west end, while there are three enormous buttresses on the north side, presumably to counteract the weight of the tower. The positioning of the tower may have something to do with the fact that the church stands on a slope, with the floor of the nave rising from west to east. As for the tower, this was built in three stages with an arched doorway and a round-headed lancet window in the first stage, two-light bell openings under round arches in the second stage, and the top stage decorated with a battlemented parapet, with each of the eight merlons surmounted by a pinnacle. Two Norman windows survive in the north wall of the nave and one in the south, while the two oldest bells of the "ring of three" date from 1615 and 1622.

Inside, the church is breath-taking. The wooden nave roof dates from the 15th century, and includes tie-beams, with collar beams on arched braces, while the lower and more ornate wooden chancel roof dates from around 1600, and includes large bosses carved with foliage and grotesques. Where the chancel and nave roofs meet, there is an impressive wooden tympanum on which there are three large coats of arms of local landowners, added in the 1860s, while there are a series of carved wooden faces along the feet of the rafters.

Elsewhere, the superb pulpit is carved with tracery and has a backplate dated to 1670, although the lower part of the pulpit is older, possibly 16th century. The north wall of the chancel is home to a 14th century

St Edith's church at Eaton-under-Heywood dates from the 12th century. Note the unusual central south tower which is early 13th century.

The north side of St Edith's church contains those three large buttresses – presumably built to counteract the central south tower.

recess with ballflower decoration, containing a 14th century life-sized wooden effigy, while the chancel also contains three widely-spaced plain lancet windows of equal height, and of a highly unusual design. The church is also home to a late medieval chest.

As for today, St Edith's is still an active Anglican parish church, and is part of a united benefice with that of St Andrew at Hope Bowdler.

The nave of St Edith's church, looking through to the chancel.

Close-up of the tympanum between nave and chancel.

This effigy set in a recess, is thought to date from the 14th century.

Eaton Historical Trivia: Middlehope Castle and Eaton Manor

A mile or so south of Eaton-under-Heywood, sited on a small ridge and bisected by a sunken lane, are the earthwork remains of Middlehope Castle, a medieval motte and bailey castle. The motte was 42ft (13m) in diameter and situated inside a 164ft (50m) bailey. The earthwork remains have been badly impacted by centuries of ploughing but there are enough to suggest that the castle was never finished.

Eaton-under-Heywood is also home to Eaton Manor, which sits across the road from the church. The building is Grade II listed and dates from the mid-to-late 18th century. It has been owned by the Madeley family since 1934, as a farmhouse. However, the current generation have diversified, converting rooms and buildings into self-catering holiday accommodation. As they went about restoring the properties, they found all sorts of hidden historic features, such as a whole inglenook fireplace, thick beams, wattle and daub walls, an old bread oven and, in another inglenook, a cooking range made at Coalbrookdale and dating from around 1900! Eaton Manor also has some rare trees, including black poplars and a 1,000-year-old oak.

Eaton Manor at Eaton-under-Heywood dates from the mid-to-late 18th century.

Eaton Quirk Alert: Road to Nowhere and the Chicken Range

St Edith's church at Eaton-under-Heywood is described on its website as "the church at the end of the road". This is because it is indeed at the end of a road where there is nowhere else to go – as Eaton is one of very few places in England that has only one route in and the same single route out – this being from the north-west. With Wenlock Edge rising behind the village, the road ends at Eaton, and no one has ever constructed a road to link Eaton to the villages on the other side of the edge.

Meanwhile, the former chicken shed at Eaton Manor was converted a few years ago into a 70-metre indoor archery range! Furthermore, it was used for training by the English team prior to the 2010 Commonwealth Games, and also hosted the Olympic squad in the run up to the London Olympics in 2012.

NAME (STATUS):	**GREAT BOLAS** (Village)
POPULATION:	320 (2001 census)
DISTRICT:	The Wrekin (1974-1998); Telford & Wrekin (post-1998)
EARLIEST RECORD:	*Belewas*, 1198; *Boulewas*, 1265
MEANING:	Riverside land liable to flooding.
DERIVATION:	The latter part of the name "Bolas" is derived from the Old English word *wæsse*, also meaning "riverside land liable to flood". The origin of the first part of the name is uncertain, but may derive from the Old English word *bogel*, meaning "small river-bend or meander", in a genitive plural form.

LEFT: *St John the Baptist's church at Great Bolas.* CENTRE: *The main road through Great Bolas.* RIGHT: *An old cross in St John's churchyard.*

Great Bolas Geographical Trivia

Great Bolas is also known as Bolas Magna, while the above river derivation relates to the village sitting between the Rivers Tern and Meese, which are less than a mile apart at Great Bolas. Just to the west of Great Bolas is the hamlet of Little Bolas, while Meeson (another hamlet) is located south of the River Meese, and was formerly a separate township of Great Bolas parish. Today, all three places are part of the civil parish of Waters Upton, which had a population of 951 at the 2011 census.

Great Bolas Church: St John the Baptist

St John the Baptist's church dates largely from the late 17th and early 18th century, although some 14th century pews survive, as do two stones in the east window which probably date back to the original 13th century church. The chancel was added in the 1690s and the tower followed in the 18th century, with the nave also being rebuilt at this time as well. The new church was opened on 23rd June 1728.

Great Bolas Historical Trivia: Origins and Foresters

Returning to the origins of the place-name, another possible source for the first syllable of the word "Bolas" is from the Old English *bold*, meaning "house". A less likely alternative is the Old Scandinavian word *ból*, meaning "farm" – less likely as the Vikings didn't settle in what would later become Shropshire territory.

At the time of Domesday Book (1086), Great Bolas was part of the manor of Isombridge, and was held by Roger de Montgomery. It was probably he, or his son, Hugh, who founded the Forestership of Shropshire and the Chief Forester lived in Great Bolas – hence the Foresters of Shropshire were also known as the Foresters of Bolas. By the end of the 13th century, Great Bolas was owned by one of the foresters who looked after the Royal Forest of Wrekin, and hence a twice-annual court, and gallows, were set up in Great Bolas to try and execute those found guilty of breaking the harsh set of forest laws, particularly poachers.

Great Bolas Quirk Alert: Henry Cecil

Henry Cecil (1754-1804), 1st Marquess of Exeter, was a man who fell into debt after his first wife eloped with another man in 1789. He sought refuge in the home of Thomas Hoggins in Great Bolas, claiming his name was John Jones. Less than a year later, in April 1790, he married Thomas's daughter, Sarah Hoggins – under the name of John Jones! Of course, as Henry Cecil, he was still married, so he got a divorce from the Consistory Court, as well as an Act of Parliament pronouncing him able to re-marry. Therefore, a year further on, in October 1791, Sarah Hoggins married the same man again, with the groom this time named as Henry Cecil! That said, the name John Jones was still used after the second marriage, as it appears in rate books as well as in Great Bolas Registers at the time!

Later, Henry Cecil bought land in the village and built Bolas Villa, eventually gifting it to his godchild, Creswell Tayleur. It was the latter who had the house enlarged and changed the name to Burghley Villa. Alfred, Lord Tennyson's poem *The Lord of Burleigh*, was based on Henry Cecil's story.

Three's-Up!

	HARTON	**HINTS**	**HOO**
POPULATION:	c.10	c.120	Lots of exotic animals!
STATUS:	Hamlet	Village	Hamlet/Farm
DISTRICT:	Shropshire	Shropshire	Telford and Wrekin
EARLIEST RECORD:	Unknown	*Hintes*, 1242	Unknown
MEANING:	Probably farmstead where harts are kept.	Place on the roads or paths.	Probably place at the spur of land.
DERIVATION:	From the Old English words *heorot* (hart or stag) and *tūn* (farmstead).	From the Welsh word *hynt* (road or path).	From the Old English word *hōh* (dative *hōe*), meaning "heel of land or projecting hill-spur".

Harton is located towards the western end of Wenlock Edge. It is also home to Harton Hollow, a wooded area located on an ancient barrier reef, where plants such as herb paris, sanicle and sweet woodruff thrive on a limestone bed, making this one of the richest areas of woodland in Shropshire. Harton Hollow lies on the brow of the ridge with the Marches Way footpath twisting its way through the woodland.

Meanwhile, the hamlet of Harton is home to only two homes, both of which are Grade II listed and both of which date from the early 17th century – these being Harton Manor and Harton Farmhouse. Bizarrely, though, there are actually more Grade II listed buildings in Harton than there are homes – as one of the barns belonging to Harton Farmhouse is also Grade II listed – and also dates from the 17th century.

The Grade II listed Harton Farmhouse in Harton dates from the early 17th century but with 19th century alterations.

Another view of Harton Farmhouse.

The barn of Harton Farmhouse is also Grade II listed and dates from the 17th century.

This is Harton Manor, a Grade II listed early 17th century house – with great chimneys – and the only other house in Harton.

Harton Hollow, just south of Harton, is one of the richest areas of woodland in Shropshire.

Next, **Hints** is a village located on the southern slopes of Clee Hill with fantastic views to the south. The name Hints derives from the Welsh Celtic word *hynt*, so it is likely that this area was occupied by Welsh speakers up until some point during the Anglo-Saxon colonisation of England. Hints belongs to the parish of Coreley, which is centred on the neighbouring village of the same name, and is also home to the Grade II listed 16th century Hints Farmhouse.

Meanwhile, **Hoo** appears on close-up maps as an area between Horton and Preston upon the Weald Moors. However, if you visit the area, the signpost that greets you is The Humbers – which *doesn't* appear on close-up maps – but which stands opposite the entrance to the 32 acres of woodland and paddocks occupied by Hoo Farm Animal Kingdom!

Hoo Farm itself is around 200 years old, and has previously been a dairy farm and a Christmas tree nursery in the 1980s. Then, in 1988, the farm was bought by the Dorrell family, who turned it into Hoo Farm Country Park, where the public were offered to cut and dig their own trees. The farm was also home to a number of native farm animals, but in the early 1990s, the Dorrells began to add others, such as ostrich, llama, deer, foxes, owls, raccoons and a small number of reptiles – and Hoo Farm Animal Kingdom was born. As the site expanded, more animals arrived and in 2008, Hoo Farm became fully zoo-licensed, making it Shropshire's first zoo. More recently, more exotic animals have arrived such as capybara, caracal, coati, lemurs, otters, servals, skunks, wallabies, warthog… and even crocodiles!

The northern entrance to the village of Hints.

The centre of Hints.

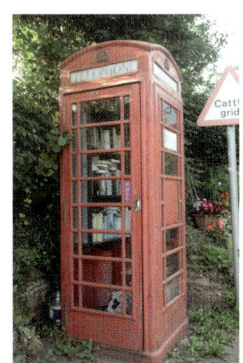

Hints Library!

NAME (STATUS):	**HIGHLEY** (Large Village)
POPULATION:	3,605
DISTRICT:	Bridgnorth (1974-2009); Shropshire (post-2009)
EARLIEST RECORD:	*Hugelei*, 1086 (Domesday Book)
MEANING:	Woodland clearing of a man called Hugga.
DERIVATION:	From the Old English personal name *Hugga*, plus the Old English word *lēah* (wood, woodland clearing or glade).
FAMOUS RESIDENTS:	Gerry Hitchens (footballer), Stan Jones (footballer), Aubrey Scriven (footballer), David Tristram (playwright).

Highley Pubs: The Ship Inn and The Malt Shovel

The Ship Inn dates from 1770, and was built alongside the River Severn, largely to serve bargemen. Meanwhile, the Malt Shovel dates from 1684 when it was built on land that was known as Little Hill. It was probably a farmhouse, as the Perry family lived and farmed here in the late 18th, century. It was believed to have been converted into a public house in 1863, but the first mention of it being called The Malt Shovel Inn is later, in 1896. The building has been altered and extended a number of times since the original 17th century farmhouse was built, as the farmhouse faced west with views over the Clee Hills.

The Ship Inn at Highley dates from 1770.

Church House at Highley dates from the 16th century.

Highley Church: St Mary's

St Mary's church dates back to Norman times, with the oldest surviving parts (the majority of the nave and chancel) built in the early 1100s. The tower was added in the 15th century, while the roof of the nave and chancel was replaced in the 16th, and includes 33 oak bosses, finely carved with Tudor flowers. Since then, the roof

St Mary's church at Highley.

has been further altered, the interior re-modelled, and a gallery fitted and later removed.

Highley Historical Trivia: Through the Ages

Highley's Norman church was built using locally quarried stone, and the quarrying industry continued here for many centuries. In fact, stone from these quarries was used in the build of Worcester Cathedral, which was built in stages between 1084 and 1504.

During medieval times, Highley prospered as a farming community, but was devastated by poor harvests and the Black Death of the 14th century. It was during this time that the village was home to William Langland (1332-1386), England's greatest medieval poet, and presumed author of the Middle English alliterative verse commonly known as *Piers Plowman*, an allegory with a complex variety of religious themes. Meanwhile, during the Wars of the Roses, Highley belonged to the

Highley railway station on the Severn Valley Railway.

powerful Mortimer family, but eventually passed to the victorious Tudors.

Coal mining arrived in Highley in the early 19th century, with mines at Stanley and nearby Billingsley, but they were closed by the 1820s. The Severn Valley Railway then arrived in 1862, but the quiet Highley was changed forever when coal mining returned in 1878. This time, the Highley Mining Company sank much deeper pits of up to 300 yards deep to get at the 4ft-thick high-quality seam of coal called the Broach Coal. The seam covered many square miles beneath Highley and a second mine was soon opened at Kinlet. Then in the early 20th century, the former mine at Billingsley was redeveloped and expanded by a rival company.

The effect on Highley was a population increase from 400 in 1871 to almost 2,000 by 1911. Many of these inhabitants were miners and their families, who lived in houses built by the mining companies – such as rows of cottages on Silverdale Terrace, built in 1885, and houses on Church Street built for the wealthier miners and officials. The Billingsley Colliery Company also started to build a new "Garden Village" at the northern end of Highley, while shops, pubs, a chapel and a cinema followed. Alas, after World War I, Billingsley Colliery closed, although Highley and Kinlet mines remained profitable. Then in 1935, a new colliery opened across the River Severn at Alveley. This was connected to Highley village by a bridge known as Pit Bridge, and to Highley Colliery by an underground tunnel.

Alveley Colliery was expanded by the National Coal Board in the 1950s and employed over 1,000 men, producing 300,000 tons of coal a year. During the 1960s, over a million pounds was spent on modernising Alveley Colliery, the intention being to sustain it for another fifty years. However, they hadn't counted on the resulting subsidence and waterlogging, and the mine had to close in January 1969. However, Pit Bridge remained open until 2006 – albeit to bridleway traffic only, due to subsidence from the steep valley sides. Meanwhile the mine area on the Alveley side was converted into an industrial estate in the late 1960s, and then was subsequently landscaped into the Severn Valley Country Park in the late 1980s. Today, it is home to public artwork and a sculpture trail, known as the Seam Pavement Trail – a series of bronze plaques depicting Highley's past and includes miner's nicknames taken from archive information within the local community. One plaque, Plough and Lady, depicts Lady Godiva, who owned Highley Manor in the 11th century.

In January 1975, serial killer Donald Nielson kidnapped seventeen-year-old Highley resident, Lesley Whittle. Nielson, later dubbed The Black Panther, had already committed several murders and an untold number of burglaries and bank robberies. Lesley was taken by Nielson from her bedroom, where he left a note demanding £50,000 for her return – but due to a series of circumstances, the money wasn't delivered on time. Poor Lesley was found strangled near Kidsgrove in Staffordshire. Nielson was captured in December 1975, and sentenced to life imprisonment.

Today, Highley also has two stations on the Severn Valley Railway, a heritage railway that runs for 16 miles (26 km) along the Severn Valley from Bridgnorth to Kidderminster. Highley Station is a decent-sized Victorian railway station and also home to a museum of village life, housed within a vintage post office sorting carriage. The other station, Country Park Halt, is an unmanned request halt near the bridge for the country park. Passengers wishing to board the train at the halt stop the train by holding out their hand, as if hailing a bus, and those wishing to alight are advised to speak to the guard of the train before it leaves the previous station.

This late medieval cross with an elaborately carved base and octagonal shaft can be found in St Mary's churchyard.

The Manor House at Highley dates from the mid-to-late 16th century.

NAME (STATUS):	**HOPE** (Village)
POPULATION:	c.50
DISTRICT:	South Shropshire (1974-2009); Shropshire (post-2009)
EARLIEST RECORD:	*Hope*, 1242
MEANING:	Small enclosed valley or enclosed plot of land.
DERIVATION:	From the Old English word *hop* (small enclosed valley or enclosure in marsh or moorland).

Hope Trivia: Holy Trinity Church, Hope Valley and Shropshire's Other Hopes

Hope is a small village located in a wooded vale in the west of Shropshire, 10 miles south-west of Shrewsbury. Four miles from the Welsh border, Hope is home to the 19th century Holy Trinity church, Hope Cemetery and Hope Primary School. Holy Trinity church belongs to the Stiperstones Group of Churches, and is part of the Pontesbury Deanery in the Diocese of Hereford.

Holy Trinity church at Hope dates from the 19th century.

The Old School House at Hope.

Meanwhile, just north-east of the village is Hope Valley, a rejuvenated oak wood which is run by the Shropshire Wildlife Trust. As their website states: "oaks do not die easily". They say this, because this steep valley wood was felled in the 1960s and conifers planted instead, so it appeared as if the old woodland had gone forever. However, from their broad and mossy coppice stools the oaks sprang back to life, sending out six or seven slender trunks each! Recognising the wood's potential for restoration, the Trust bought it in 1981. Most of the conifers have now been felled, and in late spring bluebells once again grace the woodland, with yellow archangel and early purple orchids also re-emerging.

As well as the valley in southern Shropshire known as The Hope (see page 148), Shropshire is also home to the villages of Hope Bagot and Hope Bowdler. The former lies close to the Herefordshire border, around 4 miles east of Ludlow, while the latter is a mile and a half south-east of Church Stretton. Meanwhile, Hope Bowdler Hill rises to the north of Hope Bowdler, and includes a number of summits, the tallest of which is 1,398ft (426m), while Hope Bowdler itself is situated at 728ft (222m) above sea level.

St John the Baptist church at Hope Bagot dates from the 12th century, with 13th, 14th and 17th century additions.

St Andrew's church at Hope Bowdler dates from 1862, but includes material from its 12th century predecessor, particularly in the tower.

Three's-Up!

	HOWLE	**INWOOD**	**LEIGH**
POPULATION:	c.30	c.20	Less than 10
STATUS:	Hamlet	Hamlet	Hamlet
DISTRICT:	Telford and Wrekin	Shropshire	Shropshire
EARLIEST RECORD:	*Hugle*, 1086 (Domesday Book)	Unknown	*Leigh*, early 14th century
MEANING:	Place at the mound or hillock.	Possibly wood of a man called Ina.	Usually means place at the wood or woodland clearing.
DERIVATION:	From the Old English word *hugol* (mound or hillock).	From the Old English personal name, *Ina*, plus the Old English word *wudu* (wood or forest).	From the Old English word *lēah* (wood, woodland clearing or glade).

Howle Pool.

Looking down the Inwood Valley, with Caer Caradoc in the background.

Howle is located 5 miles north-west of Newport, and is home to Howle Manor, Howle Pool Farm and Howle Pool. One alternative theory to the *hugol* name derivation above is that it may have been named after an Anglo-Saxon called Hyge. As for Howle Pool, this is a still-water fishery owned by Howle Pool Fishery, and is most noted for carp and roach. There is also a holy well south of Howle, near the road to Tibberton, while a Grade II listed windmill can be found about 400 yards south of Howle Manor.

Meanwhile, **Inwood** is a hamlet consisting of two farms, a handful of houses and The Oaks country house, all stretched out along a narrow country road which climbs up one side of the Inwood Valley. The valley, in turn, is part of the north-eastern stretch of the Long Mynd, much of which is owned by the National Trust.

Inwood is also home to a feature known as the Inwood Horse Ring, a flat, round area on the side of a hill, and which may have been used in the past for coralling or selling horses. The National Trust has cut back the bracken to ensure the feature is more easily visible.

Finally, **Leigh** is a hamlet on the B4499, 10 miles south-west of Shrewsbury and close to the Welsh border. It is comprised of a farm/Leigh Hall and one other building, along with one post box! Leigh Hall is the site of a scheduled monument – this being the earthwork and standing structural and buried remains of a medieval moated site. It is thought to be the later centre of the manor of Leigh, probably constructed in the early 14th century by Robert Corbet, who by 1324 had become the local Member of Parliament. The Corbets of Leigh held the manor until 1748 – although by 1667-68 the manor house was described as "lately burnt, destroyed or demolished", possibly the result of damage caused during the English Civil War. The adjacent Grade II listed farmhouse at Leigh Hall was constructed in the late 17th century, and replaced the former manor house.

NAME (STATUS):	**KNOCKIN (Village)**
POPULATION:	282
DISTRICT:	Oswestry (1974-2009); Shropshire (post-2009)
EARLIEST RECORD:	*Cnochin*, 1165
MEANING:	A little hillock.
DERIVATION:	From the Celtic word *cnöccïn* (hill or hillock).

Knockin Church: St Mary's

St Mary's church was founded by Ralph Le Strange between 1182 and 1195 as a chapel for nearby Knockin Castle. Prior to this Knockin was part of Kinnerley parish where there had been a church since the 6th century, but in 1197 Knockin church was separated from its mother church.

The Bradford Arms is named after the Earls of Bradford, who owned much of Knockin until recently. The family coat of arms appears on the pub sign, with the family motto: Nec temere nec timide (Neither rashly nor timidly).

St Mary's church still has its Norman chancel, nave and north aisle today, as well as a Norman doorway, while the font is Norman, too (see photo on page 35). Alas, in 1767, a terrible fire left the church gutted, resulting in the north aisle being removed and the four Norman arches filled in. The churchyard was then enclosed by a wall in 1817, and according to Arthur

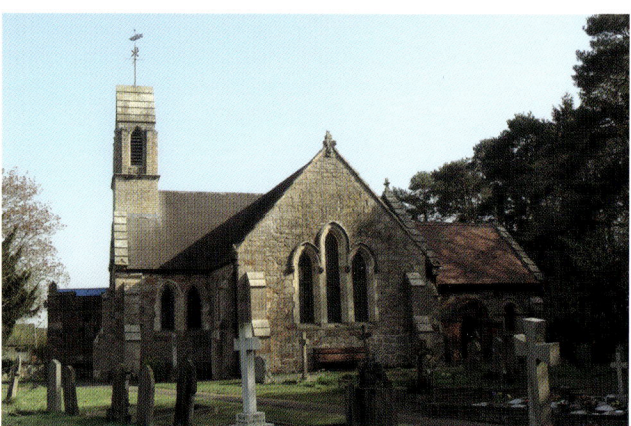

St Mary's church, Knockin dates from the 12th century.

Mee, it was built using stones from the demolished Knockin Castle. It was also in 1817 that the graveyard was first consecrated; prior to this, burials took place at neighbouring Kinnerley.

The church was then heavily restored in 1846-47, which was when the south transept was added. The lych gate was added in 1872 and the chancel enlarged between 1900 and 1910. Then in 1920, the gallery was removed, but the red sandstone porch was added in memory of the Rev N. G. Walker, while the roof was renewed in 1956 and the transept rafters altered. Finally, in 1975, the parish became part of the united benefice of Kinnerley with Melverley and Knockin with Maesbrook – with Maesbury joining the united benefice in 2011.

Today, a bricked-up doorway can still be seen in the chancel which dates back to when the priest would have entered from the castle side.

Sadly, this building is no longer The Knockin Shop! This was the affectionate local name for the village shop for many decades, but the shop recently closed down and is now in the process of being converted to a private home – although note that the post box is still in-situ!

The Old Forge at Knockin. Generations of the Maddox family were blacksmiths here. Indeed, a William Madocke was paid in the church warden's accounts as far back as 1664, this for mending the church chest!

Knockin Historical Trivia: Knockin Castle, Tornados and MERLIN

Knockin is home to a tree-covered mound that marks the location of Knockin Castle. The castle was of a motte and bailey design and was built by Guy le Strange between 1154 and 1160. The castle remained the main holding of the le Strange family for several centuries, although it was damaged in the First Barons' War (1215-1217) during the reign of King John and then repaired by John le Strange. However, by 1540, the castle was described as "ruinous", and was eventually demolished in 1817 when stone from the castle was used to build a wall around St Mary's church. Rumour also has it that many other buildings in Knockin today contain stone taken from the castle!

The Norman nave, chancel and north aisle of St Mary's church.

Records and accounts started being kept at Knockin after 1660, with the 1676 census showing the parish to be home to 65 people, all of whom were affiliated to the Church of England, with both Roman Catholic and non-conformist categories registered as zero.

In more "recent" times, Knockin and Kinnerley Cricket Club was founded in 1862, while over a century later, the cricket pitch and village were struck by an F1/T2 tornado on 23rd November 1981. Today, the cricket pitch is one of only a few areas of Knockin still owned by the Earl of Bradford – as the family recently sold off large parts of the village to finance other projects.

The remains of the motte of Knockin Castle, which dates from the mid-12th century.

Finally, Knockin is also home to one of the radio telescopes that make up the Jodrell Bank MERLIN (Multi-Element Radio Linked Interferometer Network) radio telescope array. The array is run from Jodrell Bank Observatory in Cheshire by the University of Manchester, on behalf of the Science and Technology Facilities Council (STFC) as a National Facility. The array links six observation stations in Cambridgeshire, Worcestershire, Shropshire (at Knockin) and three in Cheshire that together form a powerful telescope with an effective aperture of over 217 kilometres.

Old House at Knockin is a Grade II listed early 17th century house.

Knockin Quirk Alert: Organs, a Sheep Wash and a Conservation Area

Knockin's church organ was installed in 1907 and has always been played by a member of the Owen family. Meanwhile, built into the stream, opposite the castle mound is the old sheep wash which has recently been restored, as has the old pound which is just below the road to Maesbrook, at the other end of the village. Finally, The Avenue is an avenue of mature trees along the B4397 eastern approach to Knockin. The avenue and village centre have been designated a conservation area as a fine example of an estate village.

Knockin and Kinnerley Cricket Club was founded in 1862.

The radio telescope at Knockin forms part of the Jodrell Bank MERLIN radio telescope array.

House on the B4396 in Knockin.

NAME (STATUS):	**MORE** (Village and Civil Parish)
POPULATION:	121 (parish); village is c.25
DISTRICT:	South Shropshire (1974-2009); Shropshire (post-2009)
EARLIEST RECORD:	*La Mora*, 1181
MEANING:	The marsh.
DERIVATION:	From the Old English word *mōr* (moor, marshy ground or barren upland).

St Peter's church at More dates from the early 13th century.

St Peter's church has a large stone lychgate.

Church Farm at More dates from the early 17th century.

More Church: St Peter's

The Grade II* listed St Peter's church at More dates from the early 13th century, although its location on a raised circular enclosure suggests an earlier, perhaps pre-Norman foundation. However, the church was largely rebuilt in 1845 and then extended in 1871 – although the sturdy square tower does survive from the 13th century build, with its double pyramidal timber top and bellcote added in the 17th century; the three bells date from 1612, 1617 and 1624.

The church's oldest possessions, though, are two portions of Roman tessellated pavement inlaid into the floor (see page 20), said to have come from the Roman villa at Linley, which was excavated in 1855 – although another theory is that it was brought back from Italy by one of the More family after a European "Grand Tour". Meanwhile, the north transept is still the original, although this was added four hundred years after the tower, in 1640, and contains many memorials to the More family.

Elsewhere, the church has a black and white hammerbeam roof, old box pews, a reading desk with a Jacobean cornice and panels, an ancient chest with seven locks, and a library of old books given by Richard More during the reign of Charles II to "teach the minister sound doctrine".

More Historical Trivia: The Mores of More and Listed Buildings

The Mores of More came over with William the Conqueror in 1066, with Richard de la More falling at the Battle of Hastings. As a reward for his valour, Richard More's son received lands, including More in Shropshire. A later Sir Thomas More shared captivity with Edward II in Berkeley Castle in the early 14th century, while another Sir Thomas More was Henry VIII's famous Lord Chancellor. Meanwhile, a later Richard More was one of few Shropshire gentry to support Charles I during the English Civil War, and his son, Samuel, defended Hopton Castle, a Parliamentarian fortress. With only 31 men, he defended it for a month against a force of 500 Royalist soldiers. He did escape with his life, but the rest of the garrison were ruthlessly killed following their surrender. Finally, one of Samuel's sons, Robert (1703-1780), was a devoted botanist who returned from the Austrian Tyrol bringing with him the first larches to be planted in England.

Finally, the parish of More is home to a remarkable number of listed buildings. Linley Hall is Grade I listed, and dates from 1743-1778, while other buildings include the late 16th century Old Rectory and the 17th century Church Farm, More Farm and the Old Smithy. The Malthouse is late 18th century.

Looking from the nave through to the chancel at St Peter's church.

Some of the many memorials to the More family in the north transept, with the centrepiece in memory of Harriott Mary More (d.1851).

The heraldic arms of Richard More are also set into the chapel floor in the north transept. He was High Sheriff of Shropshire in 1619.

NAME (STATUS):	**MYDDLE** (Village)
POPULATION:	133
DISTRICT:	North Shropshire (1974-2009); Shropshire (post-2009)
EARLIEST RECORD:	*Mulleht*, 1086 (Domesday Book); *Muthla*, 1121
MEANING:	Possibly place at the confluence of streams.
DERIVATION:	From a derivative *(ge)mÿthel* of the Old English word *(ge)mÿthe*, meaning "confluence of rivers"; the Myddle village website also suggests "wood by the junction of the stream", presumably deriving part of the name from the Old English word *lēah* (wood, woodland clearing or glade).

Myddle Church: St Peter's

St Peter's church probably stands on the site of a much older church. However, the oldest part today is the 17th century tower, thought to have been built in around 1634 by John Dod, and possibly incorporating parts of its predecessor at the base to the south. The church was then largely rebuilt in 1744 by William Cooper, starting with the nave, with the chancel following in 1747. The whole church was then restored between 1857 and 1858 by John Cunningham, who also added the north porch and the south aisle, while the vestry-cum-organ chamber was added to the south-eastern corner of the church in 1877.

St Peter's church seen from the south.

The Red Lion at Myddle.

Other points of interest are the three bells and the clock. The tenor bell weighs 7cwt and was cast by Thomas Clibury of Wellington in 1668 tuned to B flat. The second bell is thought to be the work of Michael de Lichfield and cast in his Staffordshire foundry in around 1280 and tuned to C but slightly flat in pitch. Finally, the treble bell was cast in 1715 by Abraham Rudhall of Gloucester and is tuned to D. Meanwhile, the clock was erected by the parishioners of Myddle and others on August 9th, 1902, in commemoration of the coronation of Edward VII and the end of the Boer War.

Myddle Historical Trivia: Myddle Castle, Richard Gough and Treasure

Myddle has probably been the site of a settlement since at least Roman times. This is based on finds in the village which include various silver hammered coins, an axe head, and a Roman enamelled Fibula. Meanwhile, Domesday Book (1086) records the manor to be owned by Rainald the Sheriff. It was passed to the Fitz Alan family of Clun, in the 12th century, followed by John Le Strange in around 1165.

It was a later John Le Strange who built Myddle Castle between 1308 and 1310, this being a conversion of the manor house after the Le Strange family obtained a licence to crenellate from Edward II. By 1449, the castle had passed to Elizabeth Cobham as part of her dowry from Richard, 7th Lord Strange. A year after his death, Elizabeth married Sir Roger Kynaston in 1450, but died herself three years later, and the castle passed to Kynaston. Sir Roger later became the High Sheriff of Shropshire, and is rumoured to have been the man who killed Lord Audley at the Battle of Blore Heath on 23rd September 1459. It was Roger's son, Humphrey, who allowed the castle to fall into disrepair, and then abandoned it in the late 15th century (see Myddle Quirk Alert for more on Humphrey), while the castle finally collapsed during an earthquake in 1688! A few castle ruins survive today, which have Grade II listing. As for that earthquake of 1688, it also destroyed a number of other houses in Myddle.

Other historic events in Myddle include the signing of a treaty between Henry III and Welsh Prince Llewellyn in 1234, while Elizabeth I granted Thomas Barnston a licence to sell land in Myddle in 1596. Meanwhile, the English Civil War (1642-1651) saw 20 Myddle men recruited by Charles I, although 14 of them were killed. During the war, Richard Gough (1635-1723) was educated in Myddle and Broughton and lived at Newton on the Hill. It was he who wrote *Antiquities and Memoirs of the Parish of Myddle* to record 17th century life in the village, and his work has been

St Peter's church lychgate in springtime.

The ruins of Myddle Castle, just about visible through the Spring trees!

frequently used as a study of human relations. In fact, the book has been called "the greatest insight into that group in Early Modern England" – which is ironic, as "that group" in this particular context is referring to "the middle sort of people".

In 1924, Myddle manor house was destroyed and sold to pay the death duties of the 3rd Earl Brownlow, while in 1942, an RAF Whitley bomber crashed in Myddle after taking off from nearby Sleap Airfield.

More recently, metal detectorists unearthed a clutch of 600-year-old Spanish coins. Of these, five solid gold "doblas" date from Castile in the 1350s, during the reign of King Pedro the Cruel, and are believed to be the first of their kind ever discovered in the UK. Experts at the British Museum said the money, which was probably dropped by a soldier, was a rare find. It was officially declared treasure by mid and north Shropshire coroner John Ellery.

Myddle Quirk Alert: Wild Humphrey Kynaston
Earlier, we mentioned that Humphrey Kynaston abandoned Myddle Castle in the late 15th century. Despite his wealth, and being the son of the High Sheriff, "Wild Humphrey Kynaston" was also a notorious highwayman! He received his "wild" nickname as a young man, given his outrageous lifestyle and constant trouble with the law. However, on 20th December 1491, Kynaston was found guilty of the murder of John Hughes at Stretton, and declared an outlaw by Henry VII. He was also in severe debt at this time, too. Humphrey therefore moved out of Myddle Castle to a cave in Nesscliffe Rock, where he supposedly lived from 1491 to 1518, living a Robin Hood lifestyle. He certainly had a reputation for robbing from the rich, but allegedly, he did indeed give to the poor as well – although he might have had a vested interest in that, as the locals returned the favour by protecting him and providing him with food.

There were attempts to capture Humphrey, though. One occasion saw the local sheriff remove several planks from Montford Bridge in order to prevent him from crossing the River Severn. However, his horse (whom he named Beelzebub) apparently managed to jump far enough each time to clear the missing planks! Rumour also has it that he was a regular patron at the Old Three Pigeons tavern at Nesscliffe, some 6 miles to the south-west of Myddle, and his original seat is still there.

There are also stories of a royal pardon, one from Henry VII in 1493, which seems unlikely given the length of time in hiding. Another story claims that he was pardoned by Henry VIII, after he provided 100 men to aid the King in France in 1513, and was therefore pardoned a few years later.

Humphrey died in 1534, and once again, there are conflicting stories of events. Some say he lived in comfort on an estate near Welshpool, while others claim he died of illness in his cave! Either way, that cave still exists today and is known as Kynaston's Cave (see page 51 for photo). It has two rooms; Humphrey lived in one, and stabled Beelzebub in the other! The cave is also alleged to have had an iron door for an entrance, and which was later used as the door to Shrewsbury gaol! There is also an engraving in the cave, which reads "H.K. 1564". Clearly not Humphrey, as he died in 1534, but possibly his grandson, Humfridus, who was born in 1530.

The village water pump at Myddle.

Three's-Up!

	MYTTON	**NORTHWOOD**	**OVERS**
STATUS:	Hamlet	Village	Hamlet and former hundred
POPULATION:	c.50	c.200	Less than 10
DISTRICT:	Shropshire	Shropshire	Shropshire
EARLIEST RECORD:	*Mutone*, Domesday Book, 1086	Unknown	The hundred dates back to Anglo-Saxon times.
MEANING:	Farmstead where two rivers join.	Wood to the north.	Usually means "place at the ridge or slope".
DERIVATION:	From the Old English words *(ge)mȳthe* (confluence of rivers) and *tūn* (farmstead).	From the Old English words *north* (north or northern) and *wudu* (wood or forest).	From the Old English word *ofer* (flat-topped ridge, hill or promontory).

Mytton is a hamlet located around 4 miles north-west of the outskirts of Shrewsbury. Adjacent to the hamlet, in Forton Heath, is Mytton Mill Country Business Park, which is also home to Mytton Mill, a corn mill built on the River Perry in 1820 that was still operational until 1966. A fire then caused severe damage in 1982, but the mill was restored and became home to workshops for a number of small businesses. More recently, Mytton Mill has been converted into 12 luxury homes.

Elsewhere, Atcham is home to the stunning mid-to-late 18th century, Grade II listed Mytton and Mermaid Hotel. And in Shrewsbury, there is the Grade II listed Mytton Villa which dates from the late 18th century, while Habberley is home to the Mytton Arms.

However, the most famous Mytton is "Mad Jack" Mytton (1796-1834), an eccentric and rake of the Regency period who was briefly a Tory Member of Parliament.

The village water pump at Mytton.

Indeed, the Mytton and Mermaid Hotel at Atcham has a room called Mad Jack's Bar, while the 72-mile bridleway in Shropshire for riders, mountain bikers and walkers, The Jack Mytton Way, is named after him. Additionally, a racehorse was named after him, as was the Jack Mytton Run, an annual streaking event by students of the University of Minnesota following spring break. It ran from 1999 to 2009 before being discontinued on police advice!

Next, **Northwood** is located on the Welsh border, 4 miles north-west of Wem. It is home to the Horse and Jockey pub and Northwood Methodist Church, with the latter being part of the Northern Area of the Shropshire and Marches Methodist Circuit and which, in turn, is part of the Wolverhampton and Shrewsbury District. The plaque above the door states: "PRIMITIVE METHODIST Jubilee Chapel 1860. The land kindly given by W. Williams".

The bridge over the River Perry at Mytton.

Looking down the River Perry towards Mytton Mill.

The Mytton and Mermaid Hotel at Atcham.

The centre of Mytton village.

Northwood Methodist Church.

The Horse and Jockey at Northwood.

The B5063 as it heads north-westwards out of Northwood and where it also brushes against the Welsh border.

Finally, today, **Overs** is a tiny hamlet alongside the hamlet called Bridges, and which are both around 4 miles north-west of Church Stretton, at a height of around 1,000ft (300m). The "bridges" in question are over the River East Onny, where you will also find the picturesque Horseshoe Inn. Overs Wood can also be found to the east of the river. However, the most significant Overs in Shropshire history was the Anglo-Saxon Overs hundred – although it wasn't particularly near to the hamlet of Overs; the hundred was bounded to the south by Worcestershire, and contained Bitterley parish, and five other parishes.

At the time of the Norman Conquest, the lord of Overs hundred was Richard Fitz-Scrob, father of Osbern Fitz-Richard and founder Richard's Castle. In the 12th century, though, the fifteen Shropshire hundreds mentioned in Domesday Book (1086), were significantly rearranged, and only Overs, Shrewsbury and Condover retained their original names. Remarkably, those 12th century hundreds retained administrative and judicial functions until the mid-to-late 19th century, with the last aspects removed in 1895 following the passing of the Local Government Act 1894. Back in 1851, the Overs hundred amounted to 9,888 acres and had a population of 1,485. By 1861 that had risen to 2,615 people living in 522 houses.

The River East Onny at Bridges, which adjoins Overs to the north. Opposite the river here is the Horseshoe Inn.

NAME (STATUS):	**NASH** (Village and Civil Parish)
POPULATION:	405
DISTRICT:	South Shropshire (1974-2009); Shropshire (post-2009)
EARLIEST RECORD:	*La Esse*, 1242; *Nazsche*, 1391
MEANING:	Place at the ash-tree.
DERIVATION:	From the Old English word æsc, meaning "ash-tree", but with the "N" prefixed, and taken from the Middle English for *atten*, meaning "at the".

Nash Church: St John the Baptist

The Grade II listed St John the Baptist church dates from the early 14th century, although it is thought that the Norman windows in the tower date back even further to either the late 11th or early 12th century. The nave, chancel and tower, with its timber spire, are still the originals, while Arthur Mee states that the finest possession of the church is "the modern oak screen from Louvain, adorned with a wealth of leaves and floral work". When you read the word "modern", though, bear in mind that Arthur was writing in the 1930s!

St John the Baptist church at Nash dates from the early 14th century.

The church was originally used as a chapel of ease until in 1849 when it became a church in its own right. A north aisle was added in 1865, along with a north vestry, while the south porch also dates from the 19th century. In the south wall is a stained-glass window in memory of Major Sir Robert Dalrymple Arbuthnot, killed in Normandy in 1944, while a 19th century window is dedicated to Admiral Lowe, who lived in the 17th century house known as Court of Hill, a mile or so from the village.

An old wooden vertical south dial still exists on the outside of the church. And talking of Court of Hill, politician Edward Brocklehurst Fielden (1857–1942), lived there from 1926 to his death, and is buried in the churchyard.

Nash Historical Trivia: Mahorall Farm Cider

Mahorall Farm in Nash dates back to 1650, and was originally part of a country estate. Mahorall was built to specialise in livestock and horses, and in 1825, an external building was constructed on the side of the farm building to create stables, a workshop, a granary and fodder storage. Much later, in the late 1960s, the farm was converted into a dairy farm. However, the farm underwent considerable restoration in the late 20th century, and in 2000, it was re-opened as a cider farm and nature reserve. Today, the 14-acre farm hosts a range of activities for visitors and the local community, including Hawkeye Falconry – which offers a day's experience with falcons and a Hawk Walk around the farm grounds. The walk passes through 12 acres of wildlife, streams, woodland, orchards and open pastures, where you might spot the three rare Exmoor ponies that live on the land.

Arthur's Oak. But is it really a thousand years old? See Quirk Alert for more.

View from inside the church looking east from the nave towards the chancel.

Nash Quirk Alert: Arthur's Oak

Returning to Arthur Mee again, he states in the 1930s that there is a "marvellous old oak at the junction of the road to Coreley, so huge that it dwarfs the old cottages near it". He claims its "gnarled trunk is 40 feet round at the ground; about 60 feet high, it has a spread of about 90 feet". He also calls the oak a "grand veteran", suggesting that it may have been there since before the Norman Conquest. Remarkably, it is still standing today, another eighty-five years on. It isn't looking its best any more though, as the photograph, shown above, demonstrates.

NAME (STATUS):	**PANT** (Village)
POPULATION:	1,675 (civil parish of Llanymynech and Pant)
DISTRICT:	Oswestry (1974-2009); Shropshire (post-2009)
MEANING:	Probably "a hollow or a valley".
DERIVATION:	From the Old Welsh word *pant* (a hollow or valley) or the Old English word *panne*, meaning "pan" – i.e. it could have been used in a topographical sense.

The Cross Guns at Pant.

St Agatha's church at neighbouring Llanymynech is the parish church for Pant.

The 19th century limekilns at Pant, located alongside the Montgomery Canal.

Pant Pub: The Cross Guns

The Cross Guns takes its name from the army badge for a marksman, which is likely a reference to the 19th century rifle range which stood where the old first hole of the course at Llanymynech Golf Club is today. More recently, regulars at the Cross Guns acquired protected status for the pub as an asset of community value (ACV) – this after seeing two other pubs in the village close in recent years.

Pant Church: St Agatha's

The Grade II listed St Agatha's church is in Llanymynech, but is the parish church of the civil parish of Llanymynech and Pant. The current church dates from 1844-45, when it replaced a much earlier church on the same site. It was built in a striking Neo-Norman style by Thomas Pearson.

Pant Historical Trivia: Mining, Heritage Railways and Canals

Above Pant is the Ogof copper mine, originally mined by the Romans, and hence many Roman artefacts have been found in the vicinity. More recently limestone has been quarried above Pant, with tramways running from the mines down to various kilns alongside the Montgomery Canal – although these kilns were soon superseded by the more efficient Hoffman kiln at Llanymynech (see page 91 for more plus photos).

In the 19th century, Pant was on the Whitchurch to Welshpool railway line. The line closed in the 1960s, but more recently, Cambrian Heritage Railways have restored 0.75 miles (1.21 km) of the line between Llynclys and Pant as a heritage railway, and there are plans to reopen the whole line from Gobowen to Welshpool. Meanwhile, work is also under way to make the Montgomery Canal navigable through the village again, as well. "The Monty", was originally completed in 1821, and ran for 33 miles from the Llangollen Canal (at Frankton Junction) to Newtown, via Llanymynech, Pant and Welshpool. The canal fell into disuse following a breach in 1936, and was officially abandoned in 1944.

Pant Quirk Alert: Straddled and Painting in Pant

Pant is home to the Llanymynech Golf Club, which is unique in being the only 18-hole golf course in the UK to straddle the border between two countries. Meanwhile, Pant is also the location for an old love story known as "The Pant Heiress". The story tells of a young lady and painter from a wealthy Chester family who eloped to Pant with a train-worker. Alas, the husband died leaving her to bring her children up on her own, financing herself by letting out rooms in her house.

Pant Methodist Church.

The Llanymynech Rocks Reserve which sits high above Pant.

Part of Pant village to the east of the Montgomery Canal.

SHROPSHIRE: UNUSUAL & QUIRKY

NAME (STATUS):	**PRESTON** (Village/hamlet * 5)
DISTRICT:	Shropshire for four; Telford & Wrekin for Preston upon the Weald Moors
EARLIEST RECORD:	*Prestone*, 1086 (Domesday Book); *Preston Gobald*, 1292
MEANING AND DERIVATION:	Farmstead of the priests – from the Old English words *prēost* (priest) and *tūn* (farmstead). The earliest record is for Preston Gubbals, and the manorial affix *Gobald* derives from a priest called *Godebold*, who held the manor in 1086.

What is known locally as Preston Trust Homes, a Grade I listed property that was formerly Preston Hospital, founded in 1716 thanks to the will of Lady Catherine Herbert the daughter of the 1st Earl of Bradford. The whole complex is now comprised of private apartments, and one of the residents kindly gave me permission to photograph the complex in Spring 2019.

Preston Geographical Trivia: Five's Up

There are five Prestons to be found in Shropshire. Preston upon the Weald Moors is located a mile north of the outskirts of Telford. The other four Prestons circumnavigate the northern half of Shrewsbury; Preston (2 miles east of the outskirts of Shrewsbury), Preston Brockhurst (5 miles north-east), Preston Gubbals (3 miles north) and Preston Montford (2 miles west).

Preston Church: St Martin's and St Lawrence's

The Grade II listed St Martin's church is located at Preston Gubbals, and was originally a chapel of ease. However, by the early 19th century, it was just the chancel of a former medieval church. The church was then largely built anew in 1866 by Samuel Pountney Smith, and the former St Martin's (chancel only) became its south aisle. Alas, most of his work was demolished in 1973, leaving a single-cell building – which is still the old medieval chancel! The three-bay arcade of the 1866 building has been retained, though, but it has been blocked off, and forms the north wall of the present building. Also surviving is a round-arched priest's door which dates from the 12th century, while at the west end is a large round window and a doorway that formerly led to the tower staircase.

Elsewhere, a beautifully preserved 14th century engraved tomb slab and a 17th century octagonal font survived the demolition, while in the churchyard

St Martin's church, Preston Gubbals, essentially the chancel of the original medieval church.

St Lawrence's church at Preston upon the Weald Moors.

An interesting sculpture in St Martin's churchyard at Preston Gubbals.

Timber-framed house opposite St Martin's church, Preston Gubbals.

Another black and white timber-framed house in Preston Gubbals.

there is a Grade II listed sundial on the south side attached to the base of a churchyard cross dating from 1638. A bell formerly in the church is now the Sanctus bell in St Alkmund's church, Shrewsbury. St Martin's was declared a redundant Anglican church on 1st June 1973, and is now under the care of the Churches Conservation Trust.

Meanwhile, St Lawrence's church at Preston upon the Weald Moors, was built between 1739 and 1742 and replaced a medieval church that was recorded as "beyond repair" in 1736, and "so small it would not contain more than half the inhabitants of Preston". The chancel and vestry were added to the 18th century church in 1853, along with the top stage of the tower, with further restoration carried out in 1905.

Black and white timber-framed cottage at Preston Brockhurst.

Preston Farm at Preston Brockhurst.

Lady Catherine Herbert the daughter of the 1st Earl of Bradford, and left as a bequest to build almshouses in Shropshire for 12 women and 12 girls as thanksgiving for Lady Catherine's rescue when lost in the Alps. The buildings were converted into high-end apartments in 2005. The village school was built in 1898.

Meanwhile, Preston Montford Field Studies Centre is a large 18th century house with later additions, set in 30 acres (12 ha) of grassland and woodland on the banks of the River Severn. It was opened as a Field Centre in 1957, and is visited by students of Biology and Geography, as well as school groups.

Preston Historical Trivia: Preston Hospital and Preston Montford Field Studies Centre
According to the *Rotuli Hundredorum*, Preston Gobald was said to be held by Thomas de Boshall, as also mentioned in the *Nomina Villlarum* of 1316. As for Preston upon the Weald Moors, it was home to the Grade I listed Preston Hospital, known locally as Preston Trust Homes. It was founded in 1716 thanks to the will of

Preston Quirk Alert: Martin Luther
Situated in the churchyard of St Martin's at Preston Gubbals, the memorial cross lists 13 Shropshire men who fought for their country in World War I, and who sadly didn't return – including one who was called Martin Luther.

The centre of Preston upon the Weald Moors.

The village green at Preston upon the Weald Moors.

The entrance to Preston Hall at Preston Brockhurst.

SHROPSHIRE: UNUSUAL & QUIRKY

NAME (STATUS):	**RYTON** (Village)
POPULATION:	174 (Civil parish of Ryton)
DISTRICT:	Bridgnorth (1974-2009); Shropshire (post-2009)
EARLIEST RECORD:	*Ruitone*, 1086 (Domesday Book)
MEANING:	Farm where rye is grown.
DERIVATION:	From the Old English words *ryge* (rye) and *tūn* (farmstead).

Ryton Church: St Andrew's

The Grade II listed St Andrew's church was built in 1710 on a sandstone bluff overlooking the confluence of the River Worfe and Wesley Brook – although, writing in the 1930s, Arthur Mee states that the font dates from the 14th century, and that there are "two ancient corbels... and the east and south walls may be 800 years old". His theory was largely confirmed by the Grade II listing in 1984, which confirms the building as early 18th century, but with evidence of earlier medieval construction.

St Andrew's church, Ryton.

The church was extensively restored and re-modelled in 1874 by London Architects and Builders, F & H Francis & Sons, who were also responsible for the extension of the north aisle in 1886. They included sculptures by Richard Westmacott who became 'Mason for Kensington Palace' by Royal Appointment, while the churchyard was laid out by Romolo Piazzani, a famous Italian landscape architect, and reputedly the illegitimate son of the King of Italy! The original drawing for the 1886 extension hangs in the vestry.

The following year (1887), a further two bells were added to the original three to mark Queen Victoria's Golden Jubilee, and a sixth bell was added in 1993. Finally, returning to the (probably) 14th century font, it is unusual, in that it is recessed into the tower arch.

Ryton Historical Trivia: Ryton Hall and Ryton House

Ryton was part of the Anglo-Saxon parish of Shifnal, but became separate at some point during the 12th century because there is mention of a priest at Ryton named Bernard in 1186. The village was also once the site of a medieval motte and bailey castle, while key 17th century industry here came in the form of water, paper, and slitting mills. Meanwhile, it is thought that architect Romolo Piazzani also built Ryton Hall – originally as a vicarage – directly opposite the church. It then subsequently became a girl's boarding school, and then a school for children with learning difficulties, while today, it has been converted into a number of residential apartments.

The village is also home to Ryton House, built in the mid-18th century. It was home to Colonel William Kenyon-Slaney (1847-1908) in the late 19th century, a politician and footballer who scored England's first-ever goal in international football in 1873 and who is also buried in Ryton churchyard. His family home, Hatton Grange, is also in the parish. Another Ryton football connection is with George Fieldhouse Molineux, whose family gave their name to Molineux House and also the Molineux football ground, both in Wolverhampton. George Fieldhouse Molineux was the vicar of Ryton between 1798 and 1838 while the last family member to own Molineux House, Charles Edward Molineux, was born at Ryton Rectory. And sticking with Ryton rectors, Reverend Robert William Eyton (1815–1881) was the author of *The Antiquities of Shropshire*, which was published at a rate of about two large volumes annually, from 1854 to 1860.

Ryton Quirk Alert: Baron Craven

In 1643, John Craven was created Baron Craven of Ryton, named after this village – but the title only lasted for five years, as Craven died without an heir in 1648. Apparently, news of his passing didn't make it as a feature on Newsround…

The foot of the hill that climbs up to the church.

The Ryton village water pump.

Three's-Up!

	SHELVE	**SLEAP**	**STANLEY**
STATUS:	Hamlet	Hamlet and Airfield	Hamlet * 2
DISTRICT:	Shropshire	Shropshire	Shropshire
POPULATION:	c.30	Less than 10	Both less than 10 apiece
EARLIEST RECORD:	*Schelfe*, 1180	*Eslepe*, 1086 (DB); *Sleap*, 1943	*Stanley*, 1803
MEANING:	Shelf of level ground	Muddy place	Stony woodland clearing
DERIVATION:	From the Old English word *scelf* (shelf of level ground or ledge).	Probably from the Old English word *slæp*, meaning "slippery or muddy place".	From the Old English words *stān* (stone) and *lēah* (wood, woodland clearing or glade).

The hamlet of Shelve in west Shropshire.

All Saints' church at Shelve.

Shelve is a cluster of houses, two farms and All Saints' church, located in west Shropshire, at an altitude of around 1,100 feet above sea level. It is part of the civil parish of Worthen with Shelve.

Shelve All Saints' church was built in 1839 and replaced a previous medieval structure. Given Arthur Mee, in the 1930s, states that its font "may be eight centuries old", that would make it 12th century. Mee also claims that the altar table, pulpit and a reading desk are all Jacobean, meaning they all pre-date the 19th century church, too. This is confirmed by britishlistedbuildings.co.uk, which as well as confirming All Saints as a Grade II listing, also confirms that the pulpit, reading desk and panelling at the east end of the church are made up from 17th century pews from the older church. The cambered tie beam above the altar rail also comes from the previous church.

Meanwhile, **Sleap** (pronounced Slape) is a hamlet around 8 miles north of Shrewsbury consisting of a couple of farms. However, the place is far better known for its airfield and the location of Sleap Aerodrome – which has a CAA Ordinary Licence that allows flights for the public transport of passengers or for flying instruction as authorised by the licensee – which is Shropshire Aero Club.

The site originally opened as a Royal Air Force airfield, in April 1943, and was used by RAF advanced flying training units. Initially it was the base for No. 81 Operational Training Unit RAF, within No. 93 Group RAF of RAF Bomber Command, and was equipped with Armstrong Whitworth Whitley bomber aircraft. From the 1st January 1944, Sleap was assigned to No.38 Group RAF, while No. 81 Armstrong-Whitworth Whitleys towed Airspeed Horsa heavy troop-carrying gliders on training missions. The Horsas made practice formation landings at RAF Sleap to simulate attacks in enemy territory. In November 1944, Vickers Wellingtons replaced the Whitleys and by January 1945 they were being used to train Transport Command air-crew. The RAF remained at Sleap until 1964, although the site is still used as a relief airfield by nearby RAF Shawbury for Eurocopter Squirrel helicopter training.

In other news, the bar at Sleap is named after Lieutenant Eric Lock, the World War II Battle of Britain pilot who was the highest scoring British-born pilot with sixteen and a half victories during the battle. A Wartime Aircraft Recovery Group museum is also based at the site and is open at weekends.

There are two **Stanleys** in south Shropshire which are located only 5 miles apart. The more westerly Stanley is a tiny hamlet located at the end of a no-through road called Stanley Farm Lane, around a mile north of the village of Chorley. The other Stanley is located just east of Highley at the end of Station Road – the station being Highley Station on today's Severn Valley Heritage Railway.

The station originally opened in February 1862, and became a crucial transport hub during the late 19th and early 20th century, with four nearby coal mines linked to the Severn Valley line by standard and narrow-gauge lines, cable inclines and aerial ropeways. There were also extensive sidings along the line, and wagon repair works at Kinlet, half-a-mile south. The station was closed in September 1963, but was later re-opened on the heritage railway, which was secured in stages between the late 1960s and the early 1980s – and which runs today for 16 miles (26km) from Kidderminster to Bridgnorth.

The Stanley at Highley is also located alongside the River Severn, and is home to the Ship Inn which dates back to 1770 and was built largely to serve bargemen. There was also a coal mine at Stanley, opened in the early 19th century. However, by the 1820s, those mines had closed.

Light aircraft at Sleap Airfield.

Aircraft and hangars at Sleap Airfield.

Looking down towards the rear of The Ship Inn, which sits alongside the River Severn at the eastern Shropshire Stanley. It was built in 1770.

Highley Station on the Severn Valley Railway is also located at the eastern of the two Stanleys. The station was opened in 1862.

Wooden lodges on Severnside at Stanley.

NAME (STATUS):	**STOWE** (Village and Civil Parish)
POPULATION:	140 (Civil Parish of Stowe); c.20 (village)
DISTRICT:	South Shropshire (1974-2009); Shropshire (post-2009)
MEANING:	Probably assembly place or holy place.
DERIVATION:	From the Old English word *stōw* (assembly or holy place).

St Michael's church at Stowe dates from the 13th century.

Looking north towards Stowe Hill.

Knighton railway station serves the Welsh town, but is actually located over the border in Shropshire and the Stowe civil parish.

Stowe Geographical Trivia

Although Stowe only has a handful of houses, the presence of a church means that it is classed as a village. It is also fairly remote, with the road up to Stowe being single-track. The settlement is tucked away in a fold of Stowe Hill, overlooking the Teme Valley to the parish border with Wales a mile to the south along with the Welsh town of Knighton; indeed, a small part of the town actually lies within the English parish of Stowe.

Stowe Church: St Michael's

The Grade II listed St Michael's church dates from the mid-13th century. The bellcote was added in the late 17th century, and the chancel was rebuilt when the church was restored in the late 19th century. The distinctive bellcote is weather-boarded at the west end and has a pyramidal slate top. Internally, the main feature is the arch-braced collar beam roof, which has arch-braces alternating with slightly cambered moulded tie-beams having vertical struts supporting collars. The majority of the fittings and furnishings date from the mid-to-late 19th century, including the benches, pulpit and octagonal font, although the altar is Jacobean. There is also an ancient yew in the churchyard, which forms part of the boundary wall.

Stowe Historical Trivia: Listed Farmhouses and Knighton

Following excavations carried out in 1925 by the vicar of Stowe St Michael's, it is thought that Church Field at Stowe was once home to a Roman villa. A range of rectangular rooms in Church Field were excavated, while aerial photographs from 2006 also demonstrate the villa layout. The excavations revealed that the 30-36in-thick walls were covered by a blue and red plaster with spiral ornament. Roman paving, roofing and flue tiles were all found, but not pottery or other evidence that could provide a precise dating.

St Michael's church was once the mother church to Knighton, and evidence of medieval house platforms in a field close to the church suggest a once-thriving community. Meanwhile, the civil parish of Stowe is home to two Grade II listed 17th century farmhouses, a Grade II listed barn, and a Grade II listed cowhouse at a third farm. More Grade II listed buildings in the parish are covered in the Stowe Quirk Alert section!

Stowe Quirk Alert: Knighton Railway Station and K6

As mentioned earlier, the Welsh town of Knighton lies just to the south-west of Stowe, and the part that lies within Stowe parish also includes both the Grade II listed Knighton railway station, and a Grade II listed K6 telephone kiosk! Knighton railway station was built in 1865 for the London and North Western Railway, and dates from the opening of the Central Wales Railway to Llandrindod Wells. Today it is part of the Heart of Wales line. Meanwhile, the K6 telephone kiosk is located above the bridge over the station. It was designed by Giles Gilbert Scott, and was constructed in cast iron with a square plan and a dome. It also has three unperforated crowns in the top panels.

Inside St Michael's church and the impressive ceiling.

NAME (STATUS):	**THE BOG** (Former Mining Community; Visitor Centre)
POPULATION:	c.10
DISTRICT:	South Shropshire (1974-2009); Shropshire (post-2009)
EARLIEST RECORD:	*The Bog*, 1730s
MEANING AND DERIVATION:	No mysteries: the area used to be a bog! However, it dried out with the cutting of the Boat Level – an underground tunnel dug to drain the mine workings there.

The Bog Geographical Trivia

The Bog is essentially the remains of a former mining village, and is located in the north-western part of the Shropshire Hills, around 12 miles south-west of Shrewsbury. A mile or so to the north-east of The Bog, is Stiperstones, a very distinctive quartzite ridge and the second highest point in Shropshire at 1,759ft (536m) above sea level. The mine at The Bog and the adjacent Stiperstones outcrop are the result of geological movement – as millions of years ago, the outcrop was adjoined to the west by the sea! Over time movement of the tectonic plates forged the mines as softer layers of rock were worn away. Fast-forward to the 20th century, and when mining ceased it left a variety of habitats which have not been disturbed for decades. Hence old buildings have become home to nesting birds, bats have roosted in old mine tunnels, and the spoil heaps are a useful habitat for a range of invertebrates. Similarly, the old reservoirs and ponds have become an aquatic haven for newts and dragonflies. The Bog area is also one of the most important sites in Shropshire for the grayling butterfly. Bog Farm and Bog Hill Farm are also located in the area!

The Bog Historical Trivia: Lead and Baryte

The former mining village at The Bog was created in the 1730s, thanks to local mining for lead and baryte. The site would still have been boggy back then, and remained so until drains were cut to drain away much of the water; the first pumping engine was deployed in 1777. By the 19th century, the village was thriving with over 200 buildings, and during the 1870s, the Stiperstones area was one of Britain's main sources of lead, with several other small mines having opened between The Bog and Snailbeach. At the time, lead was a highly-prized metal, used for roofing and plumbing as well as paints and bullets.

Lead mining ceased at The Bog in the 1880s, but the mines were re-opened in the early 1900s to extract barytes. During World War I, German prisoners of war constructed an overhead aerial ropeway to ship the barytes down the valley; indeed, the ropeway features in Malcolm Saville's 1944 novel *Seven White Gates*. Alas, mining for barytes at The Bog soon became uneconomic and the mine was closed in 1922. The majority of the surviving village was demolished in 1972.

Today, the only survivors are the former cowhouse, and The Bog Visitor Centre, which has taken over the former Victorian school building and which is still lit by gas lamps. At one point, the schoolhouse had 106 pupils aged 5 to 14. Today, the centre tells of the 200-year mining history here and of the people who lived here who are recorded in the copies of the Census which are held at The Bog.

The Bog Quirk Alert: Eadric the Wild

The area around The Bog is rich in myth and folklore relating to the rocks of the Devil's Chair. This includes the legend of the ghost of Eadric the Wild. Eadric was a Saxon earl who held lands that were confiscated after 1066 and successfully defied the Normans, for a time at least, and the legend is that he rides the hills whenever England is threatened by invasion!

The old schoolhouse at The Bog, now The Bog Vistor Centre, which tells the 200-year-old history of this mining village.

The remains of the former Miners' Institute at The Bog.

View from the top of Stiperstones back down towards The Bog.

Three's-Up!

	THE GROVE	THE HOPE	TRENCH
STATUS:	Hamlet * 2	Hamlet, Valley	Suburb
DISTRICT:	Shropshire	Shropshire	Telford and Wrekin

Minsterley Primitive Methodist Church at The Grove in Minsterley.

Climbing up the road east of Hope Gutter is this former Methodist chapel at The Hope, now a residential home known as Hope Cottage.

Trench Pool.

There are two places called **The Grove** in Shropshire. The first is a mile north of Craven Arms along Grove Drive, named after the former country house that stood here, but which was demolished in the late 1960s. In the early 20th century, it was known as The Grove Stud, a centre of equine excellence run by founder Harriet Rowland Greene, with Welsh mountain ponies her speciality. Harriet's first Welsh mountain pony, the three-year-old Grove Ballistite, cost 36 guineas, and became the foundation stallion of the stud, winning many prizes. However, in 1914, she splashed out 280 guineas on Shooting Star, a Welsh mountain pony stallion, who had already won many prizes. Shooting Star won six times at the Royal Show and 16 championships at leading shows, while his son, Grove Sprightly, won more prizes than any other pony of his breed, being champion seven times on the trot at the Royal Welsh Show.

The other "The Grove" is named after a road of the same name on the outskirts of Minsterley. A few yards away on Horsebridge Road, but still in the area called The Grove, is Minsterley Primitive Methodist Church, which was built in 1924. It succeeded a previously demolished chapel built in 1850 on a different site at The Grove.

Next, **The Hope** (derivation *hop*, meaning "valley") is a hamlet and valley two miles north of Ludlow, through which a watercourse known as Hope Gutter flows! There is also a former Methodist chapel here, built by Mr C. T. Pugh of Welshpool, in 1882, which replaced a previous Primitive Methodist chapel nearby. The foundation stones were laid on the 11th April 1882, and it remained a place of worship until 1989. It was converted to residential use in 2005 as Hope Cottage.

Finally, **Trench** is a northern suburb of Telford. It was once the site of the Trench Inclined Plane, built in 1793, which connected the now-abandoned Shrewsbury Canal to the Wombridge Canal which was 75ft (23m) higher in elevation and part of the east Shropshire canal network. The incline was in operation until 1921, and was the last British inclined plane to close. Meanwhile, today's very urban Trench Road was once an ancient byway. Previously known as the Trench Way, it connected Newport and Wellington and was already an established route by 1288. Trench Road later became the southern boundary of the village of Horton and the northern boundary of Wrockwardine Wood, and Trench became split into two townships. It wasn't until the 1920s, though, that Trench began to see significant housing development, but by the 1960s, the area from Trench Road to Teagues Bridge Lane had become a large housing estate.

The Blue Pig at Trench Lock is located at the bottom of the former Trench Inclined Plane.

The Grade II listed Old Mill at Trench dates from 1818 when it was built as a flour mill alongside the canal between Wrockwardine Wood and Trench Link. It was operational until the 1930s, but today, it has been converted into apartments.

NAME (STATUS):	**TILLEY** (Village); **TILLEY GREEN** (Hamlet)
POPULATION:	1,659 (Wem Rural civil parish)
DISTRICT:	North Shropshire (1974-2009); Shropshire (post-2009)
EARLIEST RECORD:	Unknown, but the *lēah* element in the place-name suggests it dates back to Anglo-Saxon times
MEANING:	Probably woodland clearing of a man called Tila or Tilli.
DERIVATION:	From the Old English personal name *Tila* or *Tilli* and the Old English word *lēah* (wood, woodland clearing or glade).

Tilley Geographical Trivia

Tilley is located immediately south of Wem and is now almost conjoined. If you're heading into the village from the south along the B5476, you'll be in for a surprise if you take a first left – as that road is now a dead end, fenced off at the railway line – with the old level crossing gate still intact on the other (Tilley) side. However, if you take the road on the right off the B5476, you will find yourself in the hamlet of Tilley Green, and which is therefore disconnected from Tilley these days.

Tilley Historical Trivia: Grade II Heaven

Tilley is more hamlet than village as it doesn't have a church – which probably accounts for its absence from Domesday Book. However, Tilley is the location of an extraordinary number of centuries-old Grade II listed buildings. These include Tilley Hall, Tilley Manor, Tilley Farm, Tilley Lodge, Tilley Farmhouse, Brook Cottage and Oak Cottage, with six of those seven being black and white timber-framed houses dating from the 16th and 17th centuries. Tilley Farm and Tilley Manor are of the classic cross-wing vernacular.

In 2015, Tilley's ancient buildings were the subject of a local history project led by Dr George Nash, Visiting Fellow at the University of Bristol, and villager Alastair Reid – this thanks to a £65,500 award by the Heritage Lottery Fund for the three-year project. The aim was to archaeologically survey the village, focusing on the group of timber-framed buildings which are present on an estate map of 1631. The project, one of the largest of its kind, involved a dendrochronology survey of 28 buildings; in other words, dating the timbers of each house through calibrated tree-ring growth, which allows archaeologists to determine the date of when a tree was felled. For example, four of the seven timber samples from Brook Farm have a date range of 161 years, the earliest date being 1419, the latest from the winter of 1579/80. However, the building's boxed-framed architectural style suggests the timbers should have a much later date.

The Tilley Raven in Tilley has been a pub since the early 18th century.

The Grade II listed Oak Cottage in Tilley dates from the early 17th century with later additions and alterations.

Other facets of the project studied carpenters' marks, timber joints and decorative styles, while 3D laser scanning provided millimetre-accurate elevation surveys of each building – all complemented by a drone survey that provided a record of the upper sections of the buildings, including the roof sections. In addition, the project team applied a geophysical survey to several areas where buildings once stood

Meanwhile, to the east of the B5476, Tilley Green is also home to the Grade II listed Trench Farmhouse, another timber-framed house with brick infill, which dates from the early 17th century with later additions and alterations.

The Grade II listed Brook Farm (or Brook House) dates from the early 17th century, with eaves raised to the front in the late 18th or early 19th century.

Another Grade II listed building is Tilley Lodge, which dates from the early 17th century, again with later additions and alterations.

The Grade II listed Tilley Manor dates from the late 16th or early 17th century with later additions and alterations.

The Grade II listed Tilley Hall is next door-but-one to Tilley Manor and opposite The Tilley Raven. It dates from 1613 with later additions.

Two houses further on is this Grade II listed former farmhouse, which dates from the mid-to-late 17th century.

Tilley Farmhouse is also Grade II listed, but dates from the late 18th century; the three gabled eaves dormers date from the late 19th century.

Another view of Tilley Lodge.

Yew Tree Cottage, Tilley.

NAME (STATUS):	**TONG** (Village, Civil Parish)
POPULATION:	243
DISTRICT:	Bridgnorth (1974-2009); Shropshire (post-2009)
EARLIEST RECORD:	*Tweongan*, 10th century; *Tvange*, 1086 (Domesday Book)
MEANING:	Tongs-shaped feature – i.e. a fork in a river (two streams meet at the western end of the site of Tong Castle, both tributaries of the Worfe) or a pinched piece or spit of land.
DERIVATION:	From the Old English word *tang* or *twang* (tongs-shaped feature) with the latter probably replacing a related form, *tweonga*, of similar meaning.

St Bartholomew's church at Tong.

The nave of St Bartholomew's church.

Tong Church: St Bartholomew's

The Grade I listed St Bartholomew's church dates from the early 15th century, but is probably the third church on this site. It was Lady Isabel de Pembrugge who obtained a Royal Licence in 1409 to found Tong College and build the present Collegiate Church of St Bartholomew – this in memory of her husband, Sir Fulke de Pembrugge. The College consisted of five secular priests and two clerks, who also cared for thirteen paupers who lived in almshouses just south of the church. The College was seized by Henry VIII in 1546 as part of the Dissolution of the Monasteries, but thankfully, little was removed or destroyed.

Today, the church is notable for its architecture and fittings, including its fan vaulting in the Golden Chapel, and its numerous impressive tombs which make up one of the finest collections of alabaster effigies in the country. Indeed, with all of the male effigies clad in armour, they provide a perfect depiction of five of the seven periods into which the development of medieval armour is divided. The church has therefore been described as "The Westminster Abbey of The Midlands", and often features as one of "the best churches in England". Later patrons added further memorials, including the Stanley Monument which is inscribed with epitaphs especially written by William Shakespeare.

Tong Historical Trivia: Tong Castle, Charles II and Railways

There have been several castles at Tong with one of the earliest probably owned by Leofric, Earl of Mercia. Subsequent owners included the de Montgomery, de Belmeis, La Zouche, and de Pembrugge families, before passing to the Vernon family in 1446. By 1760, the castle belonged to George Durant, who had amassed his fortune in the West Indies, and he spent much of it building a new Tong Castle. His son, George Durant II, was a very busy man – having 14 children by his first wife, 6 by his second wife…and 32 illegitimate

LEFT: Effigies of Sir Fulke de Pembrugge (d.1409) and his second wife, Dame Isabel (d.1446), who founded the current 15th century incarnation of St Bartholomew's church in her husband's memory. CENTRE LEFT: Effigies of Sir Richard Vernon (d.1451) and his wife, Benedicta de Ludlow. CENTRE RIGHT: Effigies of Dame Anne Talbot (d.1494) and Sir Henry Vernon (d.1515). RIGHT: Effigies of Sir Richard Vernon (d.1517) and Margaret Dymoke (d.1550) – she being the daughter of the King's Champion (Sir Robert Dymoke) at the coronation of Richard III, Henry VII and Henry VIII.

SHROPSHIRE: UNUSUAL & QUIRKY

LEFT: The ruins of Tong College Hospital, and former almshouses, built in the 15th century by Isabel de Pembrugge. CENTRE: This example of fan vaulting in St Bartholomew's church can be found in the Golden Chapel, built in 1510 by Sir Henry Vernon as the Chapel of the Salutation to Our Lady. RIGHT: The Grade II listed base of a medieval preaching cross in St Bartholomew's churchyard. Note the four carved heads at the corners of the top base. The cross also used to carry a sundial made in 1776 by Thomas Ore, one of a group of Tong clockmakers.

children in the parish of Tong! The castle ceased to be occupied in 1913.

The events of Charles II's dramatic escape following the Battle of Worcester on 3rd September 1651 are described in *The Boscobel Tracts*, with Tong mentioned in a chapter called "White Ladies". While sheltering at nearby Boscobel House, Charles was said to have "had the pleasure of a prospect from Tong to Breewood (sic), which satisfied the eyes, and of the famous bells at Tong, which entertained the ear." Charles also spent the night of 4th September at Hobbal Grange in the parish of Tong, as a guest of Richard Penderel.

Moving forwards to 1840, and Tong was surveyed by two different railway companies. One – the Shrewsbury and Leicester Direct Railway – would have passed through on a north-east to south-westerly direction between Tong and Tong Norton, but was never built. Meanwhile, the Shrewsbury and Wolverhampton Railway eventually passed further south to run through Ruckley and Neachley.

Shoemakers Cottage and Old Tong House are Grade II listed and date from the mid-to-late 17th century.

The Grade II listed Church Farmhouse in Tong dates from the early 17th century, with early 19th century re-facing and late 19th century additions.

Tong Quirk Alert: Little Nell and Dame Isabel
In St Bartholomew's churchyard is the supposed grave of Little Nell, a fictional character from Charles Darwin's book, *The Old Curiosity Shop*. That said, it is thought that Charles Dickens actually visited Tong's church, while his grandmother is said to have worked at Tong Castle when she was a girl. As for Little Nell's "grave", this is probably courtesy of Americans – as it was fashionable for Americans to visit England to view scenes featured in Dickens' books, and there are references to Tong church in *The Old Curiosity Shop*. In fact, the closing chapters of the book are actually set in Tong – and hence Americans came looking for Little Nell's grave in St Bartholomew's churchyard.

Anyway, the story goes, that an entrepreneurial verger and village postmaster, George H. Boden, asked locals to pay for a headstone. He then forged an entry in the church burial register of a Little Nell, and charged people to see the grave! In doing so, though, he did make two mistakes. Firstly, it is said that he unwittingly used post office ink, which marked Nell's entry apart from the other entries, And, secondly, it clearly states in Dickens' book, that Little Nell was buried inside the church, not outside!

Starting back in around 1200, a bunch of roses used to be placed in the hands of the statue of Our Lady in the Lady Chapel of Tong church, every Midsummer's Day – the Feast of St John the Baptist. However, when the statue was removed at the Reformation, the villagers continued the custom by placing the roses on the tomb of the *other* Lady of Tong's church, its foundress, Dame Isabel de Pembrugge. If you look closely at her tomb on the previous page, you will note that she is wearing a headdress of roses!

The supposed grave of Little Nell – a fictitious character from Charles Dickens' book, The Old Curiosity Shop! *Read the Quirk Alert to find out how it became a lucrative bonus for the church coffers!*

NAME (STATUS):	**WOORE** (Village and Civil Parish)
POPULATION:	1,069
DISTRICT:	North Shropshire (1974-2009); Shropshire (post-2009)
EARLIEST RECORD:	*Wavre*, 1086 (Domesday Book)
MEANING:	Either "place by the swaying tree" or "boundary".
DERIVATION:	From either the Old English word *wæfre* (swaying tree) or from either the ancient Celtic word for "boundary" or the Anglo-Saxon word *oure* (boundary).

LEFT: *Today, Swan Court at Woore is home to a number of apartments. However, it was previously known as the Swan Inn, an 18th century coaching inn on the London to Chester post route where a change of horses was available. It remained an inn until 2016, when it closed and was redeveloped into apartments.* RIGHT: *The Coopers Arms at Woore.*

St Leonard's church at Woore was built between 1830 and 1831. It is Grade II listed, as is the old font visible in the bottom right corner of the photo.

Houses opposite St Leonard's church at Woore.

Woore Church: St Leonards

The Grade II listed St Leonard's church is relatively modern, dating back to the early 1830s, when it was built to serve what were then five townships of the ancient parish of Mucklestone. It was built to an unusual Italianate design in white plaster by George Hamilton of Stone – although the striking bell tower is actually a 1910 Edwardian addition by Chapman and Snape of Newcastle-under-Lyme. Prior to that, in 1887, the church was restored internally and the chancel was rebuilt. The present building stands near the site of an earlier chapel-of-ease, first recorded in 1552. Woore is also home to Woore Methodist Chapel.

Woore Historical Trivia: Woore Races

At the time of Domesday Book (1086), *Wavre* was held by William Malbank, as tenant-in-chief for the King. The moated manor house at that time was located on the modern-day site of Syllenhurst Farm, and was part of the hundred of Hodnet. William Malbank also held land at nearby Gravenhunger and Onneley, as well as at Dorrington in central Shropshire. Malbank, a Norman, had succeeded a Saxon lord known as Edric, while later manor ownership fell to the de Bulkeley family.

Woore parish was home to a National Hunt racecourse from the late 19th century until 1963, located 2 miles to the south-east of Woore in the hamlet of Pipe Gate. It was founded on farmland owned by Mr Icke and leased to the racecourse company, while travel to the venue was serviced by Pipe Gate railway station which was on the Stoke to Market Drayton line. The track was a mile round, with very sharp left-hand bends, while horses had to gallop over a bridge between the last two jumps.

Races are first recorded at Woore in 1883, but were moved to Pipe Gate in 1885. Early meetings were funded

LEFT: The building on the left is the Grade II listed Tudor House, and dates from the early 17th century – although it was remodelled in the 20th century. CENTRE: The Falcon Inn at Woore. RIGHT: Looking north up the A51 in Woore. This was once on the 18th century coaching route from London to Chester.

through the subscriptions of local farmers and huntsmen, but in 1905, a racecourse company was formed to manage the business. During the 1920s and '30s, the meeting became very popular, sometimes drawing crowds of over 1,500 spectators – despite only having a single, wooden grandstand. Then in 1937, King George VI attended to watch his horse, Slam, take part in the Betton Hurdle, in which it finished fourth.

By the late 1940s, Woore held three meetings a year, and in 1952, a fourth meeting was added. Nearby Mucklestone held point-to-point meetings and it was common for racegoers to attend the Mucklestone meeting on Easter Saturday and the Woore meeting on Easter Monday, when, often, the same horses would run again. During this era, the famous jockey and author, Dick Francis, had his first ride at Woore in 1946 on a horse called Russian Hero, while commentator Brough Scott debuted at Woore in March 1963.

Alas, attendances fell with the ending of passenger services to Pipe Gate station in 1956. Nevertheless, expansion of the course continued, and in 1957, buildings from Bedford Aerodrome were acquired and converted to stewards' rooms, a weighing room and a restaurant. However, on 1st June 1963 – unbeknown to most – the final meeting was held. Thousands turned up to watch Terry Biddlecombe win the opening race, and Reg Hollinshead the last. Alas, the Levy Board then withdrew funding from Woore and several other courses, although three one-day meetings were scheduled for 1964. Unfortunately, one of those meetings was scheduled for Easter Saturday, thus clashing with the nearby Mucklestone point-to-point meeting run by the North Staffordshire Hunt. When the hunt was refused permission to postpone, they instead bought the entire assets of Woore racecourse and sold them off, thus bringing racing at Woore to a close.

The bell-tower of St Leonard's church. However, those bells haven't rung since the 1980s!

Woore Quirk Alert: Shropshire Isolation, The Bells and a Pat on the Head

Woore is located in a north-eastern protrusion of Shropshire into Cheshire and Staffordshire. This means that, somewhat unusually, the two main roads that pass through Woore (the A51 and the A525), don't connect Woore to any other Shropshire place! The village is also the farthest place in Shropshire from the centre of the county near Cantlop. Meanwhile, the bells in St Leonard's church at Woore haven't actually rung since the 1980s due to safety reasons. Instead, a timed recording is used!

Finally, we return to the former Woore Racecourse. Apparently, the course had many bends and corners and hence it was advantageous to stay close to the rails. As former jockey, Bernard Wells, stated: "It felt as though you were going around on the inside of a saucepan!" However, in addition, low-hanging branches also added to the difficulty level, while the fact that the course was also used for grazing, meant that jockeys often got much more than mud splattered across their jerseys. So, caps and goggles were an essential!

The former Woore St Leonard's School, built in 1876 but now a detached, seven-bedroomed private residence.

The Best of the Rest

Name	Location and Trivia
ABBEY GREEN	A hamlet in north Shropshire around 3 miles north of Wem, and part of the civil parish of Whixall.
BAGGINSWOOD	A hamlet 3 miles north of the small market town of Cleobury Mortimer, consisting of a couple of houses and a couple of farms. Of these, Cox's Farm runs a B&B while Heath Farm is famous locally for its meat shop and has been run by the same family for over ninety years.
BETTON	Two hamlets, one in north-east Shropshire 2 miles north-east of Market Drayton and the other around 10 miles south-west of Shrewsbury. Both were mentioned in Domesday Book (1086) as *Baitune* and *Betune*, respectively, with the name meaning "farmstead or estate where beech-trees grow". The name derives from the Old English words *bēce* (beech-tree) and *tūn* (farmstead). There is also a Shropshire hamlet called Betton Strange which is located 2 miles south of Shrewsbury.
BLUEBELL	A hamlet of just three houses on the B5061, close to Uckington and Uppington. Four if you count the bus shelter there!
BOWLING GREEN	Essentially Bowling Green Farm, a mid-19th century farm which is located on The Avenue in north Shropshire, just north-west of Peplow; now also home to some beautiful converted barns.
BROAD OAK	Two places in Shropshire. One is on the border with Staffordshire on the A458 alongside the hamlet called Broad Lanes, while the other is just north of Shrewsbury.
BROUGHTON	A hamlet 2 miles north-east of the first Broad Oak mentioned above.
BRYN	A remote hamlet in south-western Shropshire, home to some lovely houses, a former Methodist chapel and Bryn farm. First recorded as *Bren* in 1272, deriving from the Celtic word *brinn* (hill).
BURLEY	A hamlet in south Shropshire comprised of just two farms, located 3.5 miles south-east of Craven Arms and alongside the hamlet of Bache.
CABIN	A hamlet consisting of a dozen houses a mile from the Welsh border. These sit at the top of the steep hill climbing in a north-westerly direction out of Bishop's Castle where you will also find a Severn-Trent Water station also called "Cabin".
CHEMISTRY	Chemistry is the name of a street in Whitchurch, and the area around that street has now also become known as Chemistry. The shropshirehistory.org.uk suggests that the area is named after a chemical works that was located here from the early 19th century to the early 20th.
CHERRY ORCHARD	A built-up housing estate in the centre of Shrewsbury. As you might expect, the area was once a cherry orchard (until 1887, in fact) – and was located on the Whitehall estate which was owned by the Earls of Tankerville until 1835. The Cherry Orchard estate was first developed by Dr Samuel Butler, headmaster of Shrewsbury School in the late 19th century.
CROSS	A hamlet in north-west Shropshire, on the A528, as it heads northwards out of Ellesmere.
EDGE	A hamlet comprised of a couple of farms and Edge Villa, home to beautiful gardens that are affiliated to the National Garden Scheme. Edge Villa's page on the NGS's website will make you smile, with a number of humorous references to local wildlife and resident pets! Edge was recorded as *Egge* in 1225, and the name means "place at the edge or escarpment", deriving from the Old English word *ecg*, meaning edge or escarpment.
FITZ	A hamlet 5 miles north-west of Shrewsbury. Appears in Domesday Book (1086) as *Witesot*. Also *Fittesho*, 1194. Means "hill-spur of a man called Fitt"; (*hōh* in Old English means hill-spur).
FOLLEY	A hamlet consisting of a handful of houses where Folley Road meets the B4176, just south of Ackleton. Is also home to The Folly Inn, which has alternated its name between Folly Inn and Folley Inn, and once had both spellings on either side of the pub sign!
FORTON	A hamlet 4 miles north-west of Shrewsbury. Half a mile further up the road is Forton Heath, a slightly larger settlement, while you will also find another Forton, a quarter of a mile over the border into Staffordshire, just north of Newport. The Shropshire Forton was recorded in Domesday Book (1086) as *Fordune*, meaning "farmstead or village by a ford", with the name deriving from the Old English words *ford* (ford) and *tūn* (farmstead or village).
FOXWOOD	An area in south Shropshire just off the A4117 between the small settlements of Doddington and Hoptonbank.
GRIMMER	A former township in the Worthen parish, but which now consists of just two houses, one of which is called Little Grimmer.
HILLSIDE	A hamlet of a dozen houses located less than a mile north of the summit of Brown Clee Hill.
HORNSPIKE	A hamlet on Shropshire's northern border with Wales, 6 miles south-west of Whitchurch.
LIGHTWOOD	A hamlet 5 miles south-west of Bridgnorth and home to a couple of farms. The farms are located around a mile or so south of Upton Cressett Hall.
LONG OAK	An area on the A5 just north-west of Shottaton where you will find a number of isolated houses alongside the busy road as well as a business selling windows and conservatories!
LOWE	A hamlet a mile north-west of Wem, and home to Low Hall Farm, which was once the home of the famous Lord Chief Justice, George Jeffreys (1645-1689) also known as "Judge Jeffreys".

SHROPSHIRE: UNUSUAL & QUIRKY

LEFT: This lovely house is at the "centre" of the hamlet of Abbey Green.

RIGHT: The Shropshire Canal as it passes under Maer Lane, a mile south of the Betton in the north-east of Shropshire.

The Wrekin, viewed from the hamlet of Bluebell.

The centre of the hamlet of Broughton in east Shropshire.

The entrance to the road known as "Chemistry" in Whitchurch at its junction with the B5398.

St Peter and St Paul's church at Fitz was built in 1722.

LEFT: The former Methodist Chapel at Forton Heath.

RIGHT: The Folly Inn at Folley. Note the different spellings!

LEFT: Lowe Hall Farm, just north of Wem was once home to Judge Jeffreys, the First Baron of Wem. The building dates from 1666 and is Grade II listed.

RIGHT: North Lynn Cottage at Lynn on the Shropshire/Staffordshire border. Next door is North Lynn Manor, while opposite is Lynn South Farm.

LYDE	A hamlet 2 miles west of Hope and around four miles from the Welsh border. Recorded as *Lude* in Domesday Book (1086), and which is named after the stream here which derives from the Old English word *hlyde*, meaning "the loud one".
LYNN	A hamlet on the border with Staffordshire, 3 miles south-east of Newport. It is composed of a handful of buildings, including North Lynn Cottage, North Lynn Manor, South Lynn House and South Lynn Farm.
MARDY	A hamlet of half a dozen houses in the far north-western corner of Shropshire, one of which is called Mardy Farm House.
MYDDLEWOOD	A hamlet of around 20 homes stretched out in a linear fashion on the main road, half a mile west of Myddle.
NEW INVENTION	A hamlet on the A488 between Knighton and Clun, consisting of four houses at a crossroads, one of which is a former Methodist chapel dating from 1874, and another the former Stag's Head. For an explanation of the name derivation, see Quirk Alert on page 71.
NOX	A hamlet on the B4386, half way between Westbury and Shrewsbury.
OAKS	A hamlet consisting of a farm and a couple of houses, around 7 miles south-west of Shrewsbury.
PATTON	A hamlet of a few isolated buildings either side of the B4378, 4 miles south-west of Much Wenlock. Eponymous buildings here include Lower Patton Farm and Patton Grange, while Patton was also an Anglo-Saxon hundred of Shropshire, covering manors in eastern central Shropshire. It was amalgamated in the early 12th century with the neighbouring hundred of Culvestan to form the Munslow hundred.
RHEWL	A housing estate at the north-eastern outskirts of the large village of Gobowen in north-west Shropshire, and which is named after Rhewl Lane.
ROUND OAK	A hamlet of pretty cottages and Round Oak Farm, 3 miles north-west of Craven Arms.
SHEET	A modern settlement along The Sheet and Sheet Road, at the south-eastern corner of Ludlow. Despite its modern feel, Sheet was actually mentioned in Domesday Book (1086) as being part of the Saxon hundred of Culvestan. Shortly afterwards, Sheet was moved to Munslow hundred.
SIX ASHES	A hamlet located on the A458 around 5 miles south-east of Bridgnorth, at a crossroads with Six Ashes Road, and right on the border with Staffordshire. It is named after the Six Ashes Inn, and the border appears to go right through the middle of the pub! A place called Four Ashes can be found less than 2 miles further south-east down the A458.
SOMERWOOD	A hamlet a mile west of Rodington Heath, although the village welcome signs for the latter from the west read as "Somerwood & Rodington Heath". However, the hamlet of Somerwood is a few yards further west and comprises a few isolated buildings, a post box, and a company who sell cabins and portable shower blocks.
STANLEY GREEN	A hamlet just north of the village of Whixall and 3 miles north of Wem, Stanley Green also lies a mile south-east of the Welsh border.
STEERAWAY	An area just south of Wellington on the south side of the M54. The only access is via Limekiln Lane, which leads you to Steeraway and Limekiln Wood.
SUTTON HALL	An 18th century Grade II listed building close to Sutton Maddock, 3 miles east of Broseley. It is a two-storey building, built of red brick with a hipped roof of old tiles, and has sash windows with plain lintels.
THE CORNER	A 90-degree corner on the only road through the village of Bushmoor. The road heading into the village from the south is a Roman road, which ran between the Roman settlements and forts at Leintwardine and Wroxeter. However, the road now deviates from its former course at The Corner and heads out eastwards towards the A49.
THE DOWN	An area on the B4364 around 4 miles south-west of Bridgnorth, and named after The Down Inn that is located there along with a couple of other houses.
THE FOXHOLES	A hamlet in the triangular space between the Shropshire villages of Silvington, Farlow and Orton.
THE GORE	A hamlet of farms and a former Methodist Chapel dating from 1869, along Thorn Lane, some 8 miles north-east of Ludlow.
THE GREEN	Two hamlets, one on the B4368 between Clunton and Clun alongside the River Clun, the other half a mile north of Wentnor. The latter is also the location of The Inn on The Green and The Green Caravan Park, with the latter a former winner of the David Bellamy Conservation Award.
THE HEM	A hamlet along Hem Lane, where you will also find the 19th century Grade II listed Hem Mill, Hem Manor Farm, Millpond Cottage and The Hem Lake, all located 2 miles south-west of Shifnal. The area also includes The Hem Farm which is now on the busy A4169.
THE HOBBINS	A housing estate to the east of Bridgnorth alongside Stanmore Country Park.
THE MARSH	Three hamlets, one 6 miles north-west of Newport, another on the Welsh border, close to Mitchell's Fold stone circle, and the third 2 miles south-west of Broseley where there is also a Grade II listed house called The Marsh which dates from 1600. One of these places was referenced in Domesday Book (1086) as *Mersse*, but it isn't clear which one.
THE NOOK	There are two places called The Nook in Shropshire. The first is a hamlet of a dozen or so houses a mile south-east of Child's Ercall, while the other is a cluster of houses on the east side of the A49 around Nook Lane, some 4 miles east of Wem.

SHROPSHIRE: UNUSUAL & QUIRKY

Looking down towards the four-house hamlet of New Invention.

Houses at Nox on the B4386.

Six Ashes Inn, 5 miles south-east of Bridgnorth is divided in half by the Shropshire/Staffordshire border! The left half (above) is in Shropshire!

Whixall St Mary's church is actually located at the southern tip of Stanley Green.

The Down Inn, at The Down, 4 miles south-west of Bridgnorth.

The Inn on The Green at the more northerly Shropshire place called "The Green".

Stanmore Country Park runs alongside The Hobbins. This includes a road called The Hobbins on which you will find The Hobbins House.

And here is both The Hobbins road and The Hobbins House.

Part of the attractive estate village of Willey.

Former chapel at The Wood, near Knockin.

Bibliography

Books
A.D. Mills, *Oxford Dictionary of British Place Names* (Oxford University Press, 1991)
Arthur Mee, *The King's England: Shropshire* (Hodder and Stoughton, 1950)
Barrie Trinder, *A History of Shropshire* (Phillimore & Co. Ltd., 1983)
The Very Reverend Dr Robert Jeffery, *St Bartholomew's Church, Tong, Shropshire* (RJL Smith & Associates, 2002)

Booklets and pamphlets at:
Berrington: All Saints' church
Bishop's Castle: Michaelmas Fair
Hope Bagot: St John the Baptist
Ironbridge: Exploring Ironbridge
Ironbridge: The Iron Trail
Knockin: A Brief History of Knockin
Lilleshall: St Michael & All Angels
Llanyblodwel: St Michaels church
Melverley: St Peter's church
More: St Peter's church
Morville: Morville Priory
Morville: St Gregory's church
Myddle: St Peter's church
Stottesdon: St Mary's church
Wroxeter: St Andrew's church

Information Panels at:
Acton Burnell Castle
Atcham, Old Malthouse
Battlefield Museum
Bedlam Furnaces
Bishop's Castle (castle)
Boscobel House
Bridgnorth Castle
Buildwas Abbey
Callow Hill hillfort
Cantlop Bridge
Church Stretton (various)
Clun Castle
Coalport
Earls Hill hillfort
Harton Hollow
Haughmond Abbey
Ironbridge (various)
Langley Chapel
Lilleshall Abbey
Llanymynech Limeworks
Ludlow, Feathers Hotel
Mitchell's Fold Stone Circle
Montgomery Castle
Moreton Corbet Castle
Much Wenlock Priory
Much Wenlock (various)
Nesscliffe Hill Country Park
Newport, Buttercross
Old Oswestry hillfort
Shrewsbury Abbey
Shrewsbury (various)
Snailbeach Mine
Stanmore Country Park
Stokesay Castle
The Bog Visitor Centre
The Stiperstones Nature Reserve
Whitchurch
White Ladies Priory
Wroxeter

Websites:
http://bogcentre.co.uk
https://churchmonumentssociety.org
https://en.wikipedia.org
https://geogeek1726.wordpress.com
https://greatenglishchurches.co.uk
https://historicengland.org.uk
https://houseandheritage.org
https://originalshrewsbury.co.uk
https://pant.today
https://parishmouse.co.uk
http://records.stiperstonesandcorndon.co.uk
http://roman-britain.co.uk
http://search.shropshirehistory.org.uk
http://shrewsburylocalhistory.org.uk
http://shropshirehistory.com
https://sites.google.com
https://theshipinnhighley.co.uk
https://traditionalcustomsandceremonies.com
https://ukga.org
https://www.aboutbridgnorth.com
https://www.achurchnearyou.com
https://www.ancient-yew.org
http://www.badgershropshire.org.uk
http://www.bbc.co.uk
http://www.bishopscastle.co.uk
http://www.bitterley.org.uk
https://www.blackandwhitetrail.org
https://www.bordercountiesadvertizer.co.uk
http://www.borderparishes.org.uk
http://www.bristol.ac.uk
https://www.britainexpress.com
http://www.british-history.ac.uk
http://www.britishlistedbuildings.co.uk
https://www.cakequirks.co.uk
https://www.cambrianrailways.com
http://www.castlesfortsbattles.co.uk
http://www.castleuk.net
http://www.castlewales.com
http://www.churches-uk-ireland.org
http://www.clivechurch.co.uk
http://www.cliveparishcouncil.org
https://www.crsbi.ac.uk
http://www.discovershropshirechurches.co.uk
https://www.eatonmanor.co.uk
https://www.ellesmere.info
http://www.english-church-architecture.net
https://www.english-heritage.org.uk
http://www.essentially-england.com
http://www.ewyaslacy.org.uk
https://www.fabulousfollies.net
http://www.familee.net
https://www.findagrave.com
http://www.fishery.co.uk
https://www.flickr.com
http://www.friendsofrytonchurch.org.uk
http://www.gatehouse-gazetteer.info
https://www.genuki.org.uk
http://www.geograph.org.uk

https://www.hereford.anglican.org
http://www.heritagegateway.org.uk
http://www.highley.org.uk
http://www.highleyshrop.co.uk
https://www.historic-uk.com
https://www.historyfiles.co.uk
https://www.hoofarm.com
http://www.hoptoncastle.org.uk
https://www.independent.co.uk
http://www.information-britain.co.uk
https://www.iwm.org.uk
https://www.joulesbrewery.co.uk
https://www.knockinchurch.co.uk
http://www.knockinparish.org.uk
https://www.ldwa.org.uk
http://www.localhistories.org
http://www.lostheritage.org.uk
http://www.megalithic.co.uk
https://www.myddle.net
http://www.myprimitivemethodists.org.uk
https://www.nationaltrust.org.uk
https://www.northshropshire.co.uk
https://www.nortoninhales.org
http://www.oldforgeknockin.co.uk
https://www.onthemarket.com
https://www.parksandgardens.org
https://www.pastscape.org.uk
http://www.pitchfordestate.com
https://www.rightmove.co.uk
https://www.samuelwood.co.uk
http://www.sfhs.org.uk
https://www.shrewsburycivicsociety.co.uk
https://www.shropshire.gov.uk
https://www.shropshireandmarches.org.uk
http://www.shropshiregeology.org.uk
http://www.shropshirelifemagazine.co.uk
https://www.shropshiresgreatoutdoors.co.uk
https://www.shropshirestar.com
https://www.shropshiretourism.co.uk
https://www.shropshirewildlifetrust.org.uk
http://www.standrewschurchshifnal.org.uk
http://www.stantonlacychurch.btck.co.uk
http://www.stmaryshighley.co.uk
https://www.streetlist.co.uk
http://www.surnamedb.com
https://www.themaltshovel.co.uk
http://www.themodernantiquarian.com
http://www.thetallyho.co.uk
https://www.towerstimes.co.uk
https://www.tripadvisor.co.uk
http://www.turnpikes.org.uk
http://www.users.waitrose.com
http://www.visionofbritain.org.uk
https://www.visitchurches.org.uk
http://www.visitoruk.com
https://www.waterways.org.uk
https://www.zoopla.co.uk

THE WOOD	Similarly, there are two hamlets called The Wood in Shropshire, too. The first is located 2 miles west of Knockin, and consists of a handful of houses, including one called The Woodlands and another called "Holly Cottage, The Wood". Meanwhile, the other is a little further north-east, just off the B4397 around 4 miles west of Wem.
THREE ASHES	We've already covered Six Ashes a couple of pages back, and mentioned it was close to another place called Four Ashes. Three Ashes can be found just south-east of the south Shropshire village of Twitchen on the B4385, and is a hamlet of five or six houses and a farm.
TWITCHEN	A hamlet of a dozen houses stretched out along the B4385 in south Shropshire, not far from the Herefordshire and Welsh borders.
WILLEY	A village just south-west of Broseley comprised of four farms, the village hall, a cricket club and Willey Hall and Park. The village was the site of one of John Wilkinson's ironworks in the 18th century, where the world's first iron boat, a barge, was built in 1787.
WOODSIDE	There are two places called Woodside. The first is a hamlet of half a dozen houses in south-west Shropshire, half a mile south-east of Clun, while the other is a southern housing estate of Telford. The latter was one of the first council house estates built in the new town of Telford in the late 1960s and early 1970s, and is now one of the largest housing estates in Shropshire.